D1037082

The Best Defense

A volume in the series
CORNELL STUDIES IN SECURITY AFFAIRS
edited by Robert J. Art *and* Robert Jervis

A full list of titles in the series appears at the end of the book.

The Best Defense

POLICY ALTERNATIVES FOR U.S. NUCLEAR SECURITY FROM THE 1950s TO THE 1990s

DAVID GOLDFISCHER

Cornell University Press

ITHACA AND LONDON

First published 1993 by Cornell University Press.

International Standard Book Number 0-8014-2570-0
Library of Congress Catalog Card Number 92-56778
Printed in the United States of America
Librarians: Library of Congress cataloging information appears on the last page of the book.

♾ The paper in this book meets the minimum requirements of the American National Standard for Information Sciences—Permanence of Paper for Printed Library Materials, ANSI Z39.48-1984.

For my parents, Barbara and Morrie

Contents

Acknowledgments

This book began at the State University of New York at Buffalo, where it was my good fortune to have had Glenn Snyder as my teacher in the field of international security. Although I benefited greatly from his scrutiny of my work, my debt to him is deeper. Whatever is of value in this book is rooted in his teaching and the insight provided by his seminal contributions to the study of deterrence and defense.

I am equally indebted to Jerome Slater, whose expertise and interest in my area of research made him an invaluable source of critical feedback. His sustained involvement and support helped me persevere through the seemingly endless process of writing and revising.

Useful comments on all or parts of my manuscript were provided by Frank Beer, Richard Betts, Robert Jervis, Peter Roman, and Claude Welch. Many others offered helpful feedback during seminar and conference presentations of various portions of my work. I first presented the basic argument of this book at a foreign policy seminar at the Brookings Institution, where suggestions by John Steinbrunner and Raymond Garthoff were particularly helpful in guiding my subsequent research. The Brookings Institution, the University of Colorado at Boulder, and the Institute for Global Conflict and Cooperation at the University of California, San Diego, provided financial support and stimulating environments in which to write.

While completing my first draft, I received greatly valued advice and encouragement from Randolf Siverson. For invaluable assistance in tracking down supporting documentation as I revised my manuscript, I thank two resourceful and gifted research assistants: Brenda Simonen and Brent Pickett. Finally, no brief acknowledgment can convey my gratitude for the editorial assistance and general guidance of my father, Morrie Goldfischer.

D. G.

Acronyms

ABM	antiballistic missile
ACD	Arms Control through Defense
ACDA	Arms Control and Disarmament Agency
AD	assured destruction
ADC	Air Defense Command
ADSEC	Air Defense Systems Engineering Committee
ALPS	Accidental Launch Protection System
ASAT	antisatellite
BMD	ballistic missile defense
C^3	command, control, and communication
CFE	Conventional Forces in Europe
CONAD	Continental Air Defense Command
DOD	Department of Defense
DPB	defense-protected build-down
GPALS	Global Protection against Limited Strikes
ICBM	intercontinental ballistic missile
INF	Intermediate Nuclear Forces
JCS	Joint Chiefs of Staff
MAD	mutual assured destruction
MaRV	maneuvering reentry vehicle
MDE	mutual defense emphasis
MIRV	multiple independently targeted reentry vehicle
NORAD	North American Defense Command
NSC	National Security Council
OSD	Office of the Secretary of Defense
OTA	Office of Technology Assessment
SAC	Strategic Air Command

SAGE	Semi-automatic Ground Environment
SALT	Strategic Arms Limitation Talks
SDI	Strategic Defense Initiative
SDIO	Strategic Defense Initiative Organization
SIOP	Single Integrated Operational Plan
SLBM	submarine-launched ballistic missile
START	Strategic Arms Reduction Treaty
THAAD	Theater High-Altitude Area Air Defense

The Best Defense

Introduction

In 1979 physicist Freeman Dyson drew a firm line between offensive and defensive weapons:

> The ground on which I will take my stand is a sharp moral distinction between offense and defense, between offensive and defensive uses of all kinds of weapons. The distinction is often difficult to make and is always subject to argument. But it is none the less real and essential. At least its main implications are clear. Bombers are bad. Fighter airplanes and anti-aircraft missiles are good. Tanks are bad. Antitank missiles are good. . . . Intercontinental missiles are bad. Antiballistic missile systems are good. This list of moral preferences goes flatly against the strategic thinking which has dominated our policies for the last forty years. And just because it goes against our accepted dogmas, it offers us a realistic hope of escape from the trap in which we are now ensnared.[1]

At the time Dyson wrote, his vision might safely have been characterized as hopelessly out of touch with postwar realities. The Soviet commitment to an offensive conventional force posture in Europe seemed as intractable as both superpowers' reliance on massive offensive nuclear capabilities. No one could have predicted that within a decade a Soviet leader would call for "a change in the entire pattern of armed forces with a view to imparting an exclusively defensive character to them"[2]—let alone have foreseen that such state-

1. Freeman Dyson, *Disturbing the Universe* (New York: Harper and Row, 1979), p. 143.

2. Mikhail Gorbachev, *Perestroika: New Thinking for Our Country and the World* (New York: Harper and Row, 1987), p. 203.

ments presaged a transformation of Soviet political and military policy in Europe.

As Europe adjusts to the dismantling of the Soviet offensive conventional threat, we should consider whether the nuclear balance of terror might also be regarded as an ephemeral by-product of the Cold War era. After all, a major impetus for the U.S. strategic offensive buildup was the need to deter an invasion of Western Europe; the radical reduction of that threat undercuts a key rationale for the nuclear deterrent strategies of the past four decades. Remember that critics of U.S. Cold War policy raised strong arguments against acquiring capabilities for total nuclear annihilation. As that conflict wanes (and new dangers arise), it is appropriate to reevaluate the merits of proposed alternatives.

In this book I examine a school of nuclear arms control that challenged the succession of U.S. nuclear doctrines accompanying the postwar nuclear buildup and shared Dyson's view that arms control agreements favoring defensive weapons offered a safer path than reliance on offense-dominant nuclear policies. I refer to that perspective here as "mutual defense emphasis" (MDE). MDE designates any superpower arms control framework using defensive weapons to reduce societal damage in a nuclear war. MDE thus belongs to the tradition of arms control and disarmament approaches that aimed to avoid—or retreat from—what Leo Szilard in 1965 called "saturation parity"[3] and that has since become known as "mutual assured destruction" (MAD).

Nuclear arms control must give first priority not to reducing offensive capabilities but to minimizing the likelihood of war. Arms control also aspires to reduce the uncertainties and costs of national security planning.[4] MDE proposals share these goals with other arms control frameworks. What is unique to MDE is the use of defensive weapons to limit the destructive consequences of a nuclear attack.

The only apparent overlap between MDE and MAD concerns the prospect of negotiated deployments of very limited nationwide ballistic missile defenses that could cope with accidental, unauthorized, or small-power nuclear strikes. Since such deployments might avoid

3. Leo Szilard, "'Minimal Deterrent' vs. Saturation Parity," in *Problems of National Strategy*, ed. Henry A. Kissinger (New York: Praeger, 1965), pp. 376–91.

4. For what remains one of the best discussions of the objectives of arms control, see Donald G. Brennan, "Setting and Goals of Arms Control," in *Arms Control, Disarmament, and National Security*, ed. Donald G. Brennan (New York: George Braziller, 1961), pp. 19–42.

substantially degrading the offensive capabilities of the nuclear superpowers, they are at least conceptually consistent with a MAD approach to arms control.

From an MDE perspective, by contrast, an agreement on limited defenses would be seen as a useful first step toward a more far-reaching defensive transition. Regardless of differences in ultimate objectives, growing recent interest in bilateral limited defense deployments reflects an ongoing shift in perspectives about the most desirable balance between offense and defense. Given these links between limited defense proposals and MDE (and even though such proposals may be consistent with MAD), here I consider arguments for limited defenses as part of the spectrum of rationales for MDE.

Despite signs of changing attitudes toward limited strategic defenses, the mainstream U.S. arms control community (which coalesced in support of MAD-based arms control in the 1960s) has generally retained its long-standing skepticism about the desirability of defensive weapons for any purpose. This book assumes that arms control rationales for "mutual assured vulnerability" may be—as Dyson claims—"dogmas." Thus, when a leading MAD advocate concedes that preserving peace by threatening mutual annihilation is "the now familiar reversal of common sense,"[5] we should consider whether we have continued to "reverse" common sense largely *because* it has become so familiar.

Common sense suggests that states wishing to cooperate in minimizing the danger of war would restrict themselves to defensive military capabilities. Since the offensive potential of nuclear weapons has made it essential to avoid war, the United States and the Soviet Union (now Russia) appear to have had a particularly strong incentive to establish such an arms control regime. In a sense, this book is concerned with one simple question: Why haven't they done so?

Some opponents of MDE (for conventional no less than nuclear forces) claim that efforts to distinguish between offensive and defensive military strength are inherently futile or misleading. Since that contention must be refuted before we even consider the possibility of MDE arms control, chapter 1 demonstrates the validity of the offense-defense distinction. I show that arguments asserting the inherent ambiguity of military capabilities are essentially polemic efforts to discourage inquiry into arms control approaches to national security.

5. Robert Jervis, "Cooperation under the Security Dilemma," *World Politics* 30 (January 1978): 206.

Demonstrating the conceptual coherence of MDE does not in itself justify exploring its applicability to the strategic environment of the nuclear superpowers. After all, nearly everyone who argues about nuclear policy claims to have a "solution" to the problem, and relatively few analysts have given serious attention to devising practical proposals for mutual defense emphasis.

Broadly speaking, there have been three prevalent schools of thought on nuclear policy: MAD advocates, who argue that defense is unnecessary because bilateral "offense-only" deterrent forces can provide a safe and durable arms control framework; "war-fighters," who claim that all forms of arms control are unnecessary because the United States can defend itself through unilateral efforts; and disarmament advocates, who maintain that the nuclear danger requires the elimination of *all* weapons, whether offensive or defensive.

In chapter 2, I argue that none of these approaches has provided an acceptable basis for addressing the nuclear danger. Although MAD advocates justifiably point out that their war-fighting and disarmament critics have failed to offer a realistic alternative to mutual assured destruction, they provide no answer to a crucial question posed by both nuclear hawks and doves: What happens if nuclear deterrence fails?

At a time when political developments have dramatically overtaken Cold War conceptions of the Soviet Union, fears of a superpower nuclear war have understandably receded. For those who have long argued for superpower acceptance of MAD, it is particularly tempting to regard arms control progress toward stabilizing the balance of terror as equivalent to resolving the nuclear danger.

This book is motivated by a belief that the preservation of "assured destruction" capabilities (defined minimally by former defense secretary Robert McNamara as the ability to kill 20 percent of the adversary's population, though in practice denoting several times that destructive capacity) should continue to be regarded as a source of incalculable danger. Theoretical rationalizations for those capabilities have exaggerated the requirements for deterring a rational adversary and ignored the political and psychological forces that can lead to violent conflict in defiance of rational calculations of risk and cost.

A long-term perspective on the nuclear age—including the proliferation of weapons of mass destruction and long-range delivery systems—should presume that no strategy of deterrence can provide permanent safety. In 1962, during his (unfortunately ill prepared and badly managed) campaign for a national effort at civil defense,

President Kennedy aptly described the tendency to allow periods of calm to lead to complacency and inaction: "These matters have some rhythm. When the skies are clear, no one is interested. Suddenly then, when the clouds come . . . then everyone wants to find out why more hasn't been done about it."[6]

In that light, the winding down of the particular conflict that made societal annihilation possible should be regarded as a potentially fleeting opportunity. A world of MAD capabilities was the inadvertent outcome of a deadly competition between great powers, and it is a reasonable premise that cooperating states might base arms control on a more reliable foundation than permanent threats of mutual annihilation.

Mutual defense emphasis advocates have claimed that their approach can satisfy the arms control requirements of nuclear parity and deterrence stability *and* provide a means to limit damage if deterrence somehow fails. The overview of the MDE approach in chapter 3 introduces some of the arguments made by U.S. and Soviet proponents at various times in the nuclear age. It also examines their underlying assumptions about the relation between politics and technology in the context of nuclear weapons.

MDE supporters since the early 1950s have offered various rationales for the value of strategic defense as a tool of arms control. Early advocates focused primarily on population defense as an alternative to a strategic bomber buildup. Proposals during the missile age included calls for defense of retaliatory forces to permit deep cuts in offensive capabilities, while envisioning societal defenses at least sufficient to offer hope of coping with limited nuclear strikes. Although some proponents emphasized strategic defense as the key to a "minimum deterrence" regime (the retention of very limited retaliatory ability), others argued that MDE offered the only technically feasible path to complete offensive disarmament. Uniting all these approaches was the goal of combining offensive limitations and defensive deployments to minimize the destructive force of both sides.

The principal explanation—and justification—for rejecting a serious effort at national defense has been the assertion that the overwhelming technological supremacy of the nuclear offense simply precludes protecting societies against nuclear attack. The balance of

6. John F. Kennedy, *Public Papers of the Presidents of the United States: John F. Kennedy, 1962* (Washington, D.C.: United States Government Printing Office, 1963), p. 543. Cited in McGeorge Bundy, *Danger and Survival: Choices about the Bomb in the First Fifty Years* (New York: Random House, 1988), p. 355.

terror is therefore regarded as an inevitable consequence of the destructive potential of nuclear weapons. Although in chapter 3 I examine the status of "technological necessity" as an explanation for decisions regarding offensive and defensive weapons, let me make one key point at the outset. Like other strong supporters of nuclear arms control, MDE advocates have consistently maintained that it is impossible to defend against the offensive forces the superpowers are capable of building. They have differed only in their claim that defense may prove possible in the context of an arms control regime that strictly limits offensive strength. Thus a great divide separates MDE from the far more familiar war-fighting rationales for strategic defense, which hold that unilateral efforts can produce a "cost-effective" defense of the U.S. homeland against a "responsive" Soviet threat.

The technological task for the defense is obviously far easier if one assumes that offenses are limited by agreement, yet MDE advocates have still had to contend with claims that defenses could be overwhelmed at very little cost, or that they could fail completely. There are, moreover, other impediments, partially rooted in technology, to devising MDE regimes: for example, the possibility that ostensibly defensive weapons might also have offensive uses; the possibility that irreducible uncertainties over defensive effectiveness, or over the relative strength of the two sides' defensive systems, might defeat the establishment of arms control standards of parity and deterrence stability; or fears that technological breakthroughs could permit a defector to achieve nuclear superiority.

Did some combination of these obstacles preclude the pursuit of MDE arms control throughout the nuclear age? I regard the role of a "technological imperative" in explaining the rejection of MDE as an open question, to be assessed by scrutinizing the history of U.S. choices between offensive and defensive strategic weapons. Subsequent chapters therefore examine why mutual defense emphasis arms control was never seriously pursued during the three periods when it was actively promoted: the early 1950s, the decade preceding the 1972 Anti-Ballistic Missile (ABM) Treaty, and the 1980s.

Those periods encompass enormous changes in strategic weapons technology—changes that affected the plausibility of claims that MDE was feasible. Yet though efforts to design an MDE arms control regime would have faced technical obstacles of varying severity, I argue that the case presented by advocates was compelling enough to merit the responses accorded any potentially advantageous arms control concept: that is, serious analytical work within the government and a dialogue on the subject with the adversary.

Yet despite its promotion by eminent experts—led by J. Robert Oppenheimer in the 1950s and Hudson Institute president Donald G. Brennan (whom McGeorge Bundy has described as "one of the first serious students of nuclear arms control")[7] in the 1960s—MDE was regarded by leading policymakers as beyond the pale of serious scrutiny. Considering its place on the margins of strategic debate, it is perhaps not surprising that MDE has received scant attention, if any, in histories of the nuclear age. That omission is unfortunate. It leaves the impression that presidents and other important actors in national security policy had no choice between the extremes of nuclear disarmament and policies that (whether deliberately or not) ensured the vulnerability of the United States to nuclear devastation. Because of the consensus among serious analysts that a verifiable regime based purely on offensive disarmament was unrealistic, the only remaining options entailed exploiting the technological supremacy of the nuclear offense.

If it can be shown that policymakers failed to engage forceful arguments for MDE, troubling questions arise about the readiness of U.S. leaders to expose their nation to a danger that, as Defense Secretary Robert McNamara put it, "could dwarf any catastrophe that has befallen man in his more than a million years on earth."[8] In that sense, the MDE critique that emerged at crucial junctures in the shaping of nuclear policy provides a unique vantage point from which to reevaluate the series of prevailing rationales for offense-dominant nuclear doctrines.

While many histories of U.S. security policy have criticized the massive strategic airpower buildup of the 1950s, their critiques have been weakened by a failure to identify and assess a clear alternative that the Truman or Eisenhower administration might have pursued.[9] For those who regard the eventual emergence of mutual assured destruction capabilities as inevitable, the question arises, Why shouldn't the United States have preserved for as long as possible any advantages conferred by nuclear superiority?

7. Bundy (n. 6), p. 553.

8. Robert S. McNamara, *The Essence of Security* (New York: Harper and Row, 1968), p. 51.

9. McGeorge Bundy is perhaps the only historian who has considered the possibility of a mutual deterrence arms control regime in the early postwar years. See Bundy (n. 6), pp. 192–96.

Chapter 4 examines the decision-making process culminating in the Eisenhower administration's policy of "massive retaliation," weighing the case made by airpower advocates against the alternative analysis offered by proponents of continental defense and arms control. The case for MDE, which then represented the *only* proposed arms control framework, was based primarily on three linked propositions: First, that relying on nuclear weapons to deter Communist aggression guaranteed that the Soviets would acquire a matching ability to destroy the United States. Second, that a rational security policy must therefore attempt to address both the threat posed by the Soviet Union *and* the common danger posed by a nuclear arms race. Third, that a realistic effort to avoid U.S. vulnerability required recognizing that strategic defense and arms control were "necessary complements."

Within a circle of informed decision makers deliberately narrowed by government secrecy on nuclear issues, none of these propositions was seriously debated. Instead, Oppenheimer and his associates confronted an insular, ideologically charged coalition that regarded unqualified support for strategic airpower and U.S. nuclear supremacy as a minimal test of patriotism. Inside that coalition, which united the bureaucratic interests of the Air Force, the preoccupation of fiscal conservatives with getting "more bang for the buck," and the political Right's equation of nuclear superiority with victory in the Cold War, it was simply deemed more acceptable to condemn nuclear arms control than to debate its merits. In sharp contrast to the more recent identification of strategic defense advocacy with hawkish anti-Communism, important elements of the airpower coalition of the early 1950s did not hesitate to denounce (with considerable effect) appeals for a serious effort at continental defense as deliberately subversive.

That U.S. leaders failed to engage the arguments for MDE hardly demonstrates that its supporters offered a viable or preferable alternative. MDE might well have foundered on the rapidly changing technological environment of the 1950s or on a Soviet rejection of any U.S. effort at serious bilateral arms control talks. One can also argue that the military threat to Western Europe—or the political requirement of reassuring U.S. allies—provided no option other than building a force capable of destroying the Soviet Union.

Pursuing MDE would have meant offering the Soviets hope of success in their determined (and otherwise futile) effort to defend their homeland against a nuclear attack. Given the absence of any serious U.S. arms control proposals during this period, it is impossible to know whether or how that chance might have altered the subsequent dynamics of the Cold War.

Although in chapter 4 I suggest that there are good reasons to doubt whether an MDE initiative would have borne fruit in the early 1950s, my central thesis is that the U.S. dismissal of MDE was not based on any clear imperatives of technology or national security. The explanation lies instead with the fact that U.S. leaders tolerated—and helped cultivate—a decision-making environment that defeated the prospects for reasoned debate.

If MDE was initially dismissed as an unwelcome challenge to the doctrine of "massive retaliation," why did the United States continue to reject the approach during the period of greater receptivity to arms control that began in the 1960s? Chapter 5 examines one critical element of the answer: the development and growing influence of a radically different approach to nuclear arms control. Many arms control theorists concluded at the onset of the missile age that complete defenselessness against the missile provided the key to establishing a "minimum deterrence" arms control system based solely on offensive strategic weapons. Such an arms control framework, they believed, could even set the stage for complete nuclear disarmament. Thus, whereas airpower supporters in the early 1950s feared the appeal of continental defense as an alternative to an offensive buildup, supporters of comprehensive arms control came to oppose defense because of its presumed incompatibility with offensive disarmament. Chapter 5 shows that proponents of "offense-only" arms control overestimated the level of strategic arms reduction achievable within their framework and misread the dynamics of technological innovation in strategic weaponry. Those errors led them to disregard the arms control opportunities represented by the maturation of antiballistic missile systems in the mid-1960s, even as Defense Secretary McNamara promoted a version of their approach that distorted their original vision of the means and ends of arms control.

Chapter 6 looks beyond the role of the offense-only arms control theorists to examine the broader forces shaping attitudes toward offense and defense in the 1960s. In contrast to the early 1950s, the need for a nationwide defense had now become the rallying point for conservative supporters of a war-fighting capability; opposing ABM could thus be regarded as a litmus test of one's commitment to arms control.

It was the effort to marshal opposition to ABM that prompted McNamara to promote the theory that forswearing defense was the key to ending the arms race on the basis of mutual assured destruction. Chapter 6 draws on the arguments of MDE advocates to question whether his position was either politically necessary (to thwart the war-fighting lobby) or based on sound strategic analysis. In terms of the latter, MDE proponents offered cogent critiques of McNamara's three key claims: first, that U.S. security required no less than "assured destruction" threats; second, that the Soviets were similarly committed to such a capability; and third, that population defense was therefore inherently incompatible with arms control. Whatever the intellectual merits of the case for MDE, McNamara and his supporters were far better positioned to shape the domestic debate. McNamara was able to use his influential role to "prove" the necessity of MAD, in part by responding to Soviet expressions of a preference for defense with a promise that the United States would expend any effort required to preserve its assured destruction potential.

An authoritative presentation of the argument that defense might prove possible in an arms control regime (and that unilateral efforts would certainly be futile) could have radically altered the ABM debates of the 1960s, providing a counterweight to equations of homeland defense with a hawkish predilection to contemplate nuclear war. Moreover, given official Soviet declarations of interest in MDE through the mid-1960s, a similar U.S. stance could have made defense emphasis the initial basis for a U.S.–Soviet dialogue on strategic arms control. In frustration over the U.S. decision to foreclose that possibility, MDE advocate Donald Brennan created the acronym "MAD" to characterize a policy of using arms control to institutionalize the balance of terror.

The mid-1980s represented a period of dramatic change in the history of MDE advocacy. In January 1985, under the label "U.S. Strategic Concept," the United States formally proposed a transition to defense dominance as the basis for subsequent strategic arms control negotiations. Chapter 7 evaluates the Strategic Concept, showing that by ignoring all the critical assumptions and criteria shared by three decades of serious MDE advocates, it provided no basis for a genuine superpower dialogue on the prospects for a defensive transition. In particular, the claim that such a transition could be driven by the technological supremacy of a "cost-effective" defense undercut the very basis for pursuing arms control negotiations with the Soviet Union. The only durable incentive for MDE arms control —as its advocates have maintained since 1952—is recognition that technology alone can provide no defense against the forces the superpowers are capable of building.

Yet the 1980s also witnessed a revival of serious advocacy of MDE from several sources, and I contrast the effort to package the Strategic Defense Initiative (SDI) as arms control with some recent mutual defense emphasis proposals that are consistent with the MDE tradition.

Although the Reagan administration failed to translate its Strategic Concept into a viable arms control initiative, the U.S. MDE proposal was not without significance. Indeed, the reintroduction of offensive disarmament as a U.S. objective—and particularly the storm of Western protest following President Reagan's assertion of that view at the 1986 Reykjavik summit—helped refocus attention on the ultimate source of the U.S. preference for offense-dominant nuclear policies: the perceived need for extended nuclear deterrence to protect and reassure Western Europe.

In principle, the collapse of the Soviet threat in Europe should make possible the first genuine effort to address the dangerous legacy of four decades of offense-dominant strategic weapons policies. If the nuclear powers wish to move toward dismantling the balance of terror, they may find themselves increasingly drawn toward using defenses as a critical tool. Yet despite the radical reformulation of Western security policy in the wake of Soviet geopolitical retrenchment and internal upheaval, only limited interest in a fundamental reappraisal of strategic arms control policy has thus far been displayed. That should not be entirely surprising, since after all the prevalent theory of arms control holds that MAD capabilities will persist whether arms control is rejected or embraced. Clearly, a belief that another type of nuclear world is possible must precede any serious search for alternatives.

In that sense, the critical role that ideas and beliefs play in shaping nuclear policy forms a central underlying theme of this book. At a historic turning point in international relations, it is essential to reexamine the intellectual origins and development of those ideas and to sort out beliefs of enduring validity from questionable judgments formed in a context of bewildering dangers and uncertainties.

I argue that decisions to rely on offense-dominant nuclear policies were based in part on flawed premises. That does not mean, of course, that at any point in the nuclear era U.S. decision makers—simply by adopting an alternative theory of nuclear weapons and national security—could have reversed the strategic arms competition in favor of defense-oriented arms control. The effort to reevaluate the range of choices between offense and defense requires detailed inquiry into the spectrum of constraints on U.S. policymakers, which include U.S. assessments of Soviet abilities and intentions, relations with allies, domestic and bureaucratic politics, and estimates of the costs and potential of existing and prospective weapons systems.

Although one or more of these types of constraints may well have precluded the adoption of an MDE arms control regime, I argue that MDE advocates in fact discerned opportunities during which their theoretically cogent approach was plausibly realistic. In that context, we can speak in terms of an intellectual failure on the part of policymakers to engage important arguments—arguments that represented an uncomfortably powerful critique of prevailing belief systems.

Since the ABM debates of the 1960s, the arms control community has successfully challenged the view that only a lack of political will prevented the development of an effective defense against nuclear weapons. Unfortunately, the strategic defense lobby's claims of limitless technological opportunity were often countered with the equally extreme assertion that choices between offense and defense are so driven by technology as to be beyond human intervention. In 1963 Warner Schilling observed that the "contributions that science and technology will bring to international politics will largely turn . . . on the purposes of statesmen and the theories they have about the political world in which they live."[10] The theory that the nuclear danger required that superpowers cooperate in emphasizing defense had little appeal for statesmen preoccupied with waging a cold war, who chose instead to overwhelm their adversary's efforts at defense. As the nuclear superpowers conceive their relationship anew, we should ask again whether and how defensive weapons might contribute to a search for mutual security. This book is written in the hope of encouraging the idea that deterrence, defense, and disarmament can be mutually reinforcing objectives.

10. Warner R. Schilling, "Scientists, Foreign Policy and Politics," in *Scientists and National Policy-Making*, ed. Robert Gilpin and Christopher Wright (New York: Columbia University Press, 1964), p. 173.

[1]

The Meaning of Offense and Defense

A fundamental criticism of defense emphasis is that one cannot distinguish meaningfully between offensive and defensive weapons and capabilities. This chapter addresses specific claims along those lines. I show that such arguments not only are flawed but are often put forth to discourage the pursuit of an arms control approach to national security.

Arguments against Distinguishing Offensive from Defensive Weapons

The first diplomatic effort to enhance international security by distinguishing between offensive and defensive military power occurred between the two world wars. Thus the agenda for the 1932–33 Geneva Disarmament Conference was based on a principle of "qualitative disarmament" presented by President Herbert Hoover: "This reduction should be carried out, not only by broad general cuts in armaments, but by increasing the comparative power of defense through decreases in the power of attack."[1]

That U.S. approach was reconfirmed a year later in President Franklin D. Roosevelt's message to the conference: "If all nations will agree wholly to eliminate from their possession and use the weapons which make possible a successful attack, defenses auto-

1. Quoted in Phillip Noel-Baker, *The First World Disarmament Conference, 1932–33* (New York: Pergamon Press, 1979), p. 81.

matically will become impregnable, and the frontiers of every nation will become secure."[2]

Even then, many participants and observers rejected the idea of a meaningful distinction between offense and defense. Robert Jervis (whose own views on this issue I will consider later) cites the following statements by European officials of that era:

> "A weapon is either offensive or defensive, according to which end of it you are looking at."
>
> "Every arm can be employed offensively or defensively in turn. . . . The only way to discover whether arms are intended for purely defensive purposes or are held in a spirit of aggression is in all cases to enquire into the intentions of the country concerned."[3]

The Disarmament Conference failed to reach agreement on which weapons could be categorized as offensive or as defensive. Two noted defense policy analysts have recently invoked that failure to show the inherent futility of all such efforts. Thus Albert Wohlstetter comments as follows and cites a passage from Winston Churchill to prove his point:

> Disarmament negotiations bogged down in a welter of ambiguities and confusion on the subject of such qualitative disarmament. Winston Churchill, it was to be expected, made the essential point with devastating wit: "The Foreign Secretary told us it was difficult to divide weapons into offensive and defensive categories. It certainly is, because almost any conceivable weapon may be used in defence or offence; either by an aggressor or by the innocent victim of his assault. To make it more difficult for the invader, heavy guns, tanks and poison gas are to be relegated to the evil category of offensive weapons. The invasion of France by Germany in 1914 reached its climax without the employment of any of these weapons. The heavy gun is to be described as an 'offensive weapon.' It is all right in a fortress; there it is

2. Quoted in Robert Jervis, "Cooperation Under the Security Dilemma," *World Politics* 30 (January 1978): 201. Jervis's source is Merle Tate, *The United States and Armaments* (Cambridge: Harvard University Press, 1948), p. 108. The interwar effort to promote defense emphasis arms control was clearly prompted by a belief that overemphasis on offense had contributed to World War I. Some recent research has reexamined that issue, arguing that the European powers' irrational attachment to offensive doctrines was a major cause of the war. See Jack Snyder, *The Ideology of the Offensive* (Ithaca: Cornell University Press, 1984), and Stephen Van Evera, "The Cult of the Offensive and the Origins of the First World War," *International Security* 9 (Summer 1984): 58–107.

3. Jervis (n. 2), p. 201.

virtuous and pacific in character; but bring it out onto the field—and of course, if it were needed, it would be brought out into the field—and it immediately becomes naughty, peccant, militaristic, and has to be placed under the ban of civilization. Take the tank. The Germans, having invaded France, entrenched themselves; and in a couple of years they shot down 1,500,000 French and British soldiers who were trying to free the soil of France. The tank was invented to overcome the fire of the machine-guns with which the Germans were maintaining themselves in France, and it saved a lot of lives in clearing the soil of the invader. Now, apparently, the machine gun, which was the German weapon for holding on to thirteen provinces in France, is to be the virtuous, defensive machine gun, and the tank, which was the means by which these Allied lives were saved, is to be placed under the censure and obloquy of all just and righteous men."[4]

Samuel Huntington has similarly assailed the utility of distinguishing offense from defense:

> At the 1932 conference, . . . the Germans and the French had differing views as to whether border fortifications were offensive or defensive. Even George Quester, who wrote an entire book based on the distinction between offensive and defensive weapons technology, had to admit that "fortifications along one frontier could be exploited to hold that sector secure with a diminished garrison, while the forces thus freed were launched on an offensive in another sector." The effort to make offense/defense distinctions in terms of weapons characteristics almost inevitably results in dubious and mystifying, if not bizarre classifications. . . . Weapons may be usefully differentiated in a variety of ways, but the offense/defense distinction is not one of them.[5]

Finally, the following observation by Theodore Draper:

> The defensive apologia that has been given to [our Star Wars Program] is a travesty of military principles and practice. There is no such thing as a pure, isolated defense or defensive weapon. Every weapon . . . can be used defensively or offensively, depending on the circumstances. An arms race to develop "defensive weapons" is just as much an arms race as one to develop "offensive" weapons.[6]

4. Albert Wohlstetter, "The Political and Military Aims of Offense and Defense Innovation," in *Swords and Shields*, ed. Fred S. Hoffman, Albert Wohlstetter, and David S. Yost (Lexington, Mass.: D. C. Heath, 1987), p. 4.

5. Samuel P. Huntington, "U.S. Defense Strategy: The Strategic Innovations of the Reagan Years," in *American Defense Annual, 1987–1988*, ed. Joseph Kruzel (Lexington, Mass.: D. C. Heath, 1987), p. 36.

6. Theodore Draper, "Pie in the Sky," *New York Review of Books*, February 14, 1985.

Before we examine the passages above, let me note that they contain three separate and inconsistent arguments. The first is that actual weapons do not lend themselves to categorization as either offensive or defensive. The second is that even when a particular weapon possesses a purely defensive capability, characterizing it as such is still inherently misleading. The reasoning here is that when combined with other weapons (i.e., in the context of a nation's overall force structure), weapons that are themselves purely defensive can contribute to the success of an offensive military strategy. Viewing defensive weapons in isolation, then, invariably provides merely a technical distinction, telling us nothing about a state's overall capabilities or objectives. The third claim, which is left implicit in the preceding citations, is that though it may be entirely possible to distinguish offensive from defensive weapons, and though it may also be possible to acquire a purely defensive military capability, states that seriously entertain such an objective do so at grave risk.

The first two claims can easily be shown to be wrong. I will provide a simple description of the attributes of a purely defensive weapon and show that it is entirely conceivable for states to adopt a purely defensive force structure. I will then consider the substantive, prescriptive core of the arguments offered by Churchill, Wohlstetter, and Huntington: the claim that a defense-dominant policy is inherently dangerous for any state that pursues it.

The Meaning of Defense

Draper has flatly maintained that there is "no such thing as a pure . . . defense or defensive weapon," since "every weapon . . . can be used offensively or defensively." Notwithstanding such sweeping assertions, several analysts have offered an obvious standard for characterizing weapons as "purely defensive." Jervis observes: "The essence of defense is keeping the other side out of your territory. A purely defensive weapon is one that can do this without being able to penetrate the enemy's land."[7] Similarly, Freeman Dyson describes as (purely) defensive "weapons which are capable of defending territory without destroying it in the process."[8] Finally, George Quester notes that "weapons become supremely defensive whenever a for-

7. Jervis (n. 2), p. 203.
8. Freeman Dyson, *Weapons and Hope* (New York: Harper and Row, 1984), p. 54.

eign decision to violate frontiers is indispensable to providing them with a target."[9]

Can this standard be applied in the real world? As Jervis notes, it is not hard to envision how a nation might rely for its security on armaments that are "only capable of being used for the defense of a State's territory. . . . The most obvious examples are fortifications. They can shelter attacking forces, especially when they are built right along the frontier, but they cannot occupy enemy territory."[10] Another example, of direct relevance to this book, would be the antiaircraft defenses protecting the homelands of both superpowers. Radar networks, antiaircraft missile installations, and fighter interceptors that are based in North America obviously cannot *themselves* initiate an attack on the former Soviet Union, nor can any component of the vast Soviet air defense system penetrate the territory of the United States.

Do current or prospective ballistic missile defense (BMD) systems also qualify as purely defensive? To decide, one must examine particular weapons in terms of the specific question Quester asked: whether a foreign decision to violate frontiers would be indispensable to providing them with a target. Certainly, none of the space-based defenses envisioned in the U.S. Strategic Defense Initiative (SDI) appears to qualify, since weapons designed to destroy enemy missiles during their "boost phase" could presumably also attack the other side's space-based defenses or satellites. Some of the envisioned "Star Wars" technology could even attack targets on Russian territory. Not all current or envisioned systems, however, possess these offensive capabilities. Specifically, ground-based BMD systems would qualify as purely defensive, provided they lacked the altitude and range to launch an attack on the adversary's satellites.

Such an apparently clear standard for a purely defensive weapons system belies Huntington's assertion about the futility of offense-defense distinctions. Huntington's own example, which depicts how a purely defensive capability can contribute to a military offensive, suggests another claim: that the distinction, though hardly mystifying, is nevertheless irrelevant. Thus he invokes Quester's "admission" that fortifications could hold one frontier while forces attacked in another sector.

9. George H. Quester, *Offense and Defense in the International System* (New York: John Wiley, 1977), p. 3.
10. Jervis (n. 2), p. 203.

That defensive and offensive forces can be combined for offensive purposes, however, does not establish that they will *inevitably* be so combined. Indeed, as Jervis shows, it is easy to imagine an alternative context in which fortifications truly reflect a defense-dominant stance: "A state with only a strong line of forts, fixed guns, and a small army to man them would not be much of a menace."[11] Clearly, the offensive menace of Huntington's example stems not from the fortifications themselves, but from the hypothetical addition of an army large enough to both man the fortifications *and* launch an invasion. Without such an army (or other offensive force), it would scarcely be mystifying or misleading to call the stance Jervis depicts defensive.

Nevertheless, in certain circumstances the defense-dominant forces in Jervis's example might, over time, be used in a transition away from pure defense. That was the point Churchill made about the heavy gun. But though he was raising an important issue, its implications are far less clear than he suggests. In the force posture Jervis depicted, would heavy guns fixed within fortifications represent a potential threat to a neighboring state? Clearly, the answer would depend on a range of factors that cannot be analyzed in the abstract. For example: Are the guns numerous and mobile enough to invade the neighbors' territory? Assuming the guns were designed for defense against an invading army, would they have any value for an offensive mission? Could they be used to overwhelm the fortifications and other defensive measures of the intended victim? If they were in fact useful for offense, how long would it take to deploy them for their new mission? What supplementary changes in one's forces (e.g., a major expansion of one's army) would be required, and over what period? Could such an undertaking be observed from the outset by the intended victim?

Finally, how robust are the victim's defenses? In the extreme case where the defenses are regarded as impregnable, the aggressor's offensive mobilization could be ignored. Or defenses may be strong enough to permit the defending state to await clear evidence of the aggressor's transition from defense to offense before abandoning its own defensive posture in favor of active preparations for war.[12]

Obviously, given enough time, even a state possessing only defensive power can restructure its force to mount an invasion.

11. Ibid.

12. For a discussion of the conditions under which a defense emphasis stance can reassure potential adversaries, see Jervis (n. 2), pp. 198–99, 211–14.

Whether another state is threatened by the mere potential for such a future shift will depend on the overall balance of power between the states, the technological balance between offensive and defensive weapons, and whether the two states have agreed on measures that either preclude or ensure sufficient warning of such a transition from defense to offense. Thus Churchill's example of heavy guns provides no basis for concluding that any defensive deployment can "immediately" become an offensive threat. Indeed, his example shows that the standard of "purely defensive" is in fact less stringent when applied to overall military capabilities than when applied to an isolated weapon. Although heavy guns cannot be characterized as purely defensive weapons, their emplacement in fortifications may reflect a purely defensive overall posture. In other words, weapons that in isolation appear to have offensive capabilities (artillery, ballistic missiles) may be embedded in weapons systems (fortifications, ballistic missile defense systems) that are manifestly incapable of an offensive mission.

Although it is not necessary for a purely defensive force to comprise solely defensive weapons, the U.S.–Soviet relationship provides a unique case in which one can envision such a "doubly" pure defense. Here, if we limit ourselves to the context of nuclear weapons and strategic airpower, we can point to a period when Soviet forces consisted solely of purely defensive weapons. Thus, from 1945 to 1949, the Soviet Union relied solely on antiaircraft defenses and civil defense for protection against air attacks by the United States. (One might extend that period to 1954, since before that time the range of Soviet bombers limited them to one-way "suicide" missions.) Although the United States had the technological capacity to overwhelm Soviet defenses and in fact made the decision to acquire that power, the Soviet Union was then relying on a purely defensive strategic force whose weapons could be used only if its territory was under attack.

Since it is so easy to conceptualize and apply the distinction between offensive and defensive weapons and forces, why do analysts such as Huntington and Wohlstetter find these categorizations "mystifying, if not bizarre"? The answer is that such highly charged condemnations of the very effort to designate certain weapons as defensive are motivated by a normative argument regarding national security policy. The officials cited from the interwar period, just like Huntington and Wohlstetter (writing in 1987), all correctly assumed that the effort simply to *define* the concept of a purely defensive weapon or force structure was inspired by a *preference* for a system of mutual security based on defense dominance. What Churchill, Wohlstetter, and Huntington have in common is that, based on their assessments of their own particular technological and political environment, they concluded that it would be futile or dangerous for their nations to endorse such a policy.

This book is not concerned with the utility of defense emphasis in the myriad historical and current circumstances in which nations have struggled to discover the best path toward safety against external threats. It is concerned instead with whether the nuclear superpowers have a common interest in redesigning one critical component of their military capabilities—their strategic forces —toward a mutual emphasis on defense.

Nevertheless, since the authors cited above denounce such an approach without qualifications based on particular circumstances, it is worth inquiring into the general conditions in which nations might wish to emphasize defense. Two basic factors must be considered. The first concerns the intentions of potential adversaries, the second the technological balance between offense and defense. As we will see, many ostensibly technological arguments against defense emphasis (including the claim that weapons characteristics preclude such distinctions) are inextricably linked to political assumptions about the behavior of states in the international system.

Beliefs about the Intentions of Adversaries

Conflicting preferences for particular types of military forces can be traced to two fundamentally opposed perspectives on international relations. The first holds that one must assume that a potential adversary in fact harbors aggressive intentions. This claim is usually supported by reference to specific statements, actions, or military preparations made by the other side. Such claims, however, are often (either explicitly or implicitly) based on the more general conviction that one must always assume such aggressive intentions, either because the intentions of other states are inherently indiscernible, because momentarily peaceful intentions are always subject to change, or because states with the power to expand will always be tempted to do so.

If one cannot exclude the prospect of military aggression, it follows that security policy must be based, if possible, on pursuing an ability both to defend one's territory and to achieve victory in war. Given these assumptions and objectives, a state may nevertheless rationally wish to pursue a defense-dominant force posture. This will be the case, however, only if military technology clearly favors the defense—a condition that was not met in Europe before World War II and is clearly not met in the current technological environment of the nuclear superpowers.

The second perspective on international relations assumes not only that a potential adversary may be content with the status quo, but that in the right circumstances the peaceful intentions of other states can reliably be inferred from the design of their military forces. This viewpoint is linked to the concept of the "security dilemma," which assumes that an apparently threatening military force may be the inadvertent by-product of a state's efforts to provide for its security rather than a signal of an aspiration to attack others.

If one subscribes to the second theory, the question arises whether states can find a means to defend themselves without simultaneously menacing others. As Jervis notes: "If all states support the status quo, an obvious arms control agreement is a ban on weapons that are useful for attacking."[13] Should such a distinction between offensive and defensive weapons not be even conceptually possible, then it follows that all such arms control efforts are doomed from the outset. Hence, one polemical tactic for those who rule out ever trusting the adversary is to attack the very idea of distinguishing offense from defense.

That an offense-defense distinction is possible does not, of course, ensure that states will attain an agreement to emphasize defenses bilaterally. Jervis, for example, has pointed out the dangers of relying on such an arrangement when offensive weapons have a technological advantage over the defense.[14] (Later I will argue that states may be able to circumvent this constraint.) Yet regardless of such obstacles to reaching an MDE arms control agreement, it is clear that those who believe an adversary might bind itself to the status quo will assess weapons with the hope of identifying and limiting those suitable for aggression rather than with the object of unilaterally maximizing their overall military strength.

Jervis has used the terms "deterrence theory" and "spiral theory" to depict and contrast the two opposed approaches described above.[15] These widely used labels can cause confusion, however. For one

13. Ibid., p. 201.

14. Ibid., pp. 186–99, 211–14.

15. Robert Jervis, *Perception and Misperception in International Politics* (Princeton: Princeton University Press, 1976), pp. 58–116.

thing, a policy of deterrence—in the general sense of seeking enough military strength to dissuade a potential aggressor—is not unique to either of the two perspectives on national security but will be pursued by all potential adversaries in an anarchic international system. Thus, even two states that agree to emphasize defensive weapons would do so only out of a belief that their defense is sufficient to deter aggression. The crucial difference between "deterrence" theorists and "spiral" theorists is that the latter will want to explore whether a policy adequate to deter might also *reassure* the other side that their intentions are peaceful.[16]

Using the term "deterrence" to designate a general approach to foreign relations can be particularly confusing in the case of nuclear policy. Many subscribers to a "spiral" interpretation of the U.S.-Soviet nuclear arms competition have hoped to resolve the security dilemma by promoting bilateral strategic force postures based *solely* on a capacity for mutual deterrence. By contrast, those who have applied a "deterrence" model to U.S. nuclear policy (those who assumed that the Soviets actively contemplated military aggression against the United States or its chief allies) commonly argued that such a "deterrence-only" policy was inadequate and must be supplemented by the power to wage and win a nuclear war.

In the following analysis, while exploring the same theoretical vantage points outlined by Jervis, I will consequently use different terms for the two approaches—terms based on the different policy preferences the two perspectives imply. Adherents of the first theory, because they see aggression as a constant threat, are drawn toward a policy based on unilateral pursuit of a military (war-fighting) strategy. Adherents of the second theory, by contrast, endorse the exploration of an arms control alternative to such unilateral efforts. The key distinction, then, is between the defense policy objectives of strategists (or "war-fighters") and those of "arms controllers." Herman Kahn outlined the distinction this way:

> Many scholars of military affairs have argued that arms control and military strategy are basically the same. One can certainly define the two to make this true, but it is more useful to distinguish rather sharply between them, even more sharply in theory then would be desirable in practice. A "strategist" seeks unilateral advantage for his

16. Thus, Michael MccGwire describes the role of "mutual reassurance" in Western arms control theory in terms of "deterrence theory and its reassurance corollary." "Deterrence: The Problem—Not the Solution," *SAIS Review* 5 (Summer–Fall 1985): 107.

> country, side, or cause. An "arms controller" seeks increased security and diminished risks and costs for all concerned. A strategist is basically competitive in his outlook; he emphasizes the "zero-sum" aspects of the situtation, i.e., his side's gains are the other side's losses. An arms controller is basically non-competitive, looking instead at mutual and shared interests.[17]

When Draper claims that labeling a weapons system defensive is a "travesty of military principles and practice," he clearly assumes the primacy of strategy over arms control. After all, the optimal unilateral advantage that strategists seek is the ability to achieve military victory over potential enemies, and they will look for the mixture of weapons that best serves the dual war-fighting requirement of protecting one's own territory and forces and also overwhelming the adversary's defenses. Given the pursuit of both offensive and defensive capabilities, Draper is right that military principles do not require that we classify weapons exclusively as offensive or defensive.

Indeed, from the strategist's point of view, the preferred weapon may well be one that can serve both missions. Thus U.S. war-fighting plans issued in June 1952 relied primarily on bombers: "(1) To defend, by both offensive and defensive air operations, critical areas in the Western Hemisphere, with particular emphasis on defense against atomic attack. (2) To conduct a strategic air offensive to destroy the vital elements of Soviet war-making capacity."[18]

In the context of those two priority missions for the Air Force, any use of active air defenses could be called "defensive" only in a very narrow sense. Assuming the nation planned its strategy rationally, the extent to which air defenses were deployed in the United States would be governed by their estimated contribution to the overall war aims of national survival and the defeat of the Soviet Union. If air strikes against Soviet territory provided the most cost-effective means of limiting damage to the United States, then bombers would be preferred over antiaircraft defenses for fulfilling the strategic mission of "defense" as well as the offensive mission.

It happened (as chapter 4 will show) that U.S. strategic planning was not completely rational in 1952. At the time, various domestic

17. Herman Kahn, *Thinking about the Unthinkable in the 1980s* (New York: Simon and Schuster, 1984), p. 194.

18. "Summary Statement No. 1—the Military Program (Prepared by the Department of Defense)," May 10, 1952, in U.S. Department of State, *Foreign Relations of the United States, 1952–1954*, vol. 2, *National Security Affairs* (Washington, D.C.: U.S. Government Printing Office, 1984), pt. 1, p. 22 (hereafter cited as *FRUS*).

political factors had yielded a war-fighting doctrine that sought to preclude *any* role for homeland defense, even though the Soviets could be expected to achieve a growing ability to strike at targets in the United States. In challenging the prevailing view, one group of strategists (on the Policy Planning Staff) thus tried to argue that "cost-effective" preparations for war required a greater emphasis on continental defense:

> Para. 27 [of the National Security Council document under discussion] does not provide for an adequate civil defense program and indeed states the American people should "avoid devoting their substance to an unrealistic concentration upon purely defensive measures." However, in light of the probability that both the Soviet Union and the United States will develop atomic stockpiles of sufficient size to permit attacks of serious and possibly catastrophic proportions, it may well be that the side with the best air and civil defense systems will be the side with the largest net capability and that greater increases in net capability can be obtained at some point by additional investments in air and civil defenses than by additional investments in offensive power.[19]

Thus, from the perspective of military strategy, debates over "purely defensive measures" are framed in terms of the issue raised above: whether a diversion of resources toward purely defensive uses (in this case antiaircraft and civil defense) would provide a net increase in overall war-fighting ability.

For the United States in 1952 to have chosen to rely *exclusively* on active and passive defenses against nuclear attack would of course have been, as Draper claimed, "a travesty of military principles and practice." The only hope the United States would have had of ensuring national survival with such a force would have been a similar Soviet decision to refrain from exploiting the revolutionary offensive potential of atomic airpower. (In other words, both states would act as "arms controllers" rather than as "strategists.") We should note, however, the conditions under which a force posture emphasizing purely defensive weapons would *not* be a travesty but would represent the most rational military strategy available.

In his seminal article titled "Cooperation Under the Security Dilemma," Jervis identified two conditions that, if met, would tend to direct a nation's military strategy toward pure defense. "Two crucial variables are involved: whether defensive weapons and policies can be distinguished from offensive ones, and whether the defense . . .

19. "Paper Drafted by the Policy Planning Staff" (undated), in *FRUS*, p. 66.

has the advantage."[20] Defense will have the advantage whenever purely defensive weapons are cost-effective at the margin or, as Jervis put it, whenever a state has "to spend . . . less than one dollar on defensive forces to offset each dollar spent by the other side on forces that could be used for attack."[21]

If such purely defensive weapons exist at all at a given point in the evolution of military technology and if, further, they are decisively superior (in terms of power and cost) to offensive weapons, then "sound military principles and practice" would impel states to forgo offense and rely for their security on a purely defensive force posture. Kenneth Waltz has characterized such a situation: "To build defenses so patently strong that no one will try to destroy or overcome them would make international life perfectly tranquil. I call this the defensive ideal. . . . The message of the strategy is this: 'Although we cannot strike back at you, you will find our defenses so difficult to overcome that you will dash yourself to pieces against them.'"[22]

Could such a strategic environment ever exist in the context of nuclear weapons? In chapter 7 I examine recent claims that new technologies in strategic defense promise to fulfill both of Jervis's criteria: that they will be both purely defensive and cost-effective at the margin. Only two points need be stressed here. First, such an outcome is at least conceivable. That is, it cannot be excluded simply by invoking a universal claim that offense and defense are inherently indistinguishable. (Of course, for a strategically acting nation the emergence of such a purely defensive capability would be an inadvertent outcome of evolving military technology, since an ideally cost-effective weapon could simultaneously perform both offensive and defensive missions.)

Second, as long as the United States (or the Soviet Union, or both) is thinking strategically, the attainment of such a defensive ideal would be endlessly provisional; that is, it would hold only as long as purely defensive capabilities remained demonstrably cost-effective at the margin. In other words, the durability of the defensive ideal would be determined by how much success strategists attained in devising an affordable means of overcoming the adversary's defense. Indeed, the strategic ideal is to combine an impregnable de-

20. Jervis (n. 2), pp. 186–87.

21. Ibid., p. 188.

22. Kenneth N. Waltz, "Toward Nuclear Peace," in *The Use of Force: International Politics and Foreign Policy*, 2d ed., ed. Robert A. Art and Kenneth N. Waltz (Lanham, Md.: University Press of America, 1982), p. 574.

fense with an unstoppable offense; an effective defense by the adversary would be a highly undesirable obstacle to a war-fighting strategy, since offensive technological innovations by the enemy could lead to one's defeat in war.

An inherent preference for defense over offense, then, is rejected by strategists but embraced by arms controllers. As a further look at the writings of Churchill, Huntington, and Wohlstetter will show, it is clearly due to their embrace of strategy (and rejection of arms control) that they deny the very possibility of distinguishing offensive from defensive weapons.

Offense and Defense: Is the Distinction Dangerous?

As I have already noted, Churchill ostensibly dismissed efforts to distinguish offense from defense because he found the distinction incoherent. Wohlstetter points out, however, that Churchill had a second reason for opposing such efforts: "Churchill challenged not only the clarity and applicability of the distinction between offense and defense to actual weapons but the political assumption implicit in the British negotiating stance: that the Third Reich . . . was no more likely [than the French Third Republic] to start a war to change the status quo."[23] In other words, Churchill was opposing the *motive* for trying to distinguish offense from defense: the pursuit of an arms control agreement between Germany and its potential adversaries. He took this position because he perceived (correctly) that Germany would eventually try to alter the status quo in Europe. Churchill concluded: "I would say to those who would like to see Germany and France on an equal footing in armaments: 'Do you wish for war?' "[24]

Which belief best explains Churchill's argument that the 1932–33 Geneva Disarmament Conference was futile: his rejection of the arms controllers' belief that military power could be categorized as offensive or defensive, or his conviction that Germany would reject or evade any arms control agreement that left it with a purely defensive capability? Although both beliefs could explain Churchill's opposition to an arms control approach to security, it is worth noting that during the interwar years France clearly adopted a defense-

23. Wohlstetter (n. 4), p. 4.
24. Ibid., p. 5.

dominant posture. Given aggressive German intentions and military preparations, this policy ultimately proved doubly disastrous. First, the decision to defend the French homeland with a defense-dominant force assumed a defensive technological advantage, when in reality German exploitation of the offensive potential of tanks and airpower had made such a policy strategically questionable. Moreover, the absence of an offensive capability left France wholly unable to honor its commitment to the defense of its allies, leading to military paralysis when Poland was invaded.

A. J. P. Taylor described the folly of France's emphasis on defense:

> France had already taken the decisive step which made action against Germany impossible. . . . France needed an active, independent and mobile army, always ready to penetrate into enemy territory. France never possessed such an army. . . . The soldiers were given purely defensive training and equipment. The Maginot line provided the eastern frontier with the most gigantic system of fortifications ever known. The divorce between French policy and French strategy was complete.[25]

Some historians (including Taylor) have maintained that the Maginot Line was impregnable and that France's inability to withstand the German attack was due only to its failure to complete the line across the Belgian frontier.[26] Nevertheless, that Germany was committed to an offensive strategy clearly made such a purely defensive stance unwise. As Bernard Brodie pointed out, "Tanks . . . spearheaded the fateful German thrust through the Ardennes in 1940, but if the French had disposed of a properly concentrated armor reserve, it would have provided the best means for their cutting off the penetration and turning into a disaster for the Germans what became instead an overwhelming victory."[27]

It is evident that in those particular circumstances tanks (a weapon with obvious offensive uses) would have been necessary for France to mount an effective defense. Yet as Jervis noted, "France would not have needed these weapons if Germany had not acquired them."[28] Put another way, a verifiable arms control regime that banned the production of tanks would have made France's purely

25. A. J. P. Taylor, *The Origins of the Second World War*, 2d ed. (New York: Fawcett Premier, 1961), p. 62.

26. Ibid., p. 113.

27. Quoted in Jervis (n. 2), p. 202.

28. Ibid., p. 205.

defensive posture entirely sufficient to defend its territory against invasion; it was inadequate only because Germany had rejected a policy of arms control in favor of an offensive military strategy.

Was such a regime technically precluded, as Wohlstetter claimed, because of an unavoidable "welter of ambiguities and confusion on the subject of such qualitative disarmament"? Here is the viewpoint expressed in 1960 by British strategist B. H. Liddell Hart:

> If tanks and bomber-aircraft had been universally abolished in 1932 as was then proposed—and nearly agreed—and a system of international inspection established as a check on their revival, there could have been no successful Blitzkrieg in 1939–40. For Hitler owed his initial victories to those particular defence-breaking weapons. Numbers of troops counted for little in comparison. . . .
>
> If the decisive weapons had once been banned, it would have been very difficult for Hitler to have developed them in secret to an adequate pitch for effectiveness—even without the check of an international inspectorate. For tanks and bombers largely depend for their effectiveness on their crews having operational practice in exercises—and such practice could hardly have been hidden.[29]

If there was confusion over the meaning of offense and defense at the 1932–33 Geneva Disarmament Conference, the source clearly lay in efforts (such as Churchill's) to prevent its success. Thus British and French military experts helped derail agreements either to ban tanks or to limit their numbers by insisting that tanks should be regarded as offensive or defensive depending on their weight (with the maximum tonnage for "defensive" tanks happening to correspond to the largest tanks each then possessed).[30] In effect, efforts by "strategists" in 1932 to obscure a distinction that was entirely clear to supporters of arms control were invoked by strategists in the 1980s to demonstrate the inherent futility of the offense-defense distinction.

Clearly, the only coherent aspect of Churchill's double assault on the validity of the offense-defense distinction *and* the value of arms control agreements with Germany was his accurate perception that Germany was not interested in forgoing offensive power. That belief was confirmed when Germany, nine months after Hitler took power, withdrew from the Disarmament Conference. (Even before Hitler, the Germans had pointed to British and French resistance to

29. B. H. Liddell Hart, *Deterrent or Defense* (New York: Praeger, 1960), p. 250.
30. Noel-Baker (n. 1), p. 78.

the proposed agreements as evidence of an effort to deny Germany the right to equality in armaments. British disarmament advocate Philip Noel-Baker, who was a participant at the conference, later argued that this perception strengthened the domestic influence of German militarists and paved the way for Hitler's rise to power.)[31]

In Wohlstetter's case it is even more apparent that denying the offense-defense distinction is merely a rhetorical effort to bolster his case against an arms control approach. Here, no sooner has he claimed that the distinction is inapplicable in practice than he offers an excellent concrete example of a contemporary defense-dominant military force structure:

> Since World War II, political elites among the democracies have often thought about reassuring potential adversaries . . . by arguing that their military forces are purely defensive or by proposing programs for making them purely defensive and incapable of launching an attack. The Japanese, very early on, in Article IX of their Constitution, formally gave up their right to use any military force. As reality impinged, they came to interpret it as saying that they could have military force to repel attack on Japan but not military force that they could use to attack others. . . . For many years they severely limited the range of their fighters to make clear that they could not attack the Asian mainland, and they even constrained navigation and guidance to make sure the fighters could not find targets even if they could reach them.[32]

Wohlstetter (writing in 1987) makes it clear that he is against this policy and still more adamantly opposed to similar proposals for NATO. Referring to "less sober factions in NATO countries," Wohlstetter notes: "Some would, like the Japanese, try to get rid of aircraft capable of bombarding the other side. . . . Tanks would have to go too, since they could be used offensively as well as defensively."[33] Wohlstetter finds it easy to imagine and describe purely defensive military capabilities. He opposes these policies because he regards them as dangerous unilateral arms control initiatives: "Democratic leaders and their publics, rather more than the dictators with whom they negotiate, tend to worry about fairness . . . and about their own power exceeding that of potential adversaries."[34]

Thus purely defensive forces are inappropriate because the adversary may well be contemplating aggression. Nowhere does Wohl-

31. Ibid., pp. 120–34.
32. Wohlstetter (n. 4), p. 5.
33. Ibid., p. 6.
34. Ibid., p. 5.

stetter consider the possibility of a corresponding unilateral decision (or arms control agreement) in which the Soviets similarly choose to emphasize defense. Strategists like Wohlstetter plausibly argued that NATO would be more secure if it increased its tank production to match Soviet deployments. Such strategic reasoning, however, left out the possibility that NATO's security might be maximized if both NATO and the Soviet Union structured their forces to ensure that neither side's defenses could be penetrated. As long as one assumes the enduring primacy of strategy over arms control, the choice of mutual defense emphasis remains beyond consideration. It follows that preferring defense over offense may well invite aggression. Trying to categorize weapons and capabilities as offensive or defensive, then, reflects a dangerous tendency to indulge in an unreciprocated policy of "reassuring" potential aggressors.

For Huntington no less than Wohlstetter, it is clear that the offense-defense distinction is "mystifying" only because of its association with a quixotic impulse to explore an arms control approach to national security. To illustrate, we need to look further at Huntington's views. Huntington explores the concepts of offense and defense in terms of four aspects of national security policy: weapons (and weapons technology); military capability; military strategy; and political goals. As I noted earlier, he maintains that "weapons may be usefully differentiated in a variety of ways, but the offense/defense distinction is not one of them." He asserts, by contrast, that "useful distinctions can . . . be drawn between offensive and defensive policy goals, strategies and capabilities."[35]

In terms of capability, however, this statement is highly qualified. To identify the misleading nature of his qualifications, let me cite his depiction of the nature of overall military capability:

> The offense/defense distinction is somewhat more useful when it comes to talking about military capabilities. Here the reference is to the overall size, organization, training, equipment, logistic support, and leadership of a military force. Depending upon how these various elements are combined, some military forces will be better prepared to fight offensive actions, while others will be better prepared to fight defensive actions. A modern army short on gasoline but well supplied with guns and shells is likely to be more effective at defense than offense. The capabilities of an air force that has many well-trained and well-equipped bomber squadrons and no interceptor squadrons will be just the reverse. Even with respect to general force capabilities, how-

35. Huntington (n. 5), p. 37.

> ever, one must be cautious about jumping to conclusions. . . . Some forms of military capability may be more useful for offensive strategies and other forms for defensive ones, but few if any military capabilities are either exclusively offensive or exclusively defensive.[36]

First, Huntington's definition of capability excludes the contribution of particular types of weapons. ("Equipment" seems at best an unnecessarily indirect reference to missiles, bombers, tanks, or antiballistic missile systems.) That omission allows him to suggest (presumably as a representative example) that the switch from a defensive to an offensive capability may be achieved merely by providing more gasoline.

His alternative example of bombers and interceptors, however, shows the inadequacy of his conception of capability. Bombers, of course, can be used "defensively," for example, to prevent an attack by destroying enemy airfields or troop concentrations, further appearing to validate Huntington's implication that offensive and defensive capabilities are inherently ambiguous. In fact, including actual weapons in his description immediately suggests the obvious possibility of an unambiguously defensive capability. One need only reverse Huntington's example of relative offensive effectiveness to note that the capabilities of an air force that has *no* bombers and *only* interceptor squadrons will be useful *only* for defense. As I noted earlier, in terms of strategic bombing, this was once precisely the nature of the Soviet capability vis-à-vis the United States.

In Huntington's subsequent discussion, it becomes clear that such a purely defensive posture should be regarded as conceptually nonexistent only because it is strategically unwise. Thus:

> Effective deterrence in an era of nuclear parity requires an across-the-board combination of offensive and defensive strategy and capability. Offensive capabilities must, however, be the dominant element in this mixture to provide maximum deterrence. A purely defensive strategy and posture in Europe will not provide the same deterrence as one that includes offensive strategy and capability. An aggressor can always find ways of overcoming or avoiding defenses.[37]

Obviously, Huntington's approach to offense and defense assumes the primacy of strategy over arms control. Since the other side is simply assumed to be an aggressor, reliance on a purely de-

36. Ibid., p. 36.
37. Ibid., p. 42.

fensive force is risky, since there is always the danger that one's defense will be overwhelmed. If we assume, alternatively, that adversaries would be willing to surrender a potential for aggression in return for security against attack, we are drawn to inquire whether they might find a way to avoid mounting threats against the other side's defenses.

Although the 1932–33 Geneva Disarmament Conference did not founder on an inability to distinguish offense from defense, its failure clearly contributed to subsequent beliefs that such a task was technically impossible. Even some arms controllers seemed to accept the intractability of the problem in the context of the conventional balance in Europe. Thus, referring to efforts in the mid-1980s by Western European analysts (on the political Left) to describe the features of a "nonprovocative defense,"[38] a 1987 study by Harvard's "Avoiding Nuclear War Project" offered the following judgment:

> Even if one could define a purely defensive military force with no capability to project itself into another country, those forces might still be used for purposes of aggression. There would be no stopping the Soviet Union from loading several divisions of border guards into Aeroflot aircraft and attempting to impose its will on a less powerful third country that had also agreed to field only border guards.[39]

By the end of the decade, one would be unlikely to encounter such apparent incomprehension regarding how states might design defense emphasis force structures. That legacy of past failure to apply the concept of mutual defense emphasis (MDE) began to break down in 1987, when Mikhail Gorbachev (speaking specifically about Europe) called for a "change in the entire pattern of armed forces with a view to imparting an exclusively defensive character to them."[40]

For a time it appeared that, as in the 1930s, strategists would suc-

38. For a presentation of these ideas, see Stanley Windass, "Essentials of Defensive Deterrence," in *Avoiding Nuclear War: Common Security as a Strategy for the Defence of the West*, ed. Stanley Windass (London: Brassey's Defence Publishers, 1985), pp. 43–62. For a critique of Western European conceptions of defense emphasis, see Stephen J. Flanagan, "Nonprovocative and Civilian-Based Defenses," in *Fateful Visions: Avoiding Nuclear Catastrophe* (Cambridge, Mass.: Ballinger, 1988), pp. 93–110.

39. Flanagan (n. 38), p. 108.

40. Mikhail Gorbachev, *Perestroika: New Thinking for Our Country and the World* (New York: Harper and Row, 1987), p. 203. For an article that anticipated the change in Soviet doctrine by arguing that Soviet interests should favor a shift to a defensive force posture in Europe, see Richard Ned Lebow, "The Soviet Offensive in Europe: The Schlieffen Plan Revisited?" *International Security* 9 (Spring 1985): 44–78.

ceed in "demonstrating" that such arms control visions were conceptually incoherent. Thus Soviet general V. G. Kulikov (then commander of the Warsaw Pact) explained Gorbachev's concept as follows: "We do realize, however, that it is impossible to defeat an enemy and destroy an aggressor through defensive actions alone. We are working out such active forms of action as offensive action, counterstrikes, and other kinds of combat action, which are in the context of the new defense doctrine."[41] Kulikov's vision of the meaning of "purely defensive" was only a mirror image of a Western strategist's application of the concept to NATO: "There is no reason why the defensive character of NATO as a *political* alliance cannot coexist with a counteroffensive approach to planning for defensive warfare" (emphasis in original).[42]

Had both sides continued to insist on regarding their "counteroffensive" forces as defensive (while predictably defining corresponding forces on the other side as unambiguously offensive), subsequent conventional arms control negotiations would have been doomed. But with discussions—unlike those of the 1930s—propelled by a genuine effort to flesh out the MDE concept, negotiators this time did not find themselves hopelessly "bogged down in a welter of ambiguities and confusion."

Thus, in his April 1988 meeting with Soviet defense minister Dmitri Yazov, U.S. defense secretary Frank Carlucci had no trouble listing the types of obviously offense-capable forces that would have to be reduced: tanks, armored vehicles, airborne and air-mobile forces, military matériel deployed in forward areas, extensive bridge-building equipment, and so forth.[43] In December 1988 Gorbachev's stated commitment to a "clearly defensive defense" was backed up by his announcement of a unilateral withdrawal of half a million troops and the disbanding of ten thousand tanks.[44] After

41. Cited in Gloria Duffy and Jennifer Lee, "The Soviet Debate on Reasonable Sufficiency," *Arms Control Today* 18 (October 1988): 19–24. In light of such inconsistent Soviet statements, and given the passage of a year before the Soviets began to implement Gorbachev's declaratory doctrine, there was debate in the West over the meaning of the Soviet endorsement of a "nonprovocative defense." For the spectrum of Western interpretations, see the articles by Raymond L. Garthoff, Andrew C. Goldberg, Jean Quantras, Michael MccGwire, and Cynthia Roberts in the section "Gorbachev and Soviet Military Power," *Washington Quarterly* 11 (Summer 1988). See also *New York Times*, March 7, 1988, p. A1.

42. Benjamin S. Lambeth, "Theater Forces," in *American Defense Annual, 1987–1988*, ed. Joseph Kruzel (Lexington, Mass.: Lexington Books, 1987), p. 110.

43. Frank C. Carlucci, "Is Moscow Really Tilting to Defense?" *New York Times*, May 6, 1985, p. A15.

44. *New York Times*, December 8, 1988, p. A1.

nearly two years of subsequent negotiations, NATO and the Warsaw Pact institutionalized the dismantling of the Soviet offensive threat with a Treaty on Conventional Armed Forces in Europe (CFE). According to NATO experts, implementing the treaty would ensure a warning period of more than two years before the Soviets could again acquire the ability to threaten Western Europe with conventional forces.[45]

One cannot regard those developments as an ultimate judgment on the competing worldviews of strategists and arms controllers. After all, arms control progress was more consequence than cause of the reduced Soviet threat to Europe. Strategists could even argue plausibly that NATO's tentative moves toward an offensive capability in the 1980s[46] (along with the U.S. readoption of a nuclear war-fighting doctrine) had helped pressure the Soviets into changing course. Certainly the success of arms control cannot be judged in isolation from the broader context of revolutionary Soviet internal change and the political liberation of Eastern Europe.

Nevertheless, there is no reason to assume that those far-reaching political events were essential for the achievement of a stable conventional arms control regime. The framework for productive negotiations (asymmetrical reductions in favor of the West, the dismantling of tanks above allowed ceilings, on-site verification, etc.) was already established at the onset of the CFE talks in March 1989. The only clearly necessary political precondition for success was recognition that current force postures created a security dilemma that needed to be resolved. The additional requirement for doing so was to draw on a simple guiding concept. That concept, based on distinguishing offensive from defensive weapons and forces, had seemed literally incomprehensible to strategists as late as 1987. Indeed, strategists—by insisting on the defensive nature of "counteroffensive" capabilities—initially tried to subvert the establishment and implementation of MDE in Europe.

In the mid-1980s, when military policy in Europe was still dominated by strategic thinking, some arms controllers had argued (to little effect) that new technological developments, notably in preci-

45. *New York Times*, November 18, 1990, p. 12.

46. The "counteroffensive" concepts promoted by NATO strategists in the 1980s were the AirLand Battle and Follow-on Forces Attack—air and land attacks on enemy territory in the event of war. For a discussion endorsing these ideas, see Lambeth (n. 42).

sion-guided munitions, were shifting the advantage to the defense.[47] Yet once a political decision had been made to embrace arms control, the irrelevance of such strategically based appeals to defense's relative cost-effectiveness became manifest. In the context of arms control, it turned out that the most critical "weapons" for providing a defensive advantage consisted of such devices as eight-ton iron balls for crushing tanks and giant vises for squashing them.[48]

The case for defensive cost-effectiveness had also been central to calls in the 1980s for a change in U.S. strategic nuclear policy. Here it was strategists who insisted on an impending technological advantage for the defense and arms controllers who countered that the offensive advantage was so great as to preclude a shift toward defense emphasis.

Although the arms controllers' assessment proved sufficiently persuasive to forestall any shift in nuclear policy, two aspects of their argument required further explanation. First, it was not obvious why arms control supporters were so preoccupied with the cost-effectiveness of competing weapons systems. After all, the arms control perspective holds that cooperating states should subordinate such considerations to the goal of restructuring their forces toward an "exclusively defensive character." Second, strategic offensive weapons were deemed preferable not only for their relative cost-effectiveness, but precisely because they were to be regarded as "defensive." In effect, nuclear arms control experts believed they had reason to reverse the definitions of "offense" and "defense" that they applied to conventional forces.

Despite that relabeling of weapons, the debate over nuclear policy retained one fundamental link to the traditional clash between "strategists" and "arms controllers." Any arms control solution to national security must require potential adversaries to structure their forces in an unambiguously defensive posture, "defensive" here being used in the general sense that both sides can be confident that they are not threatened with attack. Thus the only debate among

47. Freeman Dyson, for example (n. 8), pp. 49–52, made the case for achieving MDE in Europe based on the cost-effectiveness of precision-guided munitions over tanks. That argument was also one component of the case made for a policy of "no first use" in McGeorge Bundy, George F. Kennan, Robert S. McNamara, and Gerard Smith, "Nuclear Weapons and the Atlantic Alliance," *Foreign Affairs* 60 (Spring 1982): 767. Stephen Flanagan reasonably pointed out that "all of these concepts are premised on the realization of some immature conventional weapons technologies and on the unverifiable assumption that these emerging technologies are shifting combat advantage to the defense." Flanagan (n. 38), p. 106.

48. *New York Times*, November 18, 1990, p. 12.

those who reject strategy in favor of arms control concerns which type of bilateral force postures can best accomplish the objective of assuring both sides of their safety.

We know in retrospect that once the Nazis took power in Germany in January 1933 the only sound policy for the Western democracies would have been to follow Churchill's advice and prepare for war. Having failed to prepare adequately, they came close to total defeat at the hands of perhaps the most brutal regime in history. In the world that emerged from World War II, the United States was determined not to repeat that disastrous policy. Once it was generally perceived (whether accurately or not) that the Soviet Union was bent on aggression, any thoughts of an arms control approach to national security yielded to a deterrent strategy based on the ability to achieve victory in war.

Unfortunately, the lessons of the 1930s provided no guidance for dealing with the revolutionary change that had taken place in military technology: nuclear weapons in the hands of both major adversaries. Thus, instead of the U.S. war-fighting strategy's producing a preponderance of usable power, it yielded a "balance of terror" in which any major violation of the status quo could rapidly annihilate all the parties to the conflict. At no time in history had such an apparently compelling case for arms control ever appeared. Unlike the 1930s, the intentions of the potential aggressor now seemed irrelevant. The willingness of both sides to accept the status quo could be deduced from the fact that no remotely rational leader could now contemplate challenging the vital interests of the other side. Thus, by the mid-1960s, U.S. policymakers, without any fundamental reappraisal of the motives of the Soviet Union, began to explore the possibility of formalizing the military stalemate by an arms control agreement.

Two basic problems, however, stood in the way of such an approach. First, many strategists and their political supporters remained unconvinced that any particular change in technology could ever obviate the need to be able to prevail in a future war. Second, if strategy was to be abandoned in favor of an arms control regime, the question still remained of what types of military forces both sides would be allowed to deploy.

The answer that U.S. arms control experts provided would have profoundly shocked those who had supported the efforts of the 1932–33 Geneva Disarmament Conference. At that time, even the most pessimistic judgment about the offense-defense technological balance—a belief that "the bomber will always get through"—had led former British prime minister Stanley Baldwin to conclude that "all Disarmament hangs on the Air." Indeed, noting the "incalculable and inconceivable" future "potentialities" of air bombardment, Baldwin expressed the conviction that "on the solution of this question hangs . . . our civilization."[49]

In the third decade of the nuclear age, the earlier view that qualitative disarmament should limit offenses and favor defenses had now been completely reversed. Even as Baldwin's prophecy regarding offensive airpower had been realized (beyond any extent he could have predicted), the nuclear arms controllers of the 1960s were now maintaining that the very essence of arms control was to freeze in place the awesome offensive potential created by twenty years of preparing for war, and to do so by banning *defensive* weapons.

Whether that reversal of the meaning of qualitative disarmament represented the only available approach to the nuclear danger is the central question of this book. The next chapter looks at the controversy surrounding the effort to implement that new theory of arms control, which has acquired the label "mutual assured destruction."

49. Quoted in Noel-Baker (n. 1), pp. 119–20.

[2]

The Nuclear Policy Stalemate and the Search for Alternatives (1972–1991)

In the latter half of the 1960s, seeking to combine a stable deterrent balance with "a reasonably riskless agreement that would halt the arms race,"[1] Secretary of Defense Robert McNamara attempted to orchestrate a political consensus (extending to both superpowers) that seemingly stood conventional thinking on its head. "Security depends upon assuming a worst plausible case, and having the ability to cope with it," he wrote in 1967. "In that eventuality we must be able to absorb the total weight of nuclear attack on our country . . . and still be capable of damaging the aggressor to the point that his society would be simply no longer viable in twentieth-century terms. That is what deterrence of nuclear aggression means."[2] John Newhouse, who supported the doctrine while recognizing its brutal implications, described the logic of mutual assured destruction—MAD—as follows: "Offense is defense, defense is offense. Killing people is good, killing weapons is bad."[3]

The world of total offense dominance advocated by McNamara challenged traditional thinking in three ways. First, its reliance on threats of annihilating civilian populations seemed to defy basic standards of international law and morality. Second, it renounced what had hitherto been a universal goal of military strategy: the wartime defense of one's homeland. Finally, in seeking to prevent war

1. Robert S. McNamara, *The Essence of Security* (New York: Harper and Row, 1968), pp. 61–62.

2. Ibid., p. 53.

3. John Newhouse, *Cold Dawn: The Story of SALT* (New York: Holt, Rinehart, and Winston, 1973), p. 176.

by maximizing its destructive consequences, it represented a radical alternative to previous theories of arms control and disarmament. Advocates of nuclear arms control had argued that efforts to prevent war and limit its destructiveness not only were compatible but were equally vital goals.

Advocates of MAD, to justify the rejection of traditional views of arms control, military strategy, and morality, contended that realism in the nuclear age compelled an acceptance of threats of mass annihilation. Believing that all safe paths from the balance of terror were sealed off, they condemned the "private state of moral rectitude"[4] of those who promoted "solutions" to the enduring realities of the nuclear era. For a time, that appeal to realism seemed largely vindicated. The ABM Treaty of 1972 (which precluded meaningful population defenses) seemed to demonstrate superpower convergence around MAD and, in the wake of SALT (Strategic Arms Limitations Talks) I and the emergent superpower détente, it appeared that a jointly managed balance of terror conferred benefits that were well worth preserving.

That optimism was severely challenged by subsequent events. First, the ban on ABMs did not, as had been hoped, herald the end of the offensive arms competition. Second, the apparent acceptance of "mutual vulnerability" was belied in that the new offensive weapons on both sides were clearly of the counterforce "damage limitation" variety. Finally, MAD's status as a long-term means of coping with the nuclear threat was increasingly challenged by a broad-based coalition of political activists in Western Europe and the United States. The reemergence and growth of the antinuclear movement in the early 1980s (long tranquilized by the perception that the superpowers were making meaningful progress in arms control) offered a clear reminder that "terror" can be more than a nominal characterization of the nuclear balance.

Those related developments—MAD's failure to contain the search for damage limitation, to provide a politically viable framework for arms control, or to assure the public that it was safe from nuclear war—suggested a need to reassess the doctrine's basic assumptions.

4. Hedley Bull, "Future Conditions of Strategic Deterrence," in *The Future of Strategic Deterrence, Part I,* Adelphi Paper no. 160 (London: International Institute for Strategic Studies, 1980), p. 16. For more extensive defenses of the morality of mutual assured destruction, see Michael Walzer, *Just and Unjust Wars* (New York: Basic Books, 1977), pp. 269–83, and Arthur Hockaday, "In Defense of Deterrence," in *Ethics and Nuclear Deterrence,* ed. Geoffrey Goodwin (New York: St. Martin's Press, 1982), pp. 68–93.

In addition, other events cast doubt on the durability of any arms control framework (the Soviet invasion of Afghanistan and the election of a U.S. president with a history of animosity toward arms control). This set the stage for a renewed interest in arguments that predated the effort to "institutionalize" the balance of terror, and it increased the appeal of two radically divergent perspectives on nuclear weapons policy.

One approach held that a determined U.S. strategic arms acquisition program (including the development and deployment of a strategic defense of the United States) could substantially reduce the Soviet Union's capacity to inflict damage and could provide a chance to prevail in a nuclear war. The other approach maintained that no conceivable benefits from any policy of nuclear deterrence could compensate for the horrifying results should the policy fail; an effort must therefore be made to revive the objective of complete nuclear disarmament. Since these appeals to reject mutual vulnerability have periodically attracted considerable support, let us consider why both approaches are unsound in principle and why neither has been able to provide durable policy guidance.

MAD was the basis for U.S. declaratory policy from 1967 (when McNamara first explicitly outlined the benefits of bilateral "assured destruction only" force postures)[5] until 1981. During that period, while a succession of "flexible response" doctrines clearly deviated from a pure deterrence-only posture, U.S. policymakers consistently invoked MAD as the ultimate deterrent. Critics could rightly point to the naïveté of McNamara's original effort to educate both the Soviets and the U.S. defense establishment on the virtues of maintaining finite deterrent forces and to MAD's failure to achieve its limited aim of containing the arms race. Nevertheless, those who endorsed a renewed U.S. bid for the ability to prevail in a nuclear war might have reflected on the equally quixotic unilateral efforts at damage limitation that preoccupied policymakers (including McNamara) before the U.S. acceptance of nuclear parity.

Since the early years of the nuclear age, counterforce damage limitation had proved to be the mirage of nuclear strategy: the prospect invariably receded at least as fast as it could be approached. Two circumstances all but guaranteed that outcome. First, the essential rule of strategic deterrence—the need to avoid vulnerability to a dis-

5. McNamara publicly outlined the logic of MAD in a speech he gave in San Francisco on September 18, 1967 ("The Dynamics of Nuclear Strategy," *Department of State Bulletin*, October 9, 1967, pp. 443–51). With minor changes, that presentation is reprinted as the chapter "Mutual Deterrence" in *The Essence of Security* (n. 1), pp. 51–67.

arming first strike—was well understood by both superpowers. Second, both sides, for more than three decades, had the will, the resources, and the technical expertise to apply the rule.

From the beginning of the missile age until the development of ABM and MIRV (multiple independently targeted reentry vehicle) technologies, the superpowers' efforts to apply counterforce strategies virtually dictated a mutually counterproductive outcome. As both sides' strategic arsenals increased (to keep up with the growing number of targets), the probable number of weapons that would survive an attack by either side could only increase. That meant, in essence, an evergrowing ability to inflict retaliatory damage on the adversary's society (which was not the original priority objective) and an ever lower capacity to limit damage to one's own territory.[6]

War-fighting strategists saw the prospect of ABM territorial defense as the missing link in a successful damage-limitation strategy. But the more likely outcome of ABM deployments (as MAD advocates in the 1960s pointed out) would be simply to raise the threshold of forces required to ensure retaliation, thereby guaranteeing an open-ended arms race in both offensive and defensive weapons. ABMs might also, for the first time in the missile age, make a first strike theoretically advantageous, since defenses could more easily cope with a retaliatory force that had already been reduced by a counterforce attack.

Thus, if counterforce strategies alone were simply futile, counterforce plus active defenses could present the added danger of making it appear preferable to strike first. (MIRV compounded this danger by providing a favorable "exchange ratio" to the side that strikes first at the other's land-based forces.) This was the prospect McNamara reasonably wished to avoid, and his eventually successful effort to prevent substantive ABM deployments by either side put a first-strike capability hopelessly out of reach.

It was largely the precluding of a rational incentive to resort to strategic war that inspired the hostility of war-fighters toward restrictions on population defense. "If American nuclear power is to support U.S. foreign policy objectives," two prominent victory theorists observed in 1980, "the United States must possess the ability to

6. For a more detailed mathematical illustration of the probable futility of counterforce damage limitation (before MIRV), see Glenn H. Snyder, *Deterrence and Defense* (Princeton: Princeton University Press, 1961), pp. 97–109. For an illuminating history of the actual failure of the prolonged U.S. effort to attain a first-strike capability, see David Alan Rosenberg, "The Origins of Overkill," *International Security* 7 (Spring 1983): 4–69.

wage nuclear war rationally." Extended nuclear deterrence means, after all, an apparent willingness to initiate nuclear war, a war that "is likely to be waged to coerce the Soviet Union to give up some recent gain."[7]

Those authors were right. Unless one can reliably disarm a nuclear superpower, it is not rational to launch a nuclear attack. What victory theorists never convincingly showed is why the Soviets should tolerate the prospect of being strategically disarmed. On this point, something could be learned from the highly ambivalent attitude of U.S. war-fighters toward what they perceived as an operant Soviet victory doctrine. On one hand, they regarded the Soviet strategy (combining counterforce with strong commitments to air and civil defense and to research in ABM technologies) as dictated by common sense worthy of emulation. Alternatively, they viewed this approach as evidence of aggressive Soviet intentions toward the West, to be resisted with the full weight of U.S. economic and technological resources. Clearly, if their strategy was meant to amount to more than a doctrine of mutual provocation, it required the premise that their side could "win" an offense-defense race—the same belief, they would acknowledge, that motivated their doctrinal counterparts in the Soviet Union.[8]

Yet just as the breakdown of SALT (and détente) generated new pressures for such an open-ended arms program, an opposite reaction to the same events demonstrated the political impracticality of such an effort. Evidence that an uncontrolled nuclear arms race is in progress tends to provide a jarring public reminder that huge numbers of nuclear weapons already exist, that political leaders sometimes envision their use, and that our long-term survival would be better served by eliminating nuclear weapons than by constantly preparing for nuclear war.

Such antinuclear sentiments have been more than a nuisance to war-fighting proponents. Although antinuclear beliefs are directed in principle against both MAD and war-fighting doctrines, antinuclear activism has historically broadened the political coalition in support of MAD. MAD at least provided a coherent rationale for

7. Colin S. Gray and Keith Payne, "Victory Is Possible," *Foreign Policy* 39 (Summer 1980): 14, 26.

8. Few Western analysts pointed out that the Soviets may reasonably have viewed U.S. counterforce missile programs since the 1960s as provocative. For a discussion of probable Soviet perceptions, see John Erikson, "The Soviet View of Deterrence: A General Survey," *Survival* 24 (November–December 1982): 242–49.

halting the arms competition, a prospect that was reasonably perceived as a necessary first step toward nuclear disarmament. Thus, in the ABM debates of the 1960s, nuclear "dove" sentiment (probably heightened in reaction to the Vietnam War) readily translated into potent opposition to a major new strategic weapons system deemed crucial by the war-fighters. The same de facto alliance between MAD proponents and the antinuclear movement re-formed in the early 1980s on behalf of a "nuclear freeze"—an objective MAD advocates could rightly claim to have endorsed for the previous two decades.

War-fighters, seeking to defuse antinuclear activism, were able to draw on two powerful arguments. The first, which plausibly demonstrates why disarmament cannot happen, was expressed as follows by Albert Wohlstetter in 1983: "The uncertainty as to the number of *present* nuclear powers suggests some of the difficulty we would have in getting actionable evidence that all of the existing nuclear powers had destroyed all of their weapons. Nor are all prospective nuclear powers likely or even able to surrender the possibility of making the bomb."[9] It is interesting that Jonathan Schell, an eloquent advocate of disarmament, endorsed that reasoning and took it to its necessary and, most would agree, impossible conclusion: "As long as nations defend themselves with arms of any kind they will be fully sovereign, and as long as they are fully sovereign they will be at liberty to build nuclear weapons if they choose." Therefore, "We must lay down our arms, relinquish sovereignty, and found a political system for the peaceful settlement of international disputes."[10]

The other argument war-fighters advanced against the antinuclear movement pertained not to the futility of their ultimate aim, but to the danger of even pursuing it. Colin Gray made this point in 1982 by citing the following passage from Schell's *The Fate of the Earth*: "We do not know what the peoples of totalitarian states, including the people of the Soviet Union, may want. They are locked in silence by their own government. In these circumstances, public opinion in the free countries would have to represent public opinion in all countries, and would have to bring its pressure to bear, as best it

9. Albert Wohlstetter, "Bishops, Statesmen, and Other Strategists," *Commentary*, June 1983, p. 18.

10. Jonathan Schell, *The Fate of the Earth* (New York: Alfred A. Knopf, 1984), pp. 225–26.

could, on all governments."[11] Gray, who believed that "victory is possible," may have had good reason to be alarmed at what he described as Schell's "conscious spreading of fear and despondency asymmetrically in the West."[12] It is instructive, though, that even as U.S. victory theorists were beguiled by dreams of harnessing the West's technological and economic superiority to achieve a usable nuclear advantage, they were simultaneously beset by fear that disarmament-oriented democracies might simply relinquish parity.

Reality, they might have realized, was certain to lie between such widely divergent hopes and fears. Nuclear "hawks" and "doves," pulling at MAD with equal dedication but from opposite directions, were bound to leave it essentially undisturbed. MAD after all is more than a doctrine; it is a formidable reality. As a description of superpower capabilities, MAD came into existence during the second decade of the nuclear era even though it was advocated by nobody. It was wholly unaffected by the eight years when the Reagan administration repeatedly condemned it. The fact remained that it would take a massive shift in the strategic balance to undermine either nation's capacity to destroy the other in a retaliatory nuclear attack.

In that sense, MAD's proponents clearly "won" the nuclear policy debate that so preoccupied the nation during the final flare-up of the Cold War. Indeed, several years of living with the prospect of exchanging arms control for war-fighting policies seemed to have a sobering influence on the leadership of both superpowers. As both sides sought to shape Western public opinion, the obvious political costs of apparent intransigence on arms control promoted a softening of confrontational rhetoric and helped encourage the transition to far-reaching cooperation.

Yet if the debate shed light on the evident futility of hopes either to overturn the balance of terror with war-fighting doctrines or simply to abolish it with complete disarmament, it also focused attention on MAD's potentially catastrophic consequences. Fears of nuclear war were shared by all the protagonists in the nuclear debate. For war-fighters, the principal source of fear was U.S. military weakness in the face of Soviet aggression. For MAD advocates and the antinuclear movement, concern was focused both on the dangerous pursuit of destabilizing strategic weapons systems (the arms race itself) and on the overall deterioration in superpower relations.

11. Quoted in Colin S. Gray, "Dangerous to Your Health: The Debate over Nuclear Strategy and War," *Orbis* 26 (Summer 1982): 338.

12. Ibid.

Was the risk of war actually elevated in the early 1980s? In retrospect we know that we were witnessing not an uncontrollable spiral of mounting hostility but the last in a series of Cold War confrontations. In contrast to some of the more alarmist concerns of the time, Soviet leaders did not follow up the invasion of Afghanistan with a move against the Persian Gulf oil fields, nor did Ronald Reagan's bellicose rhetoric and limited use of American military power represent a trigger-happy readiness for the final showdown with the "evil empire."

That restraint does not mean, however, that those or other concerns were wholly irrational. No one could have precluded the possibility that aged Soviet leaders, facing intractable economic stagnation (and rapid decline relative to the West), might not have used military adventurism in a desperate effort to shore up the empire. And though actual crises turned out to be relatively minor (e.g., the shooting down of a Korean passenger plane), far more dangerous apparent provocations could certainly have occurred. Finally—in hindsight—the U.S. president seems to have pursued an artful strategy of using military and economic pressure to achieve Soviet concessions (which he then welcomed as the basis for a new relationship). At the time, however, it was not altogether irrational to fear that an aging, physically weakened leader, after a lifetime of crusading anti-Communism, might allow some crisis to escalate beyond control.

The point is that while perceptions of the danger of nuclear war are, understandably, largely a function of the state of international relations at a particular moment, the actual likelihood of war is inherently dependent on unpredictable future events. All we know with certainty is that we managed to survive the Cold War and that only once—during the Cuban missile crisis—did decision makers themselves experience a horrifying sense that they might be losing control over events.[13]

Since the cycles of fear and complacency over the nuclear threat corresponded to changes in the intensity of the superpower confron-

13. The fear experienced by President Kennedy and his advisers is captured in Robert F. Kennedy's account, *Thirteen Days: A Memoir of the Cuban Missile Crisis* (New York: W. W. Norton, 1971). As McGeorge Bundy characterized the perceptions of Kennedy and Khrushchev, "What they understood was that . . . they had come so near the precipice that there was a real chance of slipping over it." McGeorge Bundy, *Danger and Survival: Choices about the Bomb in the First Fifty Years* (New York: Random House, 1988), p. 461. For an excellent account that documents the gravity of the danger, see Raymond Garthoff, *Reflections on the Cuban Missile Crisis* (Washington, D.C.: Brookings Institution, 1987), pp. 32–60.

tation, the resolution of the principal sources of conflict predictably produced a widespread sense that we had outlasted the nuclear danger. That perception was reflected not just in a general sense of relief, but in the resurgent appeal of optimistic theories regarding the long-term direction of international political developments. Thus, while the failure of the disarmament efforts at the dawn of the nuclear age yielded dark judgments about humankind's propensity for self-destruction (symbolized by midnight's approach on the "doomsday clock" of the *Bulletin of the Atomic Scientists*), the collapse of Communism quickly inspired visionary proclamations of a prospective "perpetual peace."[14]

As long as the Cold War persisted, arguments that a global market economy and democratic institutions are the critical prerequisites for lasting peace were rarely coupled to claims of inevitable victory in the battle of ideas. Indeed, those in the West who were most emphatic in emphasizing the ideological dimension of the conflict were often particularly pessimistic about the capacity of capitalist democracies to resist the totalitarian Communist threat.[15] By contrast, Communism's economic failure, followed by the Soviet Union's tentative embrace of the Western model, inspired a wave of confidence regarding humankind's ability to transcend the historical sources of interstate violence. Since the nuclear danger was, after all, an epiphenomenon of a fateful clash of ideas, the ultimate solution to that danger would be to shore up the East's conversion to political and economic liberalism.[16]

There are certainly reasonable arguments to support both the association of Western values with the prospects for peace and the hope that the international system is evolving toward the embrace of those principles. Despite the welcome changes characterizing the

14. Thus Stanley Kober interprets Soviet change as a major step toward global embrace of democracy and free trade, identifying these as the key elements in progressing toward Kant's "perpetual peace" of a world under the rule of law. "Idealpolitik," *Foreign Policy* 79 (Summer 1990): 3–24. For an article with a similar theme (which received national attention), see Francis Fukuyama, "The End of History," *National Interest* 16 (Summer 1989): 2–18. John Mueller has recently argued that the very idea of major war—and hence its probability—is fading away. *Retreat from Doomsday: The Obsolescence of Major War* (New York: Basic Books, 1989).

15. Many leading advocates of a tough stance against the Soviets showed this pessimistic strain; e.g., Henry Kissinger, Jeane Kirkpatrick, Richard Pipes, and Colin Gray. For a particularly despairing view, see Jean-François Revel's *Why Democracies Perish* (Garden City, N.Y.: Doubleday, 1984).

16. See Kober (n. 14). See also Michael Doyle, "Liberalism and World Politics," *American Political Science Review* 80 (December 1986): 1151–69.

Gorbachev era, however, theories linking those developments to an epochal transformation of world politics should be treated with prudent skepticism.[17] For one thing, we are far from fully understanding why two societies spent decades feverishly building tens of thousands of nuclear weapons, all the while actively contemplating their use, despite compelling evidence that one accident or error in judgment could destroy civilization. A few short years after at least partially awakening from that mind-set, we can hardly take for granted our ultimate mastery of the dangerous aspects of human psychology and political organization.[18] After all, the darker potential of political

17. For a somber view of the future from a realist perspective, see John J. Mearsheimer, "Back to the Future: Instability in Europe after the Cold War," *International Security* 15 (Summer 1990): 5–56.

18. Freud argued that the psychological characteristics that allowed for the progress of civilization were counterbalanced by an instinct for aggression and self-destruction. For those who detected a natural developmental trend toward realizing humanitarian ideals, he noted, "the objection can be made . . . that in the history of mankind, trends such as these, which were considered unsurmountable, have often been thrown aside." One need not accept literally his hypothesis of two competing instincts to give credence to his conclusion (written in 1931 and even more appropriate in the nuclear age): "The fateful question for the human species seems to me to be whether and to what extent their cultural development will succeed in mastering the disturbance of their communal life by the human instinct of aggression and self-destruction. It may be that in this respect precisely the present time deserves a special interest. Men have gained control over the forces of nature to such an extent that with their help they would have no difficulty in exterminating one another to the last man. They know this, and hence comes a large part of their current unrest, their unhappiness, and their mood of anxiety. And now it is to be expected that the other of the two 'Heavenly Powers,' eternal Eros, will make an effort to assert himself in the struggle with his equally immortal adversary. But who can foresee with what success and with what result?" Sigmund Freud, *Civilization and Its Discontents* (New York: W. W. Norton, 1961), p. 92.

Even those sanguine about humankind's basic desire to survive and progress toward a less violent world need to consider psychological factors less fundamental than an instinct for aggression. In recent years some scholars have examined the "rationality" assumption underlying mainstream deterrence theory by applying experimental research in cognitive and depth psychology to case study analyses of deterrence failures. The thrust of their findings is that—particularly in stressful circumstances—assessments of prospective costs and risks may be skewed or may not be the main determinant of behavior. Attachment to goals can create wishful thinking, leading decision makers to dismiss or misinterpret credible warnings and generally to exaggerate their chance of success. Moreover, psychologically important goals (e.g., a need not to appear weak, a sense of national honor) may outweigh rational calculations of consequences. Thus interstate wars, as well as rebellions by ethnic, religious, or national minorities, have been initiated with little or no hope of success and with a high probability of catastrophe, and violent resistance has been sustained long after total defeat was certain. For a good review of the literature on psychology and deter-

change has also been amply illustrated in the post–Cold War international environment. An Iraqi leader dramatized the limits of "rational deterrence" by risking the devastation of his society, including launching missiles against the cities of a hostile nuclear power.

At least equally sobering were the events accompanying the collapse of Communism in the Soviet Union. Freed of the frightening image of a highly unified elite harnessing state power to an aggressive global strategy, we were suddenly forced to confront the political disintegration of a multinational empire. Could an internal crisis within the former Soviet Union lead to the use of strategic nuclear weapons? Just as it was during the Cold War, it is easy to imagine catastrophic scenarios, no one of which seems very likely. In the wake of the failed coup of August 1991, however, some possible elements no longer required a complete leap of the imagination: for example, the apparent seizure of the presidential briefcase containing the codes for nuclear use, and the signs of severe stress—highlighted by the suicide of Soviet interior minister Boris Pugo—as the coup unraveled.[19]

President Gorbachev later promised steps to allay concerns over a future breakdown of centralized control, including bringing "under one operational command all the strategic nuclear weapons."[20] But the fact remains that there is no organizational solution to the chaos that can be unleashed in a disintegrating society. As the Director of the Central Intelligence Agency, Robert Gates, observed: "The center is evaporating before our eyes. Those who designed the control system never anticipated this."[21] Life-and-death power struggles among extreme or desperate factions can produce risks that cannot be eliminated by any policy of nuclear deterrence, since all necessarily rely on the assumption that one is dealing with a rational, unitary adversary.

Just as few if any analysts were able to predict that a Soviet leader would initiate a revolutionary shift in domestic and foreign policy, no one can foretell the ultimate direction of the forces that have been unleashed. However one assesses prospects for stability within Russia and the Commonwealth of Independent States, the Soviet situa-

---

rence, see Richard Ned Lebow, "Deterrence: A Political and Psychological Critique," in *Perspectives on Deterrence*, ed. Paul C. Stern, Robert Axelrod, Robert Jervis, and Roy Radner (New York: Oxford University Press, 1989), pp. 25–51.

19. For an account of U.S. concerns over whose finger was on the Soviet nuclear trigger during the coup, see *New York Times*, August 24, 1991, p. 9.

20. *New York Times*, October 6, 1991, p. 11.

21. *New York Times*, December 11, 1991, p. A8.

tion demonstrated that nuclear states have no guaranteed immunity from the violent internal upheavals that societies have endured throughout history.

The combination of Saddam Hussein's actions and Soviet disintegration had a powerful effect on the domestic debate over a strategic posture of "assured vulnerability." Even as the Bush administration scaled down the original deployment goals of the SDI program, Congress moved toward endorsing a limited nationwide ballistic missile defense system, to be pursued within arms control constraints.[22] Observing the changed context of U.S. consideration of strategic defense, Gorbachev stunned the MAD arms control community by announcing Soviet willingness "to consider proposals . . . on non-nuclear anti-missile defense systems."[23]

That welcome shift in thinking represented a tentative and belated awakening to the permanent risks of offense-dominant nuclear force structures, but it falls far short of considering whether and how we might supplant MAD with a safer long-term approach to survival in a nuclear world. For much of the generation that lived through the Cold War, the balance of terror remains a fixture in the international system. As a result, there is a real risk that relaxation of the particular crises inspiring recent concerns will lead to renewed passivity toward the nuclear danger.

In the absence of certain knowledge that we are witnessing a permanent transition to a stable peace among great powers (and indeed, among all powers that have or may acquire weapons of mass destruction and the means to deliver them), we should regard complete vulnerability to nuclear devastation as inherently dangerous. As long as relations remain nonadversarial, mass annihilation capabilities and threats serve no purpose and may well perpetuate an atmosphere of residual fear and distrust. Should we return one day to a period of tension analogous to the Cold War, MAD will once again represent an incalculable threat to the survival of entire societies.

However questionable the particular assumptions of MAD's critics regarding both the sources of the nuclear danger during the Cold War and possible solutions, their common concern over a failure of nuclear deterrence was entirely justified. MAD doctrine envisions the preservation of deterrence for eternity—an eternity of rational

22. For a discussion of growing congressional interest (from 1988 to 1991) in a treaty-constrained BMD deployment, see chapter 7.

23. *New York Times*, October 6, 1991, p. 11.

leaders and stable societies, of freedom from accident and freedom from miscalculation. MAD's critics scarcely need dwell on case studies of psychopathic rulers, or of descents into "wars nobody wanted," to declare simply that nuclear deterrence—however embodied in particular doctrines and force postures—cannot be counted on to last forever.

The theorists who identified how deterrence could be preserved in what was then a newly emergent balance of terror, and the policymakers who implemented their ideas (however imprecisely), provided an imperfect strategy that nevertheless addressed a pressing concern: the removal of any conceivable rational motive to launch a nuclear attack. Yet the possibility that deterrence may nevertheless fail does not disappear in the new international context, and preoccupation with that realistic fear will continue to haunt, and influence, national leaders, defense establishments, and the public. Yet high-minded demands that all nuclear powers lay down their arms, and patriotic appeals for a unilateral effort to survive a nuclear war, are equally unrealistic. At some point (before deterrence does fail), doctrinal purity will have to give way to an approach that can reconcile the three enduring concerns generated by the nuclear threat: the need to deter, the need to defend, and the need to disarm.

[3]

The Argument for Mutual Defense Emphasis

MAD's success as a framework for the 1972 SALT agreements temporarily reduced the appeal of the war-fighting and disarmament approaches. At the same time, it all but silenced advocacy of another alternative to the balance of terror: a bilateral shift from offensive to defensive weapons. The first opportunity for active consideration of mutual defense emphasis in the missile age began with the maturation of ballistic missile defense technology in the mid-1960s, and ended with the most substantive arms control agreement of the nuclear era: the 1972 ABM Treaty.

Advocates of MDE in the 1960s shared with MAD's proponents the conviction that neither nuclear weapons nor superpower nuclear parity could realistically be dispensed with. They differed strongly, however, about two other assumptions intrinsic to MAD doctrine: first, that the United States and the Soviet Union were irrevocably committed to assured destruction criteria; second, that the success of deterrence and arms control required such a bilateral commitment.

Instead, they argued that the ongoing revolution in ballistic missile defense technology could serve three objectives:

1. To enhance the ability of the two societies to survive a nuclear attack, while avoiding provocative unilateral efforts to limit damage.
2. To provide a defensive "umbrella" that would preserve a stable deterrent balance while offensive capabilities were being reduced. (The growing capacity for both strategic offensive weapons and populations to survive an attack would compensate for the lowered capacity to inflict retaliatory damage.)

3. To create, at least potentially, the preconditions for complete nuclear disarmament. (Defensive systems would provide a safeguard against clandestine or "breakout" deployments of strategic offenses, or against any threat posed by minor nuclear powers.)

At the heart of their critique of MAD was the claim that, despite the revolutionary expansion of offensive power during the nuclear age, deterrence could still be based largely on its traditional foundation: the capacity to protect one's territory and population. Those who accept the deterrence logic of MAD, wrote a leading proponent of defense emphasis, "seem committed to support forever a strategic posture that appears to favor dead Russians over live Americans. I believe this choice is just as bizarre as it appears; we should rather prefer live Americans to dead Russians, and we should not choose to live forever under a nuclear sword of Damocles."[1]

However bizarre the choice, the ABM Treaty appeared to refute the argument for mutual defense emphasis, whose advocates seemed hopelessly out of touch with the reality of superpower policy. A retrospective look at the forging of the MAD consensus, however, indicates that U.S. policymakers overstated the role of assured destruction criteria and ignored an opportunity to retreat from the balance of terror.

In 1967 Robert McNamara and his supporters in the debate over ABM largely succeeded in portraying the issue as a stark choice between halting the arms race on the basis of preserving secure assured destruction forces and proceeding down the uncertain path of unilaterally seeking ways to limit wartime damage. As secretary of defense, McNamara had unique leverage in that debate. First, he was in an authoritative position to warn the Soviets that the United States would overcome any efforts they made to defend their population. Second, he could tell the American public that he possessed "certain knowledge" that the Soviets would react in kind to any U.S. territorial defenses.[2]

As the debate unfolded, U.S. proponents of a defense emphasis approach attempted (with little success) to draw attention to contradictory evidence. First they noted that U.S. damage-limitation programs were not limited to ABM and that a ban on ABM was unlikely to extinguish the deeply rooted identification of national security

1. Donald G. Brennan, "The Case for Population Defense," in *Why ABM? Policy Issues in the Missile Defense Controversy*, ed. Johan J. Holst and William Schneider, Jr. (New York: Pergamon Press, 1969), p. 116.

2. Robert S. McNamara, *The Essence of Security* (New York: Harper and Row, 1968), p. 65.

with defense. Second, they pointed out that, despite U.S. statements alluding to bilateral assured destruction standards, Soviet officials had been arguing that mutual defensive deployments could provide a sound basis for strategic arms control. As Raymond Garthoff noted: "The significant point is that when the U.S. proposal for BMD limitations was first being considered in Moscow, both military doctrine and "disarmament" doctrine favored BMD and other forms of active defense."[3]

Soviet interest in combining defensive deployments with offensive force reductions had first surfaced publicly in 1962, in proposals presented at the United Nations. The essence of the approach was that both nations should reduce their offensive forces to the point that they could base their security on defensive weapons. General Anatoly Gryzlov described this approach at the 1967 Pugwash Conference:

> When speaking about the danger of the arms race, people have in mind such armaments that can . . . be used for aggression by one state or a group of states against another state or a group of states. Thus, danger lies in the arms race, in the development, perfection and stockpiling of offensive weapons but not defensive weapons. . . . The anti-missile systems, the deployment of which by no means threatens the security of other states, are intended for the protection of the population. . . . The humaneness of these aims does not need any proof, it is clear and evident; they justify the system's defensive essence.
>
> . . . [T]he best approach to [nuclear] disarmament would be the destruction of offensive nuclear weapons or, at any rate, the reduction of the arsenal of the means of missile and nuclear attack to the absolute minimum, with temporary retention of a strictly limited amount of such means. Apparently, in this case no great difficulties would arise with the solution of the problem of anti-missile defense.[4]

While U.S. officials attempted to "educate" the Soviets on the threat posed by defensive weapons (and the deterrence-preserving

3. Raymond L. Garthoff, "BMD and East-West Relations," in *Ballistic Missile Defense*, ed. Ashton B. Carter and David N. Schwartz (Washington, D.C.: Brookings Institution, 1984), p. 294.

4. A. A. Gryzlov, "The Freezing of Defensive Anti-missile Systems," in *Proceedings of the Seventeenth Pugwash Conference on Science and World Affairs, Ronneby, Sweden, September 3rd–8th, 1967*, pp. 278–81. For the "Gromyko Plan," which called for combining a minimum offensive deterrent force with strategic defenses, see "Revised Soviet Draft Treaty, September 22, 1962," in *Documents on Disarmament, 1962* (Washington, D.C.: U.S Arms Control and Disarmament Agency, 1963), pp. 913–17; "Address by Foreign Minister Gromyko to the General Assembly, September 19, 1963," in *Documents on Disarmament, 1963*, pp. 509–17, and "Statement by the Soviet Representative to the Eighteen Nation Disarmament Committee: Gromyko Delivery Proposals, February 4, 1964," in *Documents on Disarmament, 1964*, pp. 23–32.

virtues of offensive weapons), their Soviet counterparts suggested that a more pertinent distinction was between counterforce "defensive" weapons and ABM or antiaircraft defenses. As Soviet general Nikolai Talensky pointed out in a 1964 article,

> Antimissile systems are defensive weapons in the full sense of the word; by their technical nature they go into action only when the rockets of the attacking side take to their flight paths, that is, when the act of aggression has been started. . . .
>
> While nuclear rockets offer only one solution to the problem of attack and defense, namely a nuclear strike, antimissile systems are a new form of nuclear rockets, namely their specifically defensive form. Their task is to destroy the nuclear rocket means of attack . . . without striking at the enemy's territory.[5]

The Soviet perspective was most widely reported shortly after McNamara personally attempted to explain the logic of MAD to Premier Alexei Kosygin at the Glassboro summit in 1967. At a press conference in London, Kosygin stated:

> What weapons should be regarded as a factor making for tension—offensive or defensive? I believe that the defensive systems, which prevent attack, are not the cause of the arms race, but constitute a factor preventing the death of people. Some argue like this: What is cheaper, to have offensive weapons which can destroy towns or whole states, or to have defensive weapons which can prevent this destruction? . . . Maybe an antimissile system is more expensive than an offensive system, but it is designed not to kill people but to preserve human lives.[6]

Other signs of Soviet interest in defense emphasis were manifested both in unofficial contacts and in a public defense of the U.S. decision to deploy Sentinel (a "light" nationwide defense system) against the criticism that it would encourage nuclear proliferation. The extent to which the Soviets in the 1960s were genuinely willing to pursue their own proposals is still unknown. Whatever factors led the Soviets to agree to forgo significant ABM deployments, high-level warnings that U.S. strategic forces would be augmented to any extent necessary to overwhelm their population defenses probably proved persuasive.[7]

5. Nikolai Talensky, "Anti-missile Systems and Disarmament," *International Affairs* (Moscow), October 1964, pp. 60–61.

6. "Remarks by Premier Kosygin at London News Conference, February 9, 1967," in *Documents on Disarmament, 1967*, pp. 60–61.

7. Those warnings included an unpublicized letter sent by President Johnson to

McNamara invoked "assured destruction" in a variety of ways. He used it retroactively to explain programs like MIRV, which he attributed solely to the need to penetrate envisioned Soviet city defenses, despite having approved MIRV development in 1961 as a counterforce program.[8] He employed assured destruction as a declaratory doctrine, even though he had presided over (and never altered) the first U.S. formulation of a specifically counterforce operational option if deterrence failed. ("We may have spread confusion," Mc-

---

Premier Kosygin, stating that domestic political reaction to a Soviet ABM deployment would force him "to increase greatly our capabilities to penetrate any defensive systems which you might establish." Lyndon Johnson, *The Vantage Point: Perspectives on the Presidency, 1963–1969* (New York: Holt, Rinehart, and Winston, 1971), pp. 479–80. Indeed, McNamara has reported that when President Johnson asked him at the 1967 Glassboro summit to "explain to Kosygin how we view their anti-ballistic missile deployment," he told the Soviet premier: "You may think, as the Congress apparently does, that a proper response to the Soviet defense is a U.S. defense; but I tell you the proper response—and it will be our response—is to expand our offensive force." Quoted in Michael Charlton, *The Star Wars History* (London: BBC Publications, 1986), p. 27. The significance of this U.S. effort to "educate" the Soviets regarding strategic doctrine is discussed further in chapter 7.

8. See James Kurth, "Aerospace Production Lines and American Defense Spending," in *Testing the Theory of the Military-Industrial Complex*, ed. Stephen Rosen (Lexington, Mass.: D. C. Heath, 1973), pp. 147–49. Kurth cites congressional testimony by then director of defense research and engineering John Foster that the "MIRV concept was originally generated to increase our targeting capability rather than to penetrate ABM defenses." In examining the origins of research and development on MIRV, Graham T. Allison and Frederic A. Morris reached the same conclusion: "Air Force sponsorship of MIRV research seems to have been motivated largely by the organization's interest in the expanded list of vulnerable targets, which had been acquired by American intelligence in the late nineteen-fifties and reinforced by McNamara's doctrine of counterforce. The Navy's interest in MIRV stemmed in large part from competition with the Air Force for the overall strategic mission, including the expanded target list authorized by McNamara's counterforce doctrine." "Armaments and Arms Control: Exploring the Determinants of Military Weapons," *Daedalus* 104 (Summer 1975): 119. For the most comprehensive study, see Ted Greenwood, *Making the MIRV: A Study of Defense Decision Making* (Cambridge, Mass.: Ballinger, 1975). Greenwood describes the pursuit of counterforce among the "disparate and frequently conflicting" interests and preferences underlying the consensus for MIRV development (see especially pp. 59–65).

Even without the overwhelming documentation amassed by researchers, that MIRV was designed with sufficient accuracy to destroy hardened targets undermines the claim that it was planned solely as an "assured destruction" weapon to be used against cities. Remarkably, in the face of abundant evidence that MIRV can be traced in part to McNamara's own support for a counterforce strategy, the former defense secretary has steadfastly denied that MIRV had *any* counterforce role. Thus, when asked in 1985 whether it was significant that MIRV development coincided with his early support for counterforce, McNamara replied: "No. It's perhaps natural that people might come to that conclusion, but I think it is wrong in fact, as I recall. There was absolutely no connection between counterforce strategy on one hand and MIRVs. The MIRV research was initiated solely as a means of countering Soviet anti-ballistic missile deployment." *Star Wars History* (n. 7), p. 26.

George Bundy wrote in 1980, "by using the measuring stick of 'assured destruction.' . . . This measurement lent itself to the erroneous conclusion that the population itself would be the preferred target of any actual attack.")[9]

Bundy also noted the one indisputable usage of the term. "Assured destruction," he observed, was in essence a "shorthand for the hideous reality of nearly any full-scale retaliation."[10] As a shorthand, assured destruction qualifies as an appropriately horrifying designation for the outcome of a nuclear war. Yet by misrepresenting the counterforce orientation of strategic planning, MAD doctrine created damaging confusion. Far more than it appeared during the negotiating process and aftermath of the ABM Treaty, the entire record of nuclear policy-making suggests that, whatever the declaratory doctrine of the moment, the pursuit of damage limitation may never be permanently contained.

Damage limitation will be sought by military establishments on both sides, who reasonably believe they must try to provide for the survival of their nation in the event of war. Even in a climate of radically improved relations, it is unlikely that civilian authorities will decisively root out such efforts. Leaders are inescapably aware that they must make fateful decisions if a nuclear attack occurs, and every U.S. president has sought alternatives to the "humiliation or holocaust" dilemma posed by MAD doctrine. Russian leaders, who have never endorsed the premise that "mutual vulnerability" is an acceptable long-term policy, are similarly unlikely to terminate their defense establishment's long-standing pursuit of homeland defense. That powerful impulse—to have some chance of survival if deterrence fails—is unlikely to be durably suppressed either by domestic efforts at persuasion or by arms control talks and treaties.

If the search persists, on both sides, to survive "beyond" deterrence (as it should, since deterrence strategies of any type may fail to prevent the catastrophic use of weapons of mass destruction), relying on counterforce weapons to defend one's country (a choice dictated by the ABM Treaty) is irrational and dangerous. First, counterforce damage limitation fails to answer the question "How much is enough?" Instead, its pursuit creates pressures for an endless competition (with ever growing "target lists" on each side) and holds little promise for reducing either nation's capacity to annihilate the other's society.

9. McGeorge Bundy, "Strategic Deterrence Thirty Years Later: What Has Changed?" in *The Future of Strategic Deterrence, Part I,* Adelphi Paper no. 160 (London: International Institute for Strategic Studies, 1980), p. 8.

10. Ibid.

Moreover, because counterforce strategies place a premium on striking first, one side's search for survival seems to the other an alarming and provocative threat. The worst thing about counterforce weapons is that they may be used to launch an attack. They can "defensively" destroy missile silos or they can "offensively" attack cities. They might well be used to do both.

MAD advocates, of course, have stressed that a competition in damage-limitation capabilities is predictably futile, costly, and possibly dangerous. They hoped that the indefinite repetition of such a compelling case would finally persuade both nuclear superpowers to abandon the effort. They have indeed been partially successful, both in winning domestic battles to curtail expansion of counterforce capabilities and in using arms control efforts to preserve a stable balance.

In an age of highly accurate strategic offenses, the operational meaning of MAD has increasingly amounted to limiting counterforce arsenals to levels far below even a theoretical capacity to succeed in their mission. A strong case can be made, in fact, that as long as strategic arsenals are limited by agreement, a capacity to target weapons is preferable to a "pure" MAD posture. After all, once nuclear weapons are launched, accurate weapons make possible a limited exchange that avoids direct attacks on cities.[11] Nevertheless, choosing limited bilateral counterforce capabilities as the ultimate goal of arms control is in one sense even more irrational than are calls for reliance on inaccurate strategic weapons aimed at cities. In effect, adopting constrained counterforce arsenals amounts to acknowledging the desirability of limiting damage without providing a reliable means to do so.

The durability of counterforce planning throughout wide swings in U.S.–Soviet relations reflects persistent resistance to the concept of cooperation in threatening mutual destruction. The dynamic of pursuing counterforce even while seeking negotiated limits is also reflected in both states' policies toward strategic defense. Thus the

11. Albert Wohlstetter argues that targeting weapons is morally superior to threatening populations and points out that increasingly accurate weapons—by requiring far lower yields to achieve their mission—have made possible steady progress in reducing the prospective destructive consequences of a superpower war. "Bishops, Statesmen and Other Strategists," *Commentary*, June 1983. A counterforce war with current arsenals, however, would kill tens of millions on both sides. See William H. Daugherty, Barbara G. Levi, and Frank von Hippel, "The Consequences of 'Limited' Nuclear Attacks on the United States," *International Security* 10 (Spring 1986): 3–45; and Barbara G. Levi, Frank von Hippel, and William H. Daugherty, "Civilian Casualties from 'Limited' Nuclear Attacks on the Soviet Union," *International Security* 12 (Winter 1987–88): 168–89.

ABM Treaty coexists with heavy Soviet air defenses and efforts by both sides to improve ballistic missile defense (BMD) technology.

Even during periods of general recognition that unilateral damage-limitation strategies are hopeless in the near term, ongoing efforts in research and development reflect the provisional nature of adherence to MAD. It is simply assumed that if one side discerned a realistic chance to escape from assured vulnerability, it would defect from a MAD-based arms control regime. Episodic (and illusory) hopes for one's own escape from MAD have therefore been coupled to constant concern about the other side's efforts and plans. The result has been an ongoing search for better ways of penetrating defenses (e.g., nuclear cruise missiles, stealth technology, maneuverable reentry vehicles) that are already hopelessly overmatched and plans for new ways to protect retaliatory forces despite their existing capacity to survive an attack and inflict assured destruction many times over.

That war-fighting strategies are unrealistic does not mean that it makes sense to cooperate in threatening mutual annihilation. The continuing interest in limiting damage, combined with the futility of doing so unilaterally, points toward a cooperative effort. If there is any hope of establishing mutual survival as a goal of strategic arms control, both sides must abandon efforts to defend themselves with weapons that "strike at the enemy's territory" and agree instead to protect themselves, at least primarily, with unambiguously defensive weapons. If the nuclear superpowers are willing at some point to reduce the level of damage they can inflict on each other, it is unlikely that they will simply agree to reduce their offensive forces to very low levels. Three reasons would prompt them to consider combining offensive reductions with greatly enhanced capability to defend both their remaining weapons and their societies.

First, low offensive levels may tempt one or both sides to seek meaningful superiority through covert production or rapid rearmament during a period of renewed tension. Although the perceived likelihood of such cheating may be small, the gravity of its consequences would likely preclude from the start an agreement to make meaningful offensive cuts. (All but very deep reductions would leave intact the danger of complete mutual destruction.) Large-scale defenses, on the other hand, might provide an essential margin of error in counting the other side's offensive forces. As J. Robert Oppenheimer observed in presenting this argument in 1953: "Steps of evasion will be either too vast to conceal or far too small to have, in view of then existing measures of defense, a decisive strategic effect."[12]

Second, in a world of nuclear proliferation, disarming superpowers would feel intolerably vulnerable to attacks by small nuclear powers. Although proliferation has occurred at a far slower pace than many originally feared, it is prudent to assume a long-term prospect of increasing numbers of states with weapons of mass destruction and delivery vehicles attaining intercontinental range. There is no fully satisfactory way to preclude that danger. Although one may hope that forswearing such weapons becomes a universal norm backed by an effective verification system, complete success probably requires the disappearance of expansionist regimes and the (potentially suicidal) self-restraint of all their prospective victims.

The persistence of regional disputes may eventually tempt many less developed states to follow in the nuclear footsteps of the superpowers, regarding weapons of mass destruction as useful for compulsion or essential for deterrence. Whether such temptations can be undercut may ultimately hinge on the ability of one or more major powers to provide reliable guarantees against aggression. Even in current circumstances it is difficult to convince prospective aggressors and intended victims that such commitments are credible and enduring. The capacity of some future regional aggressor to threaten long-range nuclear retaliation would almost certainly render big-power guarantees ineffectual. After all, dictators who rule by terror at home must be presumed willing—in the face of prospective military defeat—to inflict punitive damage on their enemies. The credibility of threats to do so would almost certainly deter interventions to protect regional allies and interests.[13]

If the "equalizing" potential of even relatively tiny mass destruction arsenals (e.g., an ability to target New York and Washington)

12. J. Robert Oppenheimer, "Atomic Weapons and American Policy," in *The Atomic Age: Scientists in National and World Affairs,* ed. Morton Grodzins and Eugene Rabinowitch (New York: Simon and Schuster, 1963), pp. 195–96. This article originally appeared in *Bulletin of the Atomic Scientists,* July 1953.

13. Speaking of the atomic scientists in prewar Nazi Germany, Paul Johnson wrote: "Perhaps deliberately, they failed to ignite Hitler's enthusiasm, though a nuclear explosive was exactly what he needed to make his rocket programme effective. . . . Even before the war he had grimly outlined to Hermann Rauschning the price of Nazi failure: 'Even as we go down to destruction we will carry half the world into destruction with us.' The atomic bomb could have brought this reckless boast closer to reality." *Modern Times: The World from the Twenties to the Eighties* (New York: Harper and Row, 1983), p. 409. Dictators facing military defeat (and their own likely death) might find such a revenge scenario genuinely tempting. Even if they do not, they could reasonably hope to exploit their enemy's fear that such threats were credible.

can erode hopes of collective security arrangements backed by the major powers, arms control reductions to below assured destruction capabilities create the long-term prospect of true nuclear equality among large numbers of nations.

Strategic defenses could help alleviate that danger. Even strategic defenses that are of questionable value against the sophisticated offensive systems of advanced nuclear powers may cope effectively with the more primitive delivery systems of less developed states. Not only could substantial strategic defenses enhance freedom of action against regional aggressors with small mass destruction arsenals, but the difficulties of overmatching such defenses may reduce the temptation to acquire such weapons in the first place. At the same time, severely threatened states may find themselves more reassured by alliances with a defended nuclear superpower, reducing their own incentives to go nuclear as well. In short, substantial defenses against aircraft and missiles can at least partially counter the incentives driving nuclear proliferation.

Similarly, without defenses, opportunities for a disarming counterforce strike (whether conventional or nuclear) against dangerous small nuclear powers may be fleeting or nonexistent. Over the long run, measures to hide or protect weapons of mass destruction (e.g., mobile land-basing and emplacement on submarines) are likely to accompany or follow their acquisition. Preventive or preemptive options against a small nuclear power will likely always be seen as a last resort in circumstances of great danger, for example, as a response to plausible threats of mass destruction. Undefended powers would have a strong incentive to risk such a dangerous action even in the face of an ambiguous threat, since a disarming attack would provide the only possible means of protecting one's society.[14] At the same time, complete vulnerability to retaliation might forestall action even if the need to act was compelling, since even a small risk of failure would direct attention to one's helplessness against retaliation.

By providing insurance against catastrophic retaliation, defenses might give the necessary margin of confidence for a disarming strike

14. In 1969, when China's newly acquired nuclear capability was combined with hostility to both superpowers, a disarming strike was discussed in the United States and actively considered by Moscow. Freeman Dyson suggested that strategic defenses could reduce that temptation: "I cannot feel at all sympathetic with the cheerfulness of those who contemplate taking out the Chinese nuclear force in China. I would much prefer to take it out over here." "A Case for Missile Defense," *Bulletin of the Atomic Scientists* 25 (April 1969): 33.

against a highly dangerous state. And defenses, one hopes, would also furnish real protection against sociopathic leaders or military commanders. At best, recognizing that superpowers feel protected against attack would dissuade a potential aggressor from actions that could make a disarming strike seem necessary.

The case for using strategic defense to preserve a usable advantage by nuclear superpowers assumes, of course, that preserving such disparities in power is a legitimate and necessary objective. Without defending that proposition at length, let me point out that it has always been a guiding principle of great power policy, and has been a major impetus for the superpowers' effort to promote nonproliferation.

Justifications for such policies rely on the reasonable premise that—in the absence of an effective world government—a potential for great power management may be critical to the pursuit of international stability.[15] That technological competition seems to favor societies with democratic, stable governance may add normative legitimacy to the preservation of substantial inequalities in military technology. Proliferation of weapons of mass destruction and long-range delivery vehicles will undercut that inequality. Coupled to a regime based purely on deep offensive cuts by current major nuclear states, it could eventually eliminate inequality altogether. In short, strategic defenses can provide an imperfect reinforcing dimension to the effort to discourage nuclear spread, to reduce its consequences for global stability, and to buttress last-resort threats to deprive small powers of such capabilities. In doing so, it can enhance the appeal of deep cuts in nuclear offenses by the nuclear superpowers.

15. The most pessimistic depiction of the international system has been its comparison to Hobbes's "state of nature." The following is from Hedley Bull's depiction of the key factors that have separated the world of states from that of individuals in the absence of a sovereign authority: "This second difference, that states have been less vulnerable to violent attack by one another than individual men, is reinforced by a third contingency of great importance; that in so far as states have been vulnerable in this sense they have not been equally so. Hobbes builds his account of the state of nature upon the proposition that 'Nature hath made men so equal . . . [that] the weakest has strength enough to kill the strongest.' It is this equal vulnerability of every man to every other that, in Hobbes' view, renders the condition of anarchy intolerable. In modern international society, however, there has been a persistent distinction between Great Powers and small. Great Powers have been secure against the attacks of small Powers; and have had to fear only other Great Powers, and hostile combinations of Powers." "Society and Anarchy in International Relations," in *International Politics: Anarchy, Force, Imperialism*, ed. Robert J. Art and Robert Jervis (Boston: Little, Brown, 1973), pp. 26–27. Although the actual consequences of a world approaching "equal vulnerability" are unforseeable, it is clearly in the interests of great powers to resist its occurrence.

Finally, defense will always be required to handle accidental or unauthorized launchings from any source. That danger alone provides a strong argument for deploying at least a light nationwide defense; intercepting a single inadvertently fired missile would avert an immediate tragedy and might prevent such an incident from igniting a nuclear war.[16]

However desirable a negotiated defensive transition might be in principle, MDE has never attracted significant interest or support. To explain why, the following chapters will explore the factors shaping nuclear policy during the three periods of MDE advocacy: the early 1950s, the decade preceding the ABM Treaty, and the 1980s. Those periods emcompass great changes in weapons technology, the strategic balance, and prevalent conceptions of how nuclear policy should relate to the broader dimensions of East-West relations. Moreover, those changes were influenced by, and in turn affected, theoretical work on the requirements of nuclear deterrence and the objectives of strategic arms control.

Inevitably, changing circumstances affected particular arguments raised by MDE advocates. Moreover, despite sharing the same basic perspective, MDE proponents have differed significantly over the means and ends of defense-oriented arms control. Although different conceptions of MDE can be evaluated only in the historical context in which they appeared, the following section provides an overview of how MDE advocates have addressed two key issues bearing on the feasibility of their approach: how best to utilize defenses in an arms control regime, and the nature of the nuclear offense-defense technological balance.

The Role of Defense in an Arms Control Regime

Although all MDE advocates are united by the goal of using defenses to reduce the damage the nuclear superpowers can inflict on each other, their approaches can be divided both according to the missions envisioned for defensive weapons and according to how far offensive capabilities might be reduced. Based on those divisions, figure 1 divides MDE proposals into four basic conceptions. Although some MDE proposals clearly belong to one type, the first

16. For a detailed argument for a negotiated superpower deployment of defenses against accidental or unauthorized launches, see Jerome Slater and David Goldfischer, "Can SDI Provide a Defense?" *Political Science Quarterly* 101, no. 5 (1986): 839–56.

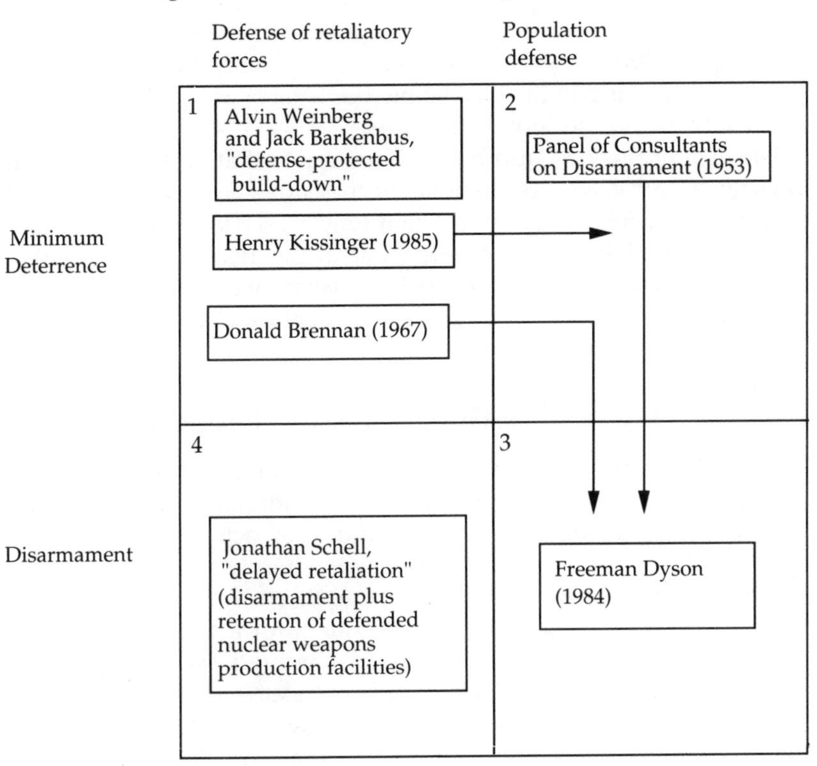

Figure 1. Approaches to mutual defense emphasis

three approaches can also be viewed sequentially as prospective stages in a defensive transition. Thus, in addition to identifying sources of proposals confined to a single conception, some proposals shown in the figure are followed by arrows to indicate their ultimate goal.

Minimum Deterrence through Hard-Point Defense

Some MDE proposals have focused on the defense of retaliatory forces (particularly land-based missiles) as a means of stabilizing deterrence. Such "hard-point" defenses are also compatible with MAD-based arms control and have occasionally been promoted by MAD supporters. The difference is that MDE supporters have claimed that heavily defended strategic forces on both sides can provide the confidence in force survivability necessary to enable the superpowers to reduce their offenses to very low levels. Thus, without any population defense at all, such a "defense-protected build-down" could bring both sides below the level of assured destruction of the adversary's society.[17]

The goal of this first approach is identical to that of the "minimum deterrence" arms control theorists of the early 1960s, who proposed that the superpowers agree to retain only a very low number of single-warhead missiles. The difference is in the means, as these MDE advocates maintained that hard-point defenses were essential to cope with the danger of hidden or "breakout" deployments of offenses sufficent to destroy a very small retaliatory force in a first strike.

Minimum Deterrence with Population Defense

Most MDE advocates who endorsed the approach described above have regarded it as only a first step, to be undertaken in preparation for (or in conjunction with) the second approach. Once highly secure retaliatory forces were coupled with sharply lowered offensive potential, they argued, only a very large disparity in population defense capabilities could provide one side with a first-strike advantage. The absolute deterrent standard of assured destruction would now be replaced by a standard based on "relative damage." Its basic meaning is that in a nuclear war, an aggressor would be deterred by the expectation of winding up worse off than the victim.[18]

At a minimum, population defenses in this approach might consist of a light nationwide defense against accidental launchings or attacks by small nuclear powers. At a higher level of defense, both sides would retain the capacity to destroy at least a few cities (e.g., by concentrating offenses to overwhelm a few heavily defended targets). Here the first approach's focus on defense of retaliatory forces would be combined with significant protection of societies against nuclear strikes arising from insane or desperate actions or catastrophic technical failures. The goal is to enhance prospects for societal survival regardless of the targeting strategy of an attacker.

17. For the "defense-protected build-down" proposal, see Alvin M. Weinberg and Jack N. Barkenbus, "Stabilizing Star Wars," *Foreign Policy* 54 (Spring 1984): 164–70. For discussion, see chapter 7.

18. For one presentation of the argument for a "relative damage" standard for deterrence, see Brennan (n. 1). For a more recent analysis supporting the view that "relative damage" could supplant "assured destruction" as a viable deterrent standard, see Charles Glaser, "Defense Dominance," in *Fateful Visions: Avoiding Nuclear Catastrophe*, ed. Joseph S. Nye, Jr., Graham T. Allison, and Albert Carnesale (Cambridge, Mass.: Ballinger, 1988). Glaser (who opposes strategic defense on other grounds) calls the standard "equal countervalue capability," overlooking the possi-

Population Defense Emphasis and Disarmament

Some MDE proponents have viewed the first and second approaches as steps toward the near or complete elimination of offensive capabilities. There are two possible versions of the third approach. The first envisions a world in which strategic nuclear offenses have been eliminated. The role of defenses (whose strength has been enhanced by a prolonged period of defense emphasis in research, development, and deployment policies) would be to provide an "insurance policy" against evasion of extensive disarmament verification measures. As I noted earlier, the reasoning was first presented by Oppenheimer in 1953: cheating through hidden offensive deployments would be either small enough to be handled by an extensive nationwide defense or large enough to be detected in time to counter the defector's bid for a strategic advantage.

A second version of the third approach would combine heavy population defenses with the preservation of small (well-protected) retaliatory forces, despite great uncertainty whether either side's population defenses could be penetrated. The three possible rationales would be (1) to ensure an ongoing capacity for offensive rearmament in the case of cheating; (2) to make it impossible for an aggressor (who has perhaps successfully hidden a small number of weapons) to fully preclude retaliation (i.e., to preserve the "residual horror" of the nuclear threat, as one analyst put it);[19] and (3) to maintain a limited nuclear deterrent against small nuclear powers and nonnuclear threats (e.g., attacks with chemical or biological weapons by Third World states).

Defense of Weapons Production Plants in a Complete Disarmament Regime

Only Jonathan Schell has proposed the fourth approach, in a concession to critics' charges that his earlier solution (which required replacing states by a world government) was utopian. Schell then called for total offensive disarmament, combined with a terminal defense limited to the protection of nuclear weapons production facilities.[20]

---

bility of designing both sides' forces to provide a prospective advantage to the victim of a first strike. The "relative damage" concept is discussed further in chapter 6.

19. See Laurence Martin, "The Determinants of Change: Deterrence and Technology," in *The Future of Strategic Deterrence, Part II*, Adelphi Paper no. 161 (London: International Institute for Strategic Studies, 1980).

20. See Jonathan Schell, *The Abolition* (New York: Alfred A. Knopf, 1984), pp. 108–37. Schell's approach is evaluated in chapter 7.

It may well be that even if the technical and political obstacles to MDE could be fully surmounted, nuclear powers might always insist on maintaining a limited offensive capability. (In other words, the second version of the third approach might be preferred over total offensive disarmament.) MDE advocates have not insisted on predetermining the ultimate objective, however. The central point is that MDE arms control theorists have provided a possible path (the sequence of the first three approaches) for moving toward a less dangerous nuclear world. The guiding principle would be simply to achieve the lowest mutually acceptable level of deliverable destructive power through some combination of offensive reductions and defensive deployments.

MDE and the Technological Balance

As those attentive to nuclear issues are well aware, "hard-point" defense is far less demanding than the defense of populations. Intercepting even a small fraction of warheads aimed at missile silos could constitute successful defensive performance. It could mean, for example, that the attacker would deplete more of its own force than it could destroy in a first strike. In a situation where, without defenses, an attacker could target the adversary's entire land-based strategic missile force, hard-point defenses could reestablish the deterring prospect of survivable forces and subsequent retaliation.

For the types of defenses envisioned in the first approach, it is generally regarded as technically feasible to aspire to a cost-effective defense. MAD supporters thus do not oppose hard-point defenses because they regard such efforts as impossible. Nor would they regard defenses designed solely to protect hardened targets as destabilizing, except in the sense that they might provide supporters of a population defense with a foot in the door. Instead, hard-point defenses are regarded as uneccessary, since both superpowers have long possessed redundant assured destruction capabilities without such defenses. Even those who see a need to address the vulnerability of land-based forces have generally endorsed means other than strategic defense as cheaper and more reliable.

If the goal is merely to preserve deterrence stability while retaining thousands of strategic weapons, it is indeed hard to justify active defenses of retaliatory forces. After all, even the elimination of land-based missiles would leave the victim with massive retaliatory power deliverable by submarine-launched ballistic missiles (SLBMs) and bombers. Moreover, hard-point defenses may well be less cost-effective than a variety of alternatives, including mobile basing, deployment of larger numbers of relatively small ballistic missiles, or greater reliance on other legs of the strategic triad (submarines and bombers).

The case for hard-point defense is thus worth considering only in the context of an arms control regime involving substantial offensive cuts. In that case, ground-based terminal defenses of missile fields and other counterforce targets could provide effective insurance against a covert buildup or "breakout" deployments by a defecting state. This safeguard could be particularly significant if both sides decided to base a mimimum deterrent system largely or exclusively on silo-based single-warhead intercontinental ballistic missiles (ICBMs). The advantages of fixed land-based missiles compared with other delivery systems include the relative ease of establishing measures of parity and verification and the relative survivability of their command, control, and communication (C^3) systems. (The great disadvantage of missiles is that, unlike bombers, they cannot be recalled once launched. That problem may be ultimately addressed by incorporating "command-destruct" mechanisms, though the longer flight time of bombers may still make them less potentially risky as a source of inadvertent attacks.)[21]

In the context of deep offensive reductions, it also becomes more feasible for point defenses to better protect hardened C^3 facilities. However small the prospect of a "decapitation strike" (preventing retaliation by striking at C^3 targets), a combination of deep offensive reductions and augmented defenses could provide reassurance against what has long been the only theoretically feasible strategy for victory in a nuclear war.[22]

21. For a discussion of the relative merits of each leg of the triad for deterrence stability and reliability of C^3, see John Steinbrunner, "National Security and the Concept of Strategic Stability," *Journal of Conflict Resolution* 22 (September 1978): 411–28. For a recent proposal by Soviet scientists arguing for limiting both sides to six hundred single-warhead ICBMs, see Committee of Soviet Scientists for Peace and against the Nuclear Threat, *Strategic Stability under the Conditions of Radical Nuclear Arms Reductions*, 2d ed. (Moscow: Committee of Soviet Scientists for Peace and against the Nuclear Threat, 1987). In October 1991 the House-Senate Conference Committee on the fiscal year 1992 defense budget called for "U.S.–Soviet discussions on . . . putting permissive action links and post-launch destruct mechanisms on all intercontinental missiles." *House Armed Services Committee, FY92 Defense Authorization Act, House-Senate Conference Summary of Major Actions*, November 1, 1991.

22. For a comprehensive look at the U.S. C^3 system, suggesting its high vulnerability to a decapitation strike with a relatively small Soviet first strike, see Paul

Given that the chief criticism of hard-point defenses has been that they are superfluous in the stable MAD environment of the missile age, the heart of the debate about strategic defense has been over the mission of using it to save lives. The strongest—and an almost certainly valid—argument against population defense is that both nuclear superpowers have the capacity to defeat such efforts. There is no need here to recapitulate the decades of technical debate on this issue. On one hand, war-fighters have long argued that some combination of counterforce offenses with active and passive defenses could provide for a victory strategy with tolerable U.S. losses. On the other side of the debate have been supporters of nuclear arms control who, no matter what their particular prescription for addressing the nuclear danger, share the common assumption that it is hopeless to try to limit damage against the forces the nuclear superpowers could deploy.

Thus the starting point for evaluating the prospects for defensive effectiveness in the context of mutual defense emphasis is the assumption that both sides are willing to adopt arms control limits on all types of strategic offenses. If such an arrangement could be designed and implemented, the technological task for the defense would obviously be far easier than coping with a responsive offensive threat.

Nevertheless, MDE arguments have still been vulnerable to claims that defenses either could fail completely or could be overwhelmed at very little cost. The MDE proposals to be considered later have relied on similar responses to such criticisms. The following discussion briefly characterizes four issues bearing on the potential effectiveness of population defense. The first three respond to claims that defenses either would be totally worthless or would be so costly (relative to the offense) as to be beyond consideration. The fourth, and most crucial, issue is the potential impact of political choices in shaping the balance between offensive and defensive capabilities.

Defenses and Unconventional Delivery Systems

One objection to MDE, widely cited by those who claim that any substantial nuclear disarmament plan poses intolerable dangers of

---

Blair, *Strategic Command and Control: Redefining the Nuclear Threat* (Washington, D.C.: Brookings Institution, 1985). Blair points out that "Soviet planners . . . could hardly fail . . . to appreciate that their only chance to block retaliation would be to paralyze U.S. C^3I" (p. 283). Although even a small likelihood that such an attack would fail provides a potent deterrent, the goal of arms control should be to remove all first-strike incentives.

cheating, is designated by the phrase "the man with a suitcase." The point is that because it is impossible to preclude the delivery of nuclear weapons by nonmilitary means, all defensive efforts are futile. The pertinent question here is, Who has sent the man with the suitcase? There are three possibilities. The first was rooted in the Cold War (though it could now be reapplied to the prospect of a newly hostile Russia): that in an arms control regime based on very low offensive capabilities, the Soviets might attempt to achieve nuclear superiority by smuggling dozens, if not hundreds, of nuclear weapons into the United States. In this case they would have been exchanging real safety against nuclear attack for a gamble that they would never be caught smuggling a single nuclear device. Detection of such an attempt would present the aggressor with a danger of incalculable magnitude. It would force the United States to conclude that the other nuclear superpower intended its destruction. The result would be a relentless nuclear and conventional buildup, conducted on a wartime footing and ending only with war or a complete change of regime in the aggressor state.

To have opposed either substantive offensive disarmament or population defenses based on visions of Soviet agents arriving with "suitcases," one needed to assume both that a significant number of Soviet leaders were deranged and that their mission would succeed. Indeed, any decision makers willing to entrust their nation's future to such a scheme would have been at least as capable of launching a counterforce attack (or "decapitation strike" at command centers) under conditions of MAD—based on a wild gamble that the United States would surrender rather than retaliate. There is a vast gap between the damage that madmen can inflict under MAD and the danger of a "suitcase" threat under MDE.

Two other possible sources for nuclear suitcases are terrorist states and terrorist groups. Neither would be either more or less deterred from such an attempt by the presence of active defenses against bombers and missiles. (In the case of states, the prospect of being identified as responsible for such an attempt would deter any remotely rational leaders.) As with efforts to smuggle conventional explosives, prevention will primarily be the task of intelligence and security at borders. The phenomenon of global terrorism has already inspired a formidable international effort to enhance those capabilities, and nuclear weapons will always be far easier to detect than plastic explosives.

Although a small nuclear power could deliver weapons on board a national airline or ship, an attempt to do so would be extremely unlikely unless in the context of deep crisis or war, producing enough concern to radically transform controls over access to borders and airspace. Even rapidly improvised measures might provide an effective defense, though at the price of massive disruption of commerce and travel. Had Saddam Hussein possessed nuclear weapons, we would already have witnessed the radical societal impact of viable threats of nuclear terrorist attacks. If proliferation of weapons of mass destruction continues, security planning may have to consider the nature and cost of steps to greatly complicate covert delivery.

If the terrorists were nonstate actors, there would be no readily available retaliatory option, whether under MAD, MDE, or a complete disarmament regime. If prevention proved impossible, and assuming such a group provided warning (since a likely objective would be nuclear blackmail), the number of lives saved would depend on the adequacy of civil defense: evacuation plans, blast and fallout shelters, and the range of preparatory measures for coping with a catastrophe. Without such preparations, the United States is probably more likely to find itself yielding one day to nuclear blackmail. In chapter 6 I describe how the same U.S. choices that marginalized the case for MDE also undercut rational debate over the value of civil defense measures in a permanently nuclear world.

None of the "suitcase" scenarios constitute serious arguments against MDE. Like the "catastrophic failure of the defense" scenario (discussed below), the "man with the suitcase" represents a tendency by some MAD advocates to substitute terrifying images for serious consideration of alternative arms control regimes.

Why Even Bad Defenses Can Save Lives

During the 1969 congressional hearings on the ABM controversy, one anti-ABM senator seemed confused when an expert witness against ABM (physicist Wolfgang Panofsky) agreed with MDE advocate Donald Brennan's assertion that an ABM system could save tens of millions of lives—provided the Soviets showed restraint in expanding their offenses. Reacting to this concession that defenses might work, physicist George Rathjens interjected: "Senator, I did want to . . . disagree with both my colleagues. To take the easy point first, Dr. Panofsky said he thought we would all agree if we had a defense . . . the defense would save some lives. . . . In my view there is a very good chance that it would fail catastrophically and would save no lives at all. That is the easy one to get out of the way."[23]

Since one cannot in fact be certain that defenses would not fail completely, invoking that prospect has provided an attractive debating point for opponents of population defense. Nevertheless, as Freeman Dyson argued at the time, the possibility of catastrophic failure is not in itself a decisive argument against deployment. Dyson pointed out that any defense that appears (to an aggressor) to have "a reasonable chance of being technically effective" *will* in fact save lives. To make clear the minimal meaning of "a reasonable chance," Dyson pointed out that "cardboard radars" would not work, since the adversary would discover that "there isn't anything behind the cardboard." Short of such obvious ineffectiveness, however, the enemy must "give the defense considerable benefit of various doubts." With a finite number of bombs and warheads, the attacker must either allocate a number that is certain to overcome the defense of particular targets (either retaliatory forces or cities) or else spare defended targets in favor of attacking undefended ones. Whatever the choice, many targets will be saved, even if the defense turns out to fail catastrophically.[24]

Thus an undefended city could be destroyed with no more than a few warheads. Ensuring destruction of a city protected by one hundred defensive interceptors (as Moscow is today) would require a far higher expenditure of weapons. If the attacker's force is limited to one thousand ballistic missile warheads targeted at the adversary's society, all of them might have to be allocated to guarantee penetration of a Moscow-scale defense of ten cities. Even if the defense fails completely, it would have prevented the destruction of the cities that could not be attacked. (If the attacker chooses to direct its forces against lightly defended or undefended targets, it will be the heavily defended areas that are spared.)

There is a second (related) way defenses fated to fail catastrophically will nevertheless save lives. This is the concept known as "virtual attrition," in which means taken to ensure penetration of defenses supplant part of the destructive power of offensive forces. Although Brennan stressed this issue in the late 1960s, the following exerpt is from a 1986 address by Herbert York:

23. In "Strategic and Foreign Policy Implications of ABM Systems," Hearings before the Subcommittee on International Organization and Disarmament Affairs of the Senate Committee on Foreign Relations, 91st Cong., 1st sess., pt. I, p. 365.

24. Dyson (n. 14), p. 31.

> Since 1965, the total megatonnage programmed for delivery by our strategic forces has dropped fivefold. . . . Several factors have contributed to this net decrease, but the largest part of it is the way we have responded to Soviet air defenses. In effect, in order to assure continued penetration, we have replaced big bombs with smaller bombs and RVs (reentry vehicles), and with stand-off missiles, ECM (electronic countermeasures), and extra fuel. In addition, much of our strategic missile attack is targeted against the numerous and widespread air defenses, leaving less for other targets. As a result, while the total weight of a potential U.S. attack is still much more than enough to kill most of the urban population and destroy most of the cities, the decrease in megatonnage—and the concomitant decrease in radioactive fallout—could mean the difference between death and life for much of the small town and rural population.[25]

Two decades after dismissing the argument that defense would save lives as an "easy one to get out of the way," Rathjens's exposure to York's explanation apparently changed his view. Acknowledging the basic validity of York's description of the virtual attrition of offenses required to ensure the failure of defense, Rathjens added: "Granted, we, and presumably they, still expect that our bombers (along with our missiles) would destroy the Soviet Union as a functioning society. If, however, defenses could reduce fatalities by several tens of millions or even just several million, ought the defensive efforts be judged 'futile'? I think not. This sounds like a pretty worthwhile defense effort to me."[26]

York may have exaggerated the role of Soviet defenses in the attrition of total U.S. megatonnage, since MIRVs (which greatly reduced the total yield per missile) were not developed solely to overwhelm prospective Soviet population defenses, and because improvements in accuracy made it possible to destroy hardened targets with far less explosive power. Nevertheless, the existence of defenses destined to fail catastrophically can still save millions of lives as offensive capabilities are depleted by the need to incorporate "penetration aids," to allocate more weapons to individual targets, and to target the defenses themselves. If the total number and weight of offenses are limited by agreement (as Brennan proposed), these factors may

25. Herbert York, *Does Strategic Defense Breed Offense?* Center for Science and International Affairs, Harvard University (Lanham, Md.: University Press of America, 1987), p. 22.

26. Ibid., p. 39. Rathjens's remarks were part of his commentary on York's address.

mean that even a "futile" defense can make the difference between life and death for society.

Obviously, supporters of MDE were not arguing for deployment of defenses that they expected to fail catastrophically. The catastrophe they feared was a human failure to avert the use of nuclear weapons. In the face of that eventuality, they pointed out that the best hope would be a regime in which both sides had long since redirected research, development, and deployment from offense toward defense, and that—in an outcome perhaps as probable as catastrophic failure—the defenses performed somewhat better than expected.

Why Good Defenses Need Not Be Cost-Effective

As Dyson conceded, the notion that even defenses prone to catastrophic failure would save lives can be taken too far. A nationwide defense would require a costly effort even if the adversary agreed to freeze its offensive force levels. If such a defense could be wholly nullified by a small increase in the other side's offensive expenditures, fear that this would occur would simply preclude deployment. In other words, the gap between the cost-effectiveness of defense and offense would have to be narrow enough to bring the issue of deployment into the arena of budget-conscious political decision making.

But how narrow would the gap have to be for it to make sense to attempt to defend? Here is part of the judgment Donald Brennan offered in 1969:

> In the actual world that is upon us of cost-exchange ratios near unity, perhaps one-half or three but not one-tenth or ten, the attitudes prevailing are not driven by the technology toward either deterrence or defense, but may (and do) go in either direction. It is much more a matter of preference and conscious decision whether we and the Soviets wish to spend our strategic-force budgets chiefly to increase the level of "hostages" on the other side, or to decrease our own.[27]

"Cost-exchange ratio" refers to the offensive expenditures necessary to nullify the amount spent on defense. As I describe in chapter 6, Brennan's claim that the ratio was small enough to permit a choice

27. Brennan (n. 1), p. 108.

was based on the estimates that Defense Secretary McNamara began presenting in 1967.

Although the MDE supporters of the 1960s relied on McNamara's estimates, expert testimony from the strategic defense lobby presented far more optimistic portraits of prospective defensive cost-effectiveness, even as the scientific opposition offered much gloomier assessments. In an article called "The Politics of ABM," Aaron Wildavsky characterized conflicting testimony about effectiveness and cost as "important arguments that do not matter—important because they appeared endlessly in the debate but that did not matter because they were inherently inconclusive."[28] It is possible to extend Wildavsky's argument to make it seem absurd. Policymakers must weigh the arguments of experts, and there are cases of weapons systems so flawed that even strong proponents of their mission may conclude that deployment is unmerited. (This was in fact the case for the earliest version of ABM: Nike-Zeus.) Yet when one encounters a technological debate in which highly qualified experts differ dramatically, it is reasonable to conclude that technological assessment alone cannot provide decisive guidance.

That is the essence of the position taken by MDE supporters throughout the nuclear age, whose advocacy corresponded to periods of promising technological innovations in strategic defense. They never questioned the premise that each superpower had the resources to overwhelm the other's defense. Instead, they argued that defensive technologies looked workable enough to make possible a bilateral "preference and conscious decision" to emphasize defense. Although any defensive advantage created by such an agreement could be overturned by either side's unilateral buildup of new offenses, MDE advocates claimed that defenses could be sufficiently robust to ensure time to react before such a defection provided a meaningful strategic advantage. Accompanying their basic technological perspective was a fundamentally political argument: that the superpowers should prefer adherence to an MDE regime over an arms competition that resulted in MAD.

Political Choices and Technological Outcomes

In 1963 Albert Wohlstetter addressed the widespread belief that, in the nuclear age, only scientific experts were qualified to make the "cardinal choices," meaning "those which determine in the crudest sense whether we live or die." Wohlstetter stated:

28. Aaron Wildavsky, "The Politics of ABM," *Commentary*, November 1969, p. 56.

> In addressing the complex cardinal choices, one of the inadequacies sometimes displayed by natural scientists is that they may ignore, or assume implicitly, or simply receive, or themselves estimate without enough study, the values of those variables which fall outside the traditional natural science disciplines. The cardinal choices . . . cannot be well made solely on estimates of the feasibility or infeasibility of some piece of hardware. They are political and military, strategic decisions. Technology is an important part, but very far from the whole of strategy.[29]

Supporters of MDE would agree with Wohlstetter's formulation: technology is important but should not determine cardinal choices. "Technology is a good servant," says Freeman Dyson, "but a bad master."[30]

One cannot begin to evaluate the feasibility of mutual defense emphasis without considering whether the cardinal choices that created the balance of terror were determined primarily by political and strategic factors or whether MAD should be regarded (to paraphrase McGeorge Bundy's characterization of the 1972 ABM Treaty) as a virtue born of technological necessity.[31] Defense emphasis might be precluded for reasons other than technology, and those reasons must also be examined to assess whether they qualify as immutable dictates of politics or strategy or fall within the boundaries of what we ordinarily regard as our freedom of choice.

But it is MAD's technological assumptions that most would accept as crucial. If technology is inescapably master rather than servant, and if technology cannot offer a workable defense, then we need think no further about diplomatic alternatives to MAD-based arms control.

Note that there is a subjective component to beliefs about the possibility of defense against nuclear weapons. For many, the image of the mushroom cloud and the memory of Hiroshima and Nagasaki (events that could never be precluded by defensive deployments) are sufficient evidence that technology has produced an "indefensible" weapon. For those to whom nuclear war is flatly unthinkable, talk about reducing—even greatly reducing—the magnitude of the disaster is unlikely to elicit sympathetic attention. Moreover, that perspective has apparently been validated by development of ever

29. Albert Wohlstetter, "Scientists, Seers and Strategy," *Foreign Affairs* 41 (April 1963): 468.

30. Freeman Dyson, *Weapons and Hope* (New York: Harper and Row, 1984), p. 293.

31. McGeorge Bundy, "Strategic Deterrence Thirty Years Later: What Has Changed?" in *The Future of Strategic Deterrence, Part I*, Adelphi Paper no. 160 (London: International Institute for Strategic Studies, 1980), p. 6.

improved methods of mass destruction throughout the 1950s (the H-bomb, the intercontinental missile), along with a progressive accumulation of bombs and warheads on both sides. That expansion of offensive capabilities, with its attendant designations of "overkill" and "nuclear winter," has seemingly proved (if further proof was necessary) the overwhelming futility of defensive efforts, thus confirming the predictions of many atomic scientists even before Hiroshima.[32]

It is hardly surprising, therefore, that the history of nuclear policymaking is commonly explained largely in terms of "technological necessity." For those who see MAD as a triumph of political accommodation to technological realities, that history can be depicted, to cite Michael Mandelbaum's 1979 account of U.S. nuclear policy, as a process wherein "technology and politics have combined to create . . . the best of all possible nuclear worlds."[33] Yet the formulation that "politics and technology have combined" glosses over the unprecedented asymmetry in the relationship—that we are admonished to accept that forces beyond human control have irrevocably narrowed the range of political possibility. Precisely that theme, the irreversible subordination of politics to technology, is the one McNamara chose to introduce his first public appeal for acceptance of MAD:

> Technology has now circumscribed us all with a horizon of horror that could dwarf any catastrophe that has befallen man in his more than a million years on earth . . . and if man is to have any future at all, it will have to be one overshadowed with the permanent possibility of thermonuclear holocaust. About that fact there is no longer any doubt. . . . Our freedom in this question consists only in facing the matter rationally and realistically.[34]

32. The "Franck Report," submitted by seven atomic scientists to the secretary of war in June 1945, contains one of the earliest statements of the argument that defense would henceforth be impossible: "In the past, science has often been able to provide new methods of protection against new weapons of aggression it made possible, but it cannot promise such efficient protection against the destructive use of nuclear power. This protection can only come from the political organization of the world." "A Report to the Secretary of War," reprinted in *The Atomic Age: Scientists in National and World Affairs*, ed. Morton Grodzins and Eugene Rabinowitch (New York: Simon and Schuster, 1963), p. 20.

33. Michael Mandelbaum, *The Nuclear Question* (New York: Cambridge University Press, 1979), p. vii.

34. McNamara (n. 2), p. 51.

It is hardly possible that McNamara meant literally that technology alone had created the world of MAD. The atomic bomb was not spawned by spontaneous generation, nor did it evolve and propagate itself into today's number and diversity of weapons. McNamara's speech argued against the utility of strategic defense, and only in that context can a plausible meaning be derived from his statement. He apparently was asserting that once both superpowers were capable of building nuclear weapons, those nations had (and would forever have) no choice but to base their security against nuclear attack on threats of assured destruction retaliation.

This was considered to be true whether or not the superpowers wished to cooperate on the nuclear danger, since the potential for a bilateral nuclear policy was reflected in McNamara's proposal, in the same speech, for a "realistic and reasonably riskless agreement that . . . would halt the arms race."[35] Thus his technological argument may be extended to assert that the nuclear superpowers, even should they wish cooperatively to base their security on defense, would be (and have been) unable to do so because of "technology." Despite its depressing consequences for "our freedom in this question," there is something reassuring about that view. It makes the history of U.S. reliance on offensive strategic weapons seem saner and more comprehensible (progress toward the "best of all possible nuclear worlds"). It invokes the image of U.S. decision makers rejecting a defense emphasis policy with great reluctance, based on the consensus of experts that defense (unless perhaps in the form of a counterforce attack) was simply beyond the reach of technology.

Those familiar with the development of U.S. rationales for favoring the strategic offense ("massive retaliation" in the 1950s, "assured destruction" and MAD in the 1960s) are aware that attributing those decisions purely to the dictates of technology is simplistic. It is also true, however, that reference to the technological imbalance between offense and defense serves for many as an adequate shorthand explanation for why U.S. policy choices never included defense emphasis.

The following look at the periods leading to the adoption of massive retaliation and MAD-based arms control is not intended to challenge the reasonable belief that a nuclear-age offense would defeat the defense in an arms race that was somehow controlled for political influence. Instead, it suggests that such a purely technological competition between offense and defense is remote from political

35. Ibid., pp. 61–62.

reality and consequently of limited use for prescribing (or retroactively explaining) fundamental policy choices. It is not a comprehensive treatment of U.S. nuclear policy-making. Rather, I aim to illustrate that the U.S. failure to explore mutual defense emphasis was due to reasons far more complex—and far less compelling—than a technological imperative.

[4]

Mutual Defense Emphasis in the Bomber Age

Historians sympathetic to MAD sometimes express regret at the early U.S. predilection to exploit the offensive potential offered by atomic energy. Thus McGeorge Bundy sees as "a missed chance" President Harry Truman's failure to propose "no first test" of the H-bomb.[1] And Jerome Kahan says of the priority given to strategic bombing capabilities in the 1950s, "U.S. defense policies made constructive negotiations difficult, if not impossible, and set no beneficial examples. . . . The administration's strategic programs clouded the international political climate, increased the risk of nuclear war, and contributed to Soviet efforts to redress the nuclear balance."[2] Critics presumably believe there once were alternatives. Clearly, both Bundy and Kahan feel that any such alternative would have made arms control (along with deterrence) a central objective.

Retrospective critiques of U.S. policy, Bundy notwithstanding, generally fail to elaborate on the form of a strategic weapons policy oriented toward arms control. Once hopes for complete disarmament had faded, three possibilities remained. The first was simple restraint; that is, deploying only a small number of bombers capable of reaching Soviet territory. But this policy would have depended on trust. It assumed that Soviet offensive and defensive forces would remain small enough to preclude a successful first strike. (Before the era of satellite surveillance, even unconcealed Soviet deployments could go undetected.)

1. McGeorge Bundy, "The Missed Chance to Stop the H-Bomb," *New York Review of Books*, May 13, 1982.

2. Jerome Kahan, *Security in the Nuclear Age: Developing U.S. Strategic Arms Policy* (Washington, D.C.: Brookings Institution, 1975), p. 73.

The second possibility was to agree with the Soviet Union to build *up* to the level of MAD. Such a negotiated buildup might at least have reduced the intense fears of preemptive or preventive war that accompanied the inadvertent achievement of MAD. In practice, however, even those who foresaw a stable balance of terror were not so fervent as to recommend—in the name of arms control—that both sides cooperate to build a secure capacity for mutual annihilation.[3]

Only the third possibility avoids obvious strategic incoherence and manifest unrealism; in fact, it was the only arms control approach that U.S. analysts actually proposed to avoid an unrestrained buildup of strategic airpower. This proposal emphasized continental defense to preserve deterrence as it created conditions for an eventual agreement on offensive disarmament.

The argument for defense emphasis in the pre-MAD era originated in April 1952, when Secretary of State Dean Acheson set up the Panel of Consultants on Disarmament. The chairman was J. Robert Oppenheimer, still a principal adviser on U.S. nuclear policy. The consultants included Vannevar Bush, the dean of American scientific advisers at the time, according to McGeorge Bundy,[4] and Allen Dulles, then deputy director of the Central Intelligence Agency. The panel's initial purpose was to review the U.S. disarmament proposals submitted by the Disarmament Commission of the United Nations. Thus its earliest meetings included briefings and discussions on the comprehensive disarmament plans being debated inside the government.

On May 6 a briefing by officials (most notably Paul Nitze, then head of the State Department's Policy Planning Staff) broadened the panel's objectives. Nitze conveyed his belief that genuine U.S. interest in nuclear disarmament was contingent on first resolving the

3. McGeorge Bundy has speculated on the possibility of an early agreement in which the "great powers . . . limit themselves to some finite number" of nuclear weapons and impose constraints on technological advances. He argues that such an approach would have been highly desirable and implies that it might have been feasible. The possibility of a mutual deterrence arms control system in the late 1940s was overlooked, Bundy suggests, because of President Roosevelt's failure to plan for the postwar world and President Truman's inability to come to grips with the dangers of a nuclear arms race. McGeorge Bundy, *Danger and Survival: Choices about the Bomb in the First Fifty Years* (New York: Random House, 1988), pp. 192–96, 222–29.

4. McGeorge Bundy, "Early Thoughts on Controlling the Nuclear Arms Race," *International Security* 7 (Fall 1982): 3. For a discussion of Acheson's possible motives in creating the panel, see Barton J. Bernstein, "Crossing the Rubicon: A Missed Opportunity to Stop the H-Bomb?" *International Security* 14 (Fall 1989): 140–41.

political conflicts between the superpowers.[5] Nevertheless, U.S. reliance on nuclear weapons presented an obvious problem. According to the minutes of the meeting: "Nitze stated that two forces seem to be running in opposite directions. First the fact that our forces in being are constantly being increased, and secondly that the Soviet capabilities of waging atomic warfare are also being increased."[6]

The consultants then began to discuss how to limit the expansion of nuclear capabilities on both sides, or at least to test whether the Soviets might be interested in bilateral constraints. In a sense this moment marked the birth of U.S. consideration of an arms control approach to national security. Among other ideas, Vannevar Bush suggested a "test case" that could help determine the feasibility of future progress: "Such a test case which would not require inspection and control could possibly be provided by telling the Soviets that we would agree not to test an 'H' bomb providing we have their assurance that they likewise would not test an 'H' bomb. This would provide an opportunity for us to know whether or not the Soviets keep their word without requiring us to inspect their territory."[7]

Two days after the May 6 meeting, the members of the panel met privately to reconsider its objectives. They decided, with the subsequent approval of Secretary of State Acheson, to consider the broader issue of the "relationship between serious disarmament work and U.S. security."[8] Over the next several months, the consultants searched for an approach that could reconcile those two objectives. By November they had agreed on what qualifies as the first coherent approach to arms control in the nuclear age. Their findings were debated in the waning months of the Truman administration, but the final report was submitted after Dwight Eisenhower was elected president, leaving its recommendations to the new administration.

In their initial effort to alter U.S. nuclear policy, the consultants attempted unsuccessfully to postpone the first test of the hydrogen bomb, scheduled for November 1952. Their lengthy memorandum

5. "Minutes of Meeting with the Panel of Consultants on Disarmament at the Department of State, May 6, 1952, 10 a.m.," in U.S. Department of State, *Foreign Relations of the United States, 1952–1954*, vol. 2, *National Security Affairs* (Washington, D.C.: United States Government Printing Office, 1984), pt. 2, p. 919 (hereafter cited as *FRUS*). Enrico Fermi and I. I. Rabi had come very close to calling for such a no-first-test agreement in 1949. See Bundy (n. 3), pp. 214–19.

6. "Minutes of Meeting" (n. 5), p. 921.

7. Ibid., p. 924. See Bundy (n. 3), pp. 201–19, and Bernstein (n. 4), pp. 135–39.

8. "Memorandum for the Files," May 8, 1982, *FRUS*, pt. 2, p. 925.

on this subject establishes the intellectual context that led the panel to conclude that continental defense and strategic arms control were "necessary complements." Noting that a thermonuclear weapon could have an explosive power "one thousand times as great as that of the atomic bomb used at Hiroshima," the consultants argued that "it will be impossible to conceal the fact that this event has taken place, and very difficult to conceal the fact that it is an event of great portent for all men."[9] Under the heading "A Thermonuclear Arms Race May Not Be in the American Interest," the panel noted:

> A successful test will mark our entrance into a new order of destructive power, and this is the last point of departure now in sight. . . . If the test is conducted, and if it succeeds, we will lose what may be a unique occasion to postpone or avert a world in which both sides pile up constantly larger stockpiles of constantly more powerful weapons. . . .
>
> . . . Until we have tested thermonuclear devices there remains one opportunity for an international agreement on armaments which would avoid the overwhelmingly difficult problem of disclosure and verification. An international agreement to conduct no more atomic tests could be monitored by each major government on its own. . . . An agreement of this character has the unique characteristic that it separates the problem of limitation from the problem of "inspection."
>
> . . . For a limited period such an agreement would provide a reasonable assurance against the hazards of a stockpile of hydrogen bombs. In such a period the very existence of an agreement might be an occasion to move forward to more comprehensive and durable areas of agreement.[10]

These arguments were stressing critical new concepts in arms control thought: that limitations on nuclear weapons might be a viable alternative to complete disarmament, and that the standard for acceptability would be "reasonable assurance" against meaningful cheating—in contrast to the unrealistic level of inspection required by complete disarmament.

These authors understood, however, that their proposal would be judged not only by its technical feasibility, but in terms of a fundamental appraisal of the value of nuclear arms control:

> Our basic assignment has been to consider this larger question. We have been forced to recognize the strength of the following three prop-

9. "Memorandum by the Panel of Consultants on Disarmament: The Timing of the Thermonuclear Test" (undated), *FRUS*, pt. 2, pp. 995–96.

10. Ibid., pp. 999–1002.

ositions which are exceedingly hard to reconcile with one another. First, no limitation of armament is feasible unless it becomes a part of a larger understanding of some sort. Second, most sorts of understanding with the Kremlin are either impossible or undesirable or both; we do not know that peaceful co-existence is possible, but it is plain that even if it be possible, it cannot be comfortable. . . . Third, unless armaments are in some way limited, the future of our whole society will come increasingly into peril of the gravest kind.

. . . It is the reality of this third proposition which makes inapplicable the flawless logic that can be built on the first two propositions taken alone. . . . What is necessary is . . . that we should lose no chance that is not totally foreclosed by the irreducible necessities of our defense of freedom. Before we test a thermonuclear device, we should be quite certain that this moment does not offer us some chance of recognizing all three of the hard realities of our time.[11]

The memorandum ended with an implicit recognition that their arguments would not be sympathetically received:

We cannot by a prejudgment of the temper of the Government excuse ourselves from the obligation to record our considered opinion that under the conditions we have stated, the postponement of the scheduled test not only is desirable, but could become a decisive act of statesmenship.[12]

There is little chance that the members of the panel, and most notably its chairman, could have foreseen the ferocity of the attacks on those who combined support for such efforts to limit offensive capabilities with a corresponding arms control proposal to emphasize defense.

On September 17, McGeorge Bundy (the panel's secretary) met with a member of the Bureau of United Nations Affairs Planning Staff to explain the panel's evolving perspective. Noting that its five members think "astonishingly alike," Bundy stated that the panel was "unable to persuade itself that disarmament is not of major importance." Bundy also conveyed the panel's conclusion that "real agreements can only be developed outside of the publicity attending United Nations discussions." Finally, he indicated the panel's belief that the U.S. approach (the Baruch Plan), with its premise that disarmament could be safeguarded by a comprehensive scheme of international control and inspection, was unrealistic. Instead, the panel

11. Ibid., pp. 1006–7.
12. Ibid., p. 1008.

had concluded that "if agreements ever become possible, reliance will have to be placed on broad safeguards aginst big violations."[13] This latter point became a central rationale for the panel's proposal of a strong emphasis on continental defense.

By the time the panel submitted its final report, the attack on rationales for an unconstrained offensive buildup had been sharpened. In effect, it took Nitze's earlier observation that "two forces seem to be running in opposite directions" to the logical conclusion that there was an obvious *need* for strategic arms control:

> Official comment on atomic energy has tended to emphasize the importance of the atomic bomb as part of the American arsenal. There is altogether insufficient emphasis upon . . . the fact that no matter how many bombs we may be making, the Soviet Union may fairly soon have enough to threaten the destruction of our whole society. . . . Beyond a certain point we cannot ward off the Soviet threat merely by keeping ahead of the Russians.[14]

Its second premise was that the deepening Cold War did not mean that arms control negotiations were forever precluded; the United States should therefore aim for a deterrent posture that was compatible with that prospect:

> Even negotiation, which seems so remote, so unmanageable at present and unlikely in the immediate future, is not to be wholly dismissed. . . . It seems important that American policy should not permit the continuance of a situation in which our own rigidities would inhibit us from creating an opportunity to negotiate. . . .
>
> Any development which gives us freedom to reduce our own commitment to the use of atomic weapons will tend to decrease the possibility of an atomic war. So too will measures which combine a defensive character with a deterrent effect upon the Soviet Union.[15]

By this time the panel had concluded that this combination of goals—minimizing the danger of nuclear war and providing a deterrent whose "defensive character" could promote future arms control agreements—required a U.S. emphasis on continental defense.

> No problem has forced itself upon us more insistently and regularly, in the course of our work, than that of the defense of the continental

13. "Memorandum of Conversation by Lincoln P. Bloomfield of the Bureau of United Nations Affairs Planning Staff," September 17, 1952, *FRUS*, pt. 2, p. 1015.
14. "Report by the Panel of Consultants of the Department of State to the Secretary of State: Armaments and American Policy," January 1953, *FRUS*, pt. 2, p. 1080.
15. Ibid., p. 1077.

United States. Nominally this question would seem to fall outside the range of our assignment, but in fact it is impossible to consider the problem of armaments and policy without giving careful attention to the whole subject of defense against weapons of mass destruction. Arms regulation and continental defense are complementary methods of achieving the goal of safety against the danger of a surprise knockout blow. They are thus interlocked in a variety of ways, and no policy can be consistent and effective unless it applies to both subjects the same fundamental attitude. It is not too much to say, in our view, that unless continental defense is taken seriously, arms regulation must seem a foolish goal, while if real attention is given to defensive measures, the whole approach to moderating the dangers of the arms race may become more manageable.[16]

Defense and arms control were seen as "interlocked" in several ways. First, emphasizing continental defense could demonstrate U.S. interest in arms control: "It cannot be read as an aggressive move, and it should constitute real evidence of the fact that we believe atomic weapons to be dangerous for all concerned."[17] As was described in chapter 1, this notion of conveying nonaggressive intentions by emphasizing purely defensive capabilities dated back to the disarmament negotiations of the interwar period. The conceptual continuity between the 1932–33 Geneva Disarmament Conference and the 1952 Panel of Consultants on Disarmament may be due to Allen Dulles's participation in both. Thus, at the first meeting of the panel, Dulles noted that the defense emphasis approach to arms control retained potential value. An excerpt from the minutes of that meeting reads:

Mr. Dulles indicated his hesitation and skepticism of any success in the work, referring to himself as one of the few living relics of the extensive and fruitless disarmament discussions between World Wars I and II. However he agreed upon the importance of presenting our present buildup as defensive in character and agreed that our disarmament work should help in that connection. . . . He remarked . . . that so long as the Soviets continue as at present to put great emphasis in their buildup on such weapons as MIG 15's and not on TU 4's [long-range bombers] there is some hope that Soviet intentions are defensive and not offensive.[18]

16. Ibid., p. 1083.
17. Ibid., p. 1084.
18. "Minutes of the Meeting of the Secretary of State with the Panel of Consultants on Disarmament," April 28, 1952, *FRUS*, pt. 2, p. 900.

Although it hoped that each side could draw inferences about the other's intentions from a shared emphasis on defensive weapons, the panel believed that any such tacit agreements would have to be grounded in bilateral superpower negotiations. The Soviets might well refuse a frank private exchange, but "if communication should prove possible, it would have just that real relationship to the dangers of our present situation which the present discussions in the United Nations lack."[19]

Thus, beyond demonstrating defensive intentions, the second rationale for defense emphasis was its possible contribution to a realistic arms control regime based on what would later be called "minimum deterrence": "Since the peculiar danger of the present arms race derives from the growing possibility that the two great Powers may soon be able to strike each other direct and crippling blows, the basic objective of any scheme of arms regulation should be to eliminate this capability. This is not the same thing as eliminating all atomic bombs."[20] Whereas their call to negotiate "a reduction in the size of stockpiles and bombing fleets" would require some verification ("there can be no arms regulation without some sort of inspection"), insistence on comprehensive inspection would "defer all hope of arms regulation until after a revolution had occurred in Russia—and perhaps still further."[21] In the meantime, "each improvement in continental defense may make it less necessary to insist on totally ironclad schemes of arms regulation."[22]

Like the failed proposal for no first test of the H-bomb, in the short run an emphasis on defense was aimed at restraining the superpowers' offensive capabilities while providing greater freedom to negotiate substantive agreements. Even if the Soviets rejected the U.S. approach, greater emphasis on defense could delay "the time at which the Soviet Union will be able to strike a knockout blow."[23] Moreover, defenses could enhance deterrence, serving, "in the measure of its apparent effectiveness, to dissuade Soviet leaders from attempting any catastrophic attack."[24]

19. "Report by the Panel of Consultants" (n. 14), p. 1087.

20. Ibid., p. 1089. (This arms control objective is set forth in annex I of the report, "Some Possible Characteristics of a Realistic Agreement on the Regulation of Armaments.")

21. Ibid., pp. 1089–90.

22. "Memorandum by the Panel of Consultants on Disarmament: A Draft Summary of the Line of Argument Agreed on November 15 (1952) at a Partial Meeting of the Panel in New York City," undated, *FRUS*, pt. 2, p. 1040.

23. "Report by the Panel of Consultants" (n. 14), p. 1083.

24. Ibid., p. 1084.

The final, and most ambitious, link envisioned between defense and arms control was an eventual role for defense as a vital component of an offensive disarmament regime. As Oppenheimer explained this view in a later article, a future disarmament agreement would require large-scale defenses, so that "steps of evasion will be either too vast to conceal or far too small to have . . . a decisive strategic effect."[25] As one historian of nuclear policy, Robert Gilpin, summarized the overall argument: "While the ultimate defense would be disarmament, an effective continental air defense would enhance American freedom to negotiate a disarmament agreement."[26]

Despite their enthusiasm for defense as an instrument of arms control, the consultants sharply rejected the view that defense represented a technological solution to the emergent Soviet nuclear threat:

> Important and valuable as air defense may be, however, it will be a pleasant surprise if the defense is ever able to knock down or deflect as many as four out of five of the attackers. . . . Even a combination of the most optimistic assessments leads to the theoretical conclusion that, if she is willing and able to build a sufficient strategic air force, the Soviet Union may be able to destroy our economy beyond the hope of recovery when . . . she has as few as 600 [atomic bombs].[27]

Despite the impossibility of defending against an unconstrained Soviet offensive buildup, the panel did not fully share the early fears of many atomic scientists that a failure to avert an arms race made a catastrophic war virtually inevitable. Instead, they were confident that both sides would develop a secure "second-strike" capability (though that term was not yet in use). In other words, they sought to avoid what would later be called mutual assured destruction:

> If the atomic arms race continues . . . the two great powers will each have a clearcut capacity to do very great damage to the other, while each will be unable to exert that capacity except with the gravest risk of receiving similar terrible blows in return. . . . There is likely to be a point in our time when the Soviet Union will have "enough" bombs—no matter how many more we ourselves may have.[28]

25. J. Robert Oppenheimer, "Atomic Weapons and American Policy," in *The Atomic Age: Scientists in National and World Affairs*, ed. Morton Grodzins and Eugene Rabinowitch (New York: Simon and Schuster, 1963), pp. 195–96. This article originally appeared in the *Bulletin of the Atomic Scientists*, July 1953.

26. Robert Gilpin, *American Scientists and Nuclear Weapons Policy* (Princeton: Princeton University Press, 1962), p. 126.

27. "Report by the Panel of Consultants" (n. 14), p. 1067.

28. Ibid., p. 1067.

That prediction corresponds exactly to the world McNamara described in 1967 when he appealed for permanent superpower acceptance of MAD. The crucial difference is that the call for defense emphasis and arms control was based on the belief that it would be folly to entrust survival even to a "stable" balance of terror: "It is conceivable that a world of this kind may enjoy a strange stability arising from general understanding that it would be suicidal to 'throw the switch.' On the other hand it also seems possible that a world so dangerous may not be very calm, and to maintain peace it would be necessary for statesmen to decide against rash action not just once, but every time."[29] In the meantime, the "transition" to MAD would be fraught with danger: "Since the coming of such a world will be gradual and since its coming may or may not be correctly estimated in all countries, there is a possibility that one nation or another may be tempted to launch a preventive war 'before it is too late,' only to find out that the time for such a blow has already passed."[30]

Eight months later, having rejected the appeals of the Panel of Consultants on Disarmament, President Eisenhower indeed experienced that temptation. In a memorandum to Secretary of State John Foster Dulles, he wrote that "if the contest to maintain this relative position should have to continue indefinitely, . . . we would be forced to consider whether or not our duty to future generations did not require us to *initiate* war at the most propitious moment we could designate" (emphasis in original).[31]

Maintaining that offensive arms control was essential for the long-term effectiveness of strategic defense, the panel was also convinced that a shift in research and development priorities toward defensive weapons would affect the technological offense-defense balance: "If research and development in this whole area are given a proper priority, still more impressive gains will become likely; the pattern of scientific research on military problems has regularly indicated that we tend to make most progress in those areas where we care most and try hardest."[32]

29. Ibid., p. 1068.
30. Ibid.
31. "Memorandum by the President to the Secretary of State," September 8, 1953, *FRUS*, pt. 1, p. 461. For discussions of this issue, see Bundy (n. 3), pp. 251–55, and David Alan Rosenberg, "The Origins of Overkill," *International Security* 7 (Spring 1983): 33.
32. "Report by the Panel of Consultants" (n. 14), pp. 1084–85.

A year later, in an article titled "Ban H-Bomb Tests and Favor the Defense," physicist David Inglis (later president of the American Federation of Scientists) based his argument on the same premise the panel used. Although defensive technology was promising, arms control was essential for redressing the technological imbalance between offense and defense:

> Even though it provides no disarmament and provides arms limitation only indirectly by limiting the development of new types of arms, this agreement would have a very important value to both sides. Its chief value is that *it would slow down the rate of development of new techniques of offense and allow the techniques of defense to come closer to catching up*. The most explosive feature of the dangerous international situation arises from the undisputed supremacy of offense over defense. To lessen this without giving either of the contenders a distinct advantage over the other is to make a more stable world.
>
> . . . If both sides should discontinue H-bomb tests by agreement . . . the bombs in the stockpiles would gradually become more and more old-fashioned relative to what they would have been if the tests had continued. Advances in long-range rockets and other vehicles for delivery would have to contend with clumsy, old-fashioned warheads. Meanwhile, on the defense, development of radar screens and interceptor missiles would go on unhampered by the agreement. (Emphasis in original)[33]

If there was a technological explanation for the repudiation of defense emphasis arms control in the bomber age, one would expect to find a record of expert testimony pointing out the futility of defense, or at least an indication of such widespread despair over the prospect that hopes for continental defense and arms control would yield to the greater realism of those promoting an offensive buildup. Instead, one encounters technical studies reinforcing the argument for defense emphasis, and attacks against pro-defense scientists not primarily for their technical findings, but for their underlying interest in strategic arms control. The following section depicts the highlights of what one Air Force publicist called a "life and death struggle" against proponents of defense emphasis and examines technology's place in the range of factors that led to the first clear policy choice of offense over defense.

33. David Rittenhouse Inglis, "Ban H-Bomb Tests and Favor the Defense," in *To End the Arms Race: Seeking a Safer Future* (Ann Arbor: University of Michigan Press, 1986), p. 51. This article originally appeared in *Bulletin of the Atomic Scientists*, October 1954.

Significantly, the best single source for the then prevalent U.S. attitude toward defense emphasis arms control is testimony presented before the Gray Board, which met in 1954 to consider whether J. Robert Oppenheimer was a security risk, and whose judgment ended Oppenheimer's career as an adviser on nuclear policy. There it is clearly and repeatedly indicated that the Air Force leader considered defense emphasis proposals prima facie evidence of questionable loyalty. The role of such advocacy in Oppenheimer's purportedly disturbing "pattern of activities" can be illustrated in testimony by Air Force chief scientist David Griggs:

> It became apparent to us—by that I mean to Mr. Finletter [secretary of the Air Force], Mr. Borden and Mr. Norton [Finletter's two assistants] that there was a pattern of activities all of which involved Mr. Oppenheimer. . . . We were told that in . . . 1951, Mr. Oppenheimer and two other colleagues formed an informal committee of three to work for world peace or some such purpose, as they saw it. We were also told that in this effort they considered that many things were more important than the development of the thermonuclear weapon, specifically the air defense of the continental United States.[34]

There was, in fact, a "pattern" to the activities of Oppenheimer and several other scientists. (Air Force officials claimed that the scientific leaders of the defense emphasis school had formed a secret group of four that called itself "ZORC"—an acronym based on the initials of Jerrold Zacharias, Oppenheimer, Isadore Rabi, and Charles Lauritsen.) Some of the same scientists (whose general approach Robert Gilpin has characterized as the "finite containment school") who advocated continental defense had also favored the "no-first-test" H-bomb proposal, as well as supporting the Project Vista argument that Europe could be defended with tactical rather than strategic nuclear weapons.[35] Whatever these proposals conveyed about the patriotism of their advocates, they clearly posed a

34. *In the Matter of J. Robert Oppenheimer: Transcript of Hearings before Personal Security Board and Texts of Principal Documents and Letters* (Cambridge: MIT Press, 1970), p. 749.

35. Project Vista was a 1951 study commissioned by the three military services. For a review depicting Air Force fears that its recommendations would undermine the Strategic Air Command, see Matthew Evangelista, *Innovation and the Arms Race: How the United States and the Soviet Union Develop New Military Technologies* (Ithaca: Cornell University Press, 1988), pp. 133–45.

basic challenge to Air Force doctrine and an immediate threat to the Air Force budget.

Until 1954 the Air Force was preoccupied with fending off a range of assaults on the wisdom (and morality) of relying on strategic airpower—attacks emanating from the other armed services (whose institutional survival hinged on demonstrating limits to the utility of strategic bombing) as well as the "finite containment" arms control supporters. Continental defense, however, represented a special case, since it was the Air Force itself that was then primarily responsible for that mission. It is not hard to discern the impact of that allocation of roles on the military's receptivity to emphasizing defense. Not only would the Air Force be unlikely to lead a struggle to change its own doctrine, but the other services likewise would see no organizational benefits in backing a major effort at continental defense.

In the absence of intervention from outside the military, inquiry into the problem of air defense proceeded at a leisurely pace.[36] After the 1949 Soviet A-bomb test, the Air Force Science Advisory Board proposed that a committee be formed to study the problem. A year later, the committee (which included two future Air Force chief scientists) reported that an effective defense was feasible, leading to a subsequent study known as Project Charles.

In 1951 a concerted, centralized research effort was finally begun when the Air Force established Lincoln Laboratory at Massachusetts Institute of Technology. Given Air Force concern with persuading civilian policymakers that there were no alternatives to a strategic offensive buildup, there was an inherent risk of tension between Lincoln and its bureaucratic sponsor: optimistic evaluations of air defense would not be welcomed by the Air Force leadership. When approximately thirty scientists met in the summer of 1952 to assess

36. Apparently the first study examining U.S. vulnerability to atomic attack was done in September 1945 by the Army's Air Intelligence Division. It had no impact on subsequent policy. In general, the air defense effort before 1949 was inadequate to the point of meaninglessness. After 1947 the Air Force had primary responsibility for continental defense, to be implemented through its slowly expanding Air Defense Command (ADC). The opportunity for a coordinated national effort did not appear until mid-1951, when the Army (whose Anti-Aircraft Command controlled antiaircraft artillery) agreed to coordinate activities with the ADC. For a review of early efforts to plan a continental defense, see Joseph T. Jockel, "The United States and Canadian Efforts at Continental Air Defense, 1945–1957" (Ph.D. diss., Johns Hopkins University, 1978). The 1949 committee referred to in the text was called the Air Defense Systems Engineering Committee (ADSEC). For a brief summary of the 1949–51 studies of air defense prospects, see Herbert York, *The Advisors: Oppenheimer, Teller, and the Superbomb* (Stanford: Stanford University Press, 1989), pp. 114–15.

Lincoln Laboratory's progress, the Air Force leaders became concerned over their anticipated recommendations. That fear prompted a series of preventive measures (which came to light at the Oppenheimer trial).[37]

First, Secretary Thomas Finletter expressed concern to MIT president James Killian that the "Lincoln Summer Study" might make too strong a case for active defense. Despite advance reassurance from MIT, the study nevertheless concluded that technological advances (in radar, data processing, interceptor aircraft, and missiles) were sufficiently promising to warrant a major U.S. effort—with a prospective increase in the probable rate of interception from near zero to a range of 60 to 80 percent. The study also stressed the still unwelcome fact that the United States was becoming increasingly vulnerable, so that there was a *need* to step up work on defense.[38]

In response the Air Force, with the cooperation of the Department of Defense, attempted to prohibit circulation of the Lincoln Summer Study findings. That effort failed in September 1952 when the director of the National Security Resources Board (Jack Gorrie) presented the findings directly to the National Security Council (NSC). Gorrie, whose particular bureaucratic concern was lack of support for civil defense by the administration, explained to President Truman that "many of these scientists and technicians had changed their minds and abandoned their previously pessimistic estimates about the possibility of developing a more adequate . . . system for the defense of the Continental United States."[39] In response, Truman authorized an NSC briefing on the Lincoln Summer Study findings.

One might think that, in light of growing Soviet nuclear capabilities, a strongly favorable technical evaluation of prospects for air defense (particularly for an effective early warning system) would have been enthusiastically received by the Truman administration. Instead, the Lincoln Summer Study findings were presented to the

37. *Summer Study Group 1952 Final Report*, Lincoln Laboratory, Massachusetts Institute of Technology, February 10, 1953. Volume 1 contains the study's summary and recommendations, including the group's "basic philosophy of a sound defense." Volume 2 contains selected working papers on technical issues. Most of the report was declassified in 1978. For descriptions of Air Force interference with the Lincoln Summer Study see Philip M. Stern, *The Oppenheimer Case: Security on Trial* (New York: Harper and Row, 1969), pp. 192–94, and Samuel P. Huntington, *The Common Defense: Strategic Programs in National Politics* (New York: Columbia University Press, 1961), pp. 329–35.

38. Huntington (n. 37), p. 329.

39. "Memorandum for the President of Discussion at the 123d Meeting of the National Security Council on Wednesday, September 24, 1952," *FRUS*, pt. 1, p. 138.

NSC a month later by an Air Force general (serving simultaneously as spokesman for the Department of Defense), who presented the technical data and then recommended not implementing the study's recommendations.[40]

Two years later, Lloyd Berkner (who had headed the Atomic Energy Commission–sponsored East River study of civil defense) wrote: "For reasons known only to the Armed Forces . . . many efforts were made to ignore or suppress the findings of the Lincoln Summer Study and little effort was made to demonstrate how the ideas might work out. . . . The Armed Forces refused to recognize the serious state of the air-defense problem or to admit that it could be improved by radical measures."[41] The reasons for the hostility to the Lincoln Summer Study would have been clearer to Berkner had he known of the following testimony (at the Oppenheimer hearings) by the Air Force chief scientist: "It was further told me by people who were approached to join the summer study that in order to achieve world peace . . . it was necessary not only to strengthen the Air Defense of the continental United States, but also to give up something, and the thing that was recommended that we give up was the Strategic Air Command, or more properly I should say the strategic part of our total air power."[42]

The subsequent fate of the Lincoln Summer Study report, as Samuel Huntington noted, was "almost a classic case of a proposal which was studied to death."[43] During the first year of the Eisenhower administration, at least four groups deliberated over its find-

40. "Memorandum by the Under Secretary of State (Bruce)," October 14, 1952, *FRUS*, pt. 1, p. 164.

41. Huntington (n. 37), p. 335. Advocates of civil defense were, if anything, more frustrated than the air defense advocates by the prevailing attitudes toward strategic defense. Air defense was a military mission, and the existence of the Continental Defense Command within the Air Force at least ensured the appearance of a national effort, however subordinated to the offensive mission. Civil defense was a civilian operation with no political base or influential promoter inside the government. Moreover, those who studied the problem quickly concluded that their task was hopeless in the absence of a major air defense effort, and their promotion of active defense guaranteed the animosity of the airpower lobby. The link between active and passive defense was stressed by Project East River, the government's major air defense study, which submitted a series of reports during the summer and fall of 1952. Its first recommendation called for "a military defense of such a character as to prevent a 'saturation' attack so that the task of civil defense is kept within manageable bounds. P.E.R. [Project East River] concludes that such a defense is feasible." Joseph E. McLean, "Project East River—Survival in the Atomic Age," *Bulletin of the Atomic Scientists* 9 (September 1953): 247.

42. *In the Matter of J. Robert Oppenheimer* (n. 34), p. 749.

43. Huntington (n. 37), p. 330.

ings. Although no new comprehensive technical evaluation was undertaken, subsequent recommendations increasingly reflected the linked priorities of the new administration: limiting the budget and relying on strategic airpower as the major means to contain Communism. While the last of these groups, the Kelly Commission, was still working, Oppenheimer described the climate of hostility surrounding consideration of continental defense: "This panel, it would appear, has been oppressed and troubled by the same overall oppression which any group always finds when it touches seriously any part of the problem of the atom."[44]

In the same article (published in July 1953), Oppenheimer launched a strongly worded attack on the Air Force, attributing to "a high officer of the Air Defense Command" the statement that "it was not really our policy to protect this country, for that is so big a job it would interfere with our retaliatory capabilities." Oppenheimer added: "Such follies can occur only when even the men who know the facts can find no one to talk to about them, when the facts are too secret for discussion and thus for thought."[45]

44. Oppenheimer (n. 25), p. 195. The Kelly Commission (headed by Bell Telephone Laboratories president Marvin J. Kelly) was formed in December 1952 to consider the implications of Project Lincoln and the Lincoln Summer Study recommendations. Its report was submitted in July 1953. The summary released to the public indeed confirmed Oppenheimer's fears about the official "oppression" that was preventing informed debate over the need for strategic defense. In November the presidents of MIT and Lincoln Laboratory complained: "When the recent Kelly Report on continental defense was summarized in part in a news release, certain of its grim conclusions about the present threat to America were made less grim. . . . The American public is not well served by withholding facts that are vital to the decision-making of a democracy and to its self-preservation." James R. Killian, Jr., and A. G. Hill, "For a Continental Defense," *Atlantic*, November 1953, p. 41. According to the published summary of the Kelly Report, a Soviet nuclear attack could "possibly temporarily lessen U.S. capability . . . to support a major war effort." "Air Defense: Kelly vs. 'Summer Study' Group," *Fortune* 48 (July 1953): 40. By contrast, the classified perception was that "the present continental defense programs are not now adequate . . . to ensure the continuity of government, the continuity of production, or the protection of the industrial mobilization base and millions of citizens in our great and exposed metropolitan centers." "Report of the Continental Defense Committee" (NSC 159, July 22, 1953), p. 4. Citation is from "Statement of Policy by the National Security Council: Continental Defense," September 25, 1953, *FRUS*, pt. 1, p. 478.

45. Oppenheimer (n. 25), p. 193. A similar complaint had been made in the published summary of the Project East River civil defense study: "Defense should include not merely defense of military bases and the direct support of an offensive force; it should also include the transcending, overriding responsibility to defend the nation—its citizens and its institutions. To do less would be to sacrifice our civilians and civilian institutions to the support merely of our military offensive forces." McLean

The Air Force responded with great effect to Oppenheimer's attacks. An anonymous Air Force–sponsored article in *Fortune* proclaimed a "life and death struggle" over national military policy, concerning "whether a strategy shaped around the 'retaliatory deterrent' principle embodied in the Strategic Air Command shall be discarded, or at least drastically modified, in favor of a defensive strategy" that envisioned "a renunciation of atomic-offensive power by both major adversaries."

In part this article (which came under prolonged scrutiny during the Oppenheimer hearings) addressed the technical dimension of defense, (falsely) attributing to the Lincoln Study a claim of offering a "near leakproof defense." Dismissing this purported finding, it charged that the members of "ZORC" had merely "confirmed . . . what they had set out to prove." But the article's primary concern was to repudiate "the ZORC idea . . . that the fortress concept offers a more moral solution to the dilemma of Cold War strategy than does SAC (Strategic Air Command)." In advocating "this mutual foreswearing of strategic air warfare," it said, ZORC failed to recognize that "for the U.S. . . . to throw away its strongest weapon merely because it is an offensive weapon is a naive way to go about ridding the world of war: The atomic advantage constitutes a 'shield' behind which the American people can work steadily for peace—until Mr. Eisenhower's proposals for world disarmament are universally accepted." Retrospectively, the article's final paragraph appears ominous: "Meanwhile, there was a serious question of the propriety of scientists trying to settle such grave national issues alone, inasmuch as they bear no responsibility for the successful execution of war plans."[46]

(n. 41), p. 250. Two months after Oppenheimer's public complaint, the head of the Federal Civil Defense Administration reacted with similar frustration over the nearly nonexistent civil defense effort: "And to me that is not only pitiful, but it is nearly criminal in its implications, because it is, in my judgment, just as important to learn how to protect 160 million Americans as it is to learn how to fight the enemy." "An Interview with Governor Val Peterson," *Bulletin of the Atomic Scientists* 9 (September 1953): 238.

46. "The Hidden Struggle for the H-Bomb," *Fortune* 47 (May 1953): 108–10, 230. Another account, also highly sympathetic to the Air Force position, attributed the origins of the purported "ZORC" conspiracy to Lloyd Berkner, who had headed the East River study of civil defense. The authors, in this case, backed up their accusation that Berkner and ZORC were claiming to offer a "near leakproof defense" by attributing to Berkner the claim that "active defense measures [would be] able to reduce enemy bomber penetrations to mere 'leakage.'" James R. Shepley and Clay Blair, Jr.,

Six months later William Borden—one of the earliest and most extreme advocates of atomic airpower—would charge that "more probably than not" Oppenheimer was acting "under a Soviet directive in influencing United States military, atomic energy, intelligence and diplomatic policy."[47] This began the formal process of discrediting Oppenheimer. Describing this period, George Quester wrote:

> In effect, there was a race between the funding and deployment of population-protecting air defense equipment on one hand and Soviet and American progress in the development of the hydrogen bomb and jet bombers on the other. The President's decision to go ahead with the bomb in 1950 had not been a final defeat for the defense advocates, but [the H-bomb tests] were more serious setbacks, showing perhaps that "nature" was on the offensive weapons side, since any big program of early-warning radar and jet interceptor protection had still only reached the proposal stage.[48]

Given the level of political intrusion into the technological "race" between offense and defense, Quester was right to put "nature" in quotation marks. Whatever the actual merits of a defensive alternative to a nuclear arms race, the U.S. fixation on expanding offensive capabilities was not driven by a scientific consensus that defense was impossible. Had policymakers been interested in the simultaneous pursuit of defense emphasis and offensive arms control, hopes of thereby preventing the emergence of a Soviet assured destruction capability would have been supported by the most authoritative study of defensive technologies during this period.

The discussion above illustrates one important aspect of the political opposition to defense emphasis: the determined effort by the Air Force to discredit supporters of continental defense. Yet though the attitude of Air Force officials can be explained in terms of bureaucratic interests, their influence on policy required the acquiescence of the Truman and Eisenhower administrations. Among the political factors that stood between technological assessments and selection of policy, it was the views of these two presidents on the role of

---

The Hydrogen Bomb: The Men, the Menace, the Mechanism (New York: David McKay, 1954), p. 184.

47. Stern (n. 37), p. 217. See also Gilpin (n. 26), p. 132.

48. George Quester, *Nuclear Diplomacy: The First Twenty-five Years* (New York: Dunellen, 1970), p. 76.

nuclear weapons that were clearly most crucial in shaping choices between offense and defense.

Presidential Leadership

As I noted earlier, the argument that continental defense and arms control were "necessary complements" was presented during the closing months of the Truman administration. Formal consideration of the panel's arguments occurred during the first six months of the Eisenhower administration. Nevertheless, it was President Truman who bore responsibility for the initial "cardinal choices" regarding nuclear policy. Given that Soviet strategic nuclear capabilities were barely emerging by the end of his administration, the technological environment of near-total offense dominance is largely a legacy of Truman's personal decision to exploit the offensive potential of atomic and thermonuclear weapons.

To President Truman, the atomic bomb was a weapon so horrendous ("it murders the civilian population by wholesale")[49] as to require international control of atomic energy. He also saw it as an irresistible military alternative (e.g., Hiroshima and Nagasaki, U.S. war-fighting plans after 1948) to costly conventional warfare. Swinging between the extremes of complete disarmament and usable superiority, Truman betrayed no familiarity with the notion that intermediate measures (i.e., arms control) were conceivable, and he certainly displayed no interest in investigating what sort of force posture might enhance future U.S. "freedom of action" to negotiate. "Since we can't obtain international control," he told his advisers in 1949, "we must be strongest in atomic weapons."[50]

Characterizing Truman's failure to consider an H-bomb test ban, McGeorge Bundy has aptly written: "When conflicting claims of common danger and national defense are presented as a crude choice between racing ahead and falling behind, it is the President above all others who should ask for something better."[51]

That failure to grasp long-term nuclear issues might be explained by reference to the novelty of the weapons and the immediacy of concern over defending Europe. Nevertheless, one might have expected active presidential attentiveness to the likelihood that a

49. Quoted in Rosenberg (n. 31), pp. 26–27.

50. Ibid., pp. 21–22.

51. Bundy (n. 1), p. 20. For more extensive speculation on how "a different president" might have avoided the nuclear arms race, see Bundy (n. 3).

meaningful U.S. nuclear advantage was unsustainable and that pursuing it would guarantee the growing vulnerability of the U.S. homeland. Truman's rejection of appeals to seek alternatives to an unrestrained atomic airpower buildup can only be regarded as a scarcely considered political choice.

In this context, Truman's lack of interest in continental defense seems at odds with his own nuclear policy objectives. After all, a decision to reject arms control all but ensured a steadily growing Soviet offensive threat. Even if one considered only the possibility that the United States would strike first (in the event of a war in Europe), such an attack could not indefinitely preclude devastating retaliation. Although the Air Force, driven by its "life and death" struggle for bureaucratic supremacy, might be expected to neglect the obvious need for active defense in a nuclear war, it is hardly obvious why the president would endorse that position. In short, Truman delayed initiating a major effort at improving U.S. air defenses even though a defense policy predicated on nuclear threats seemed to mandate it.

In this context also, it is significant that government advocates of a coherent nuclear war-fighting doctrine considered the technological prospects for defense far more promising than did those who promoted defense-emphasis arms control. Whereas the latter group assumed that offensive arms control was necessary for a meaningful defense, these war-fighters held (as some continue to hold) that defense might well outstrip the offense even in an unconstrained arms race.

During the Truman years, the State Department's Policy Planning Staff (under the strong direction of Paul Nitze) was the major government source arguing that strategic defense was central to an overall war-fighting strategy. For the last two years of the Truman administration, Nitze and his staff sought to persuade the president of the need for an effective defense. Their first assumption was that though the prospect for an effective defense was unknown, it was entirely possible that one could be developed, if only the effort was made: "New weapons are constantly being developed, and . . . in the past, new defensive weapons which could successfully challenge new offensive weapons have invariably been produced. . . . That the possibilities are great is evidenced, in one important instance at least, by the fact that the atomic bomb itself was designed, developed and used within a four-year period."[52]

52. "Memorandum by the Executive Secretary of the Policy Planning Staff (Schwartz) to the Counselor (Bohlen), May 12, 1952, *FRUS*, pt. 1, pp. 14–15.

The second justification for defense was that it was vital to ward off a Soviet surprise attack:

> We believe that the present state of international tensions . . . require[s] us to assume that the risk of war remains great. We believe it would be imprudent to make a contrary assumption so long as we do not have the capability of successfully defending areas of vital interest—including the defense of the United States against "direct attack of serious and possibly catastrophic proportions."[53]

> It has been estimated that if the Soviet Union should drop 500 or more atomic bombs on targets in the United States, our ability to recover from the attack would be destroyed. . . . To prevent such a national tragedy of this sort, it is clear that the United States must develop a combined system of air defense and civil defense. . . .
>
> The inadequacy of military measures precedent to a manageable civil defense and of our civil defense system, including early warning, constitute [*sic*] a startling weakness in our national defense at the present time. Our civilians and our industrial establishment would suffer terrible losses as a consequence of enemy atomic attack.
>
> On the other hand, an effective defense would be a powerful deterrent to war; the enemy would be reluctant to strike if its blows would not be effective against us. Furthermore, an adequate defense would increase tremendously our security, add to our power position with respect to the Soviet Union, and give us a sounder base for speaking with assurance in international affairs.[54]

Toward the end of the Truman administration, then, appeals for a continental defense were emanating from two disparate groups: those who thought it essential for arms control, and those who saw it as necessary (and feasible) in the absence of arms control. The former group held that defensive technology could at least delay emergent U.S. vulnerability; the latter believed that a concerted effort at defense might even reverse the nuclear revolution. Although the technical studies of defense only justified the more limited goal of forestalling U.S. vulnerability, supporters of defense could accurately refer to broad support—within the community of scientists who had studied the problem—in favor of a major U.S. effort.[55]

53. "Paper Drafted by the Policy Planning Staff: Basic Issues Raised by Draft NSC 'Reappraisal of U.S. Objectives and Strategy for National Security,'" undated, *FRUS*, pt. 1, p. 61.

54. "Paper Drafted by Paul H. Nitze and Carlton Savage of the Policy Planning Staff," November 11, 1952, *FRUS*, pt. 1, pp. 182–83.

55. In their opposition to a major effort at continental defense, the Joint Chiefs of

Nevertheless, President Truman was simply not interested in continental defense, either as an alternative to an airpower buildup or to complement it. In effect, Truman had made his own "estimate" of the prospects for defense, indicated by his response when Jack Gorrie informed him of the optimistic reports of the scientists working on the problem. From the minutes of that NSC meeting: "As far as he could see, said the President, there wasn't very much in prospect except a vigorous offense." A moment later, Secretary of Defense Robert Lovett echoed the president's sentiments: "The defensive weapon of today was almost always an offensive weapon also."[56] Thus Truman bequeathed to his successor a policy that, by rejecting both arms control and a commitment to continental defense, seemed designed to hasten the emergence of United States vulnerability to complete annihilation.

In contrast to his predecessor, Dwight Eisenhower undertook an early effort to formulate a coherent nuclear policy, a process that spanned most of his first year in office. Thanks to the timing of its report, the Panel of Consultants on Disarmament was able to make its case to the president and his top advisers during the first weeks of the new administration. Largely as a result of the consultants' efforts, continental defense quickly became the subject of intense discussion within the narrow group responsible for shaping nuclear policy.

The relative prominence of continental defense on the presidential agenda also reflected the fact that Eisenhower, unlike Truman, did not have any preconceived technical judgments regarding the prospects for air defense. Indeed, by October 1953 his administration had fully accepted the technological assessments and recommendations of the Lincoln Summer Study. Finally, the Soviet's detonation of a hydrogen bomb in August provided a shocking reminder of America's growing vulnerability that effectively silenced Air Force opposition to a meaningful effort at strategic defense.

Nevertheless, by the end of that year, the policy that emerged differed drastically from that advocated by the panel. The decision

---

Staff (JCS) were able to draw on one study (produced by the RAND Corporation in 1952) identifying possible countermeasures to a prospective early-warning system. Based on that study, the JCS argued that "spoof raids and false alarms . . . could eventually reduce the effectiveness of this great investment to a low level." JCS 1899/22, December 22, 1952, "Memorandum for the Secretary of Defense, Subject: Early Warning System," /s/J. Lawton Collins, Chief of Staff, U.S. Army, "for the Joint Chiefs of Staff." Files of the Joint Chiefs of Staff. Cited in Jockel (n. 36), p. 185.

56. "Memorandum for the President of Discussion at the 122d Meeting of the National Security Council on Wednesday, September 3, 1952," *FRUS*, pt. 1, p. 121.

to rely on strategic nuclear bombing culminated in John Foster Dulles's public enunciation of the "massive retaliation" doctrine in January 1954. Continental defense was indeed given a far higher priority, though scarcely in pursuit of defense emphasis arms control. As Glenn Snyder has explained, "Greater effort in the air defense field was a logical complement to the strategy of 'instant, massive retaliation,' for the credibility of such a threat would be small indeed if the United States were to leave itself wide open to retaliatory air attacks by the Soviet's long-range air force."[57]

The Eisenhower administration's rationale for strategic defense meant a victory for those who (like Nitze) had promoted defense as a vital component of a nuclear war-fighting capability. It set the stage for the later association of strategic defense with the rejection of arms control, in stark contrast to the (now largely forgotten) earlier identification of defense as a means to make arms control possible. The end of Eisenhower's tenure found the United States with three thousand nuclear-capable bombers, the beginnings of ICBM deployment, a substantial early warning and antiaircraft network in the United States, and a growing belief on the president's part that further pursuit of a war-winning strategy was in fact "crazy."[58]

Eisenhower's last position on nuclear strategy as president envisioned use of the new Polaris fleet to "disrupt and knock out" Soviet defenses, followed by a SAC assault that would obliterate Soviet society. "All we really have that is meaningful," he told his advisers in 1960, "is a deterrent."[59] Having largely despaired of massive retaliation, he left no record of regret over past failure to come to grips with the 1953 observation of the report of the Panel of Consultants on Disarmament, that "beyond a certain point we cannot ward off the Soviet threat merely by 'keeping ahead of the Russians.'" The message had been even more simply stated in the same report: "The atomic bomb works both ways."[60]

President Eisenhower in fact met several times with the consultants during his first few months in office. On different occasions, Allen Dulles, Vannevar Bush, and Oppenheimer each attempted to explain the futility and risk of pursuing an offensive strategic arms race, while making the case for continental defense.

President Eisenhower's rejection of their recommendations, cou-

57. Glenn H. Snyder, "The 'New Look' of 1953," in *Strategy, Politics and Defense Budgets*, ed. Warner R. Schilling, Paul Y. Hammond, and Glenn H. Snyder (New York: Columbia University Press, 1962), p. 462.

58. Rosenberg (n. 31), pp. 62–63.

59. Ibid.

60. "Report by the Panel of Consultants" (n. 14), p. 1079.

pled with his acceptance of defense as an integral component of a nuclear war-fighting posture, seems to reflect considerable initial optimism regarding the prospects for national survival and victory in a war with the Soviet Union. In other words, the president appeared to reject the panel's prediction that a nuclear arms race would nullify any U.S. effort at homeland defense. Yet Eisenhower often privately acknowledged the futility and danger of pursuing meaningful nuclear superiority over the Soviet Union—even during the first years of his presidency. Since he nevertheless chose massive retaliation, it is necessary to look further for plausible explanations of the choice to reject exploration of mutual defense emphasis in favor of an airpower buildup.

National Security Rationales for Relying on Strategic Airpower

Reflecting on the fact that both superpowers "possess power to destroy the world," MAD supporter Leon Wieseltier has written: "We are stuck with it; there are grounds for a certain amount of fatalism about history after Hiroshima."[61] Such fatalism might be justified had decision makers been ignorant of the insight that MAD was a predictable outcome of the U.S. offensive buildup. It could also be explained by an expert consensus that technology precluded an arms control approach combining defense emphasis and offensive constraints. But both those explanations are at odds with reality.

There are other factors, however, that might retrospectively justify fatalism regarding U.S. adoption of massive retaliation. First, had the Soviets demonstrated an unshakable commitment to a massive offensive buildup in the 1950s, one could argue that simple prudence would have driven U.S. decision makers to fully exploit the offensive potential of nuclear weapons. (Unless one is utterly convinced that the defense is technologically dominant, the other side's pursuit of a disarming first-strike capability all but compels the potential victim to expand its offenses.)

Second, massive retaliation could be justified if decision makers had concluded that only a capacity to annihilate the Soviet Union could forestall an invasion of Europe. Despite recognition that nu-

61. Leon Wieseltier, "A Defense of Nuclear Realism," *The Nuclear Predicament: A Sourcebook*, ed. Donna Gregory (New York: St. Martin's Press, 1986), p. 296. This article originally appeared in the *Los Angeles Times*, October 7, 1984, sec. 4, p. 1.

clear superiority was a "wasting asset" (as Richard Betts has described Eisenhower's own perception of his policy),[62] a short-term ability to defeat the Soviets in a nuclear war could be seen as a vital stopgap measure for the protection of Europe, even though the explicit first-strike threat underlying the massive retaliation doctrine would eventually compel Soviet leaders to build a devastating retaliatory capability. It would simply have to be left to future administrations to find new approaches for reliably protecting Europe, while being endlessly careful not to somehow trigger the complete destruction of the United States. Despite those dismal implications, President Eisenhower could hardly be blamed if the choice was between a near-certain catastrophe in the present (the loss of Western Europe) and possible catastrophe, even of far greater magnitude, in the future.

The fact is, however, that the strategic airpower buildup of the Eisenhower years was driven neither by Soviet nuclear policy nor by any apparent conviction on President Eisenhower's part that he faced a stark choice between building thousands of strategic weapons and losing Western Europe.

Soviet Strategic Policy

Those arguing for defense emphasis envisioned at least a tacit arms control agreement with the Soviet Union, to be pursued by a combination of offensive restraint and private dialogue. In the long run they hoped that a combination of verification measures and mutual defense emphasis could provide the basis for an enduring disarmament agreement. Since their receptivity to this approach was never tested, one can hardly assume that the Soviets would have rejected a serious U.S. proposal for MDE. Although the United States exaggerated Soviet offensive strength through most of the 1950s, it became increasingly clear that in their deployment policy the Soviets had in fact emphasized antiaircraft capabilities, persisting in this approach despite the growing U.S. capacity to overwhelm their defense.

The Soviets began constructing an early warning radar network in 1946.[63] Two years later they began deploying jet-powered MIG-15s—designed primarily for high-altitude interception of bombers—pro-

62. Richard K. Betts, *Nuclear Blackmail and Nuclear Balance* (Washington, D.C.: Brookings Institution, 1987), p. 154.

63. Asher Lee, *The Soviet Air and Rocket Forces* (New York: Praeger, 1959), p. 121.

ducing approximately 15,000 by 1954.[64] In 1948 the Soviet Air Defense (PVO Strany) became an independent branch of the armed services. Its manpower (according to Western estimates) was in the 500,000 to 600,000 range, about half assigned to ground forces (manning antiaircraft artillery to defend economic centers) and half to fighter interception.[65] In 1952 the Soviets began deploying their first all-weather and night interceptors (the YAK-25)[66] and an improved, supersonic version of the MIG-15 (the MIG-19).[67] Close to 4,000 of these two fighter interceptors had been produced by 1955,[68] with most of the Soviets' elite pilots assigned to the strategic defense mission.[69] By this time they possessed multitiered lines of radar stations,[70] had deployed about 10,000 radar-guided antiaircraft guns, and had begun a massive deployment of surface-to-air missiles.[71]

By contrast, the United States had in effect no air defense before 1950. President Truman did not authorize work on a comprehensive early warning radar network until December 1952, and a significant commitment to a national air defense system began only in late 1953. Even after that, funding limitations and inadequate centralized management continued to retard implementation of planned improvements; a February 1955 study showed persisting gaps in radar coverage and major shortfalls in production and quality of defensive weaponry. Moreover, in contrast to the Soviet Union, the United States simply failed to lay the groundwork for a meaningful program in civil defense.[72]

64. Ibid., p. 107. For a discussion of the role and capabilities of the MIG-15, see Matthew A. Evangelista, "The Evolution of Soviet Tactical Air Forces," in *Soviet Armed Forces Review Annual*, ed. David R. Jones (Gulf Breeze, Fla.: Academic International Press, 1982–83), pp. 454–55.

65. Matthew A. Evangelista, "Stalin's Postwar Army Reappraised," *International Security* 7 (Winter 1982–83): 132. The author points out that these forces were misleadingly included in estimates of Soviet offensive forces, contributing to significant exaggeration of Soviet capabilities for an invasion of Europe.

66. Lee (n. 63), p. 141, and Evangelista (n. 64), p. 457.

67. Robert P. Berman, *Soviet Air Power in Transition* (Washington, D.C.: Brookings Institution, 1978), p. 25.

68. Robert A. Kilmarx, *A History of Soviet Airpower* (New York: Praeger, 1962), p. 226.

69. Lee (n. 63), pp. 124–25.

70. Johan Holst, "Missile Defense: The Soviet Union and the Arms Race," in *Why ABM? Policy Issues in the Missile Defense Controversy*, ed. Johan J. Holst and William Schneider, Jr. (New York: Pergamon Press, 1969), pp. 146, 154.

71. Ibid.; Lee (n. 63), pp. 124–25.

72. See n. 36. The first aircraft control and warning system (called Lashup) was deployed in 1950. With huge gaps in its coverage, the Defense Department Weapons System Evaluation Group concluded that all Soviet bombers might reach their targets. Jockel (n. 36), p. 114. In July 1953, in a SAC drill that sent ninty-nine bomber sorties

Instead, the United States concentrated on overwhelming the rapidly expanding Soviet air defense. By 1955 the United States had acquired a stockpile of 2,250 nuclear bombs (the largest with a yield of fifteen megatons)[73] and had produced approximately 2,000 bombers. (These included intercontinental-range B-36s and the new B-52, as well as medium-range B-29s and B-47s, which could be launched at the Soviet Union from thirty-two overseas bases.) A 1954 SAC war plan called for a near simultaneous first strike by 735 bombers, after which (according to a summary of the classified SAC briefing) "virtually all of Russia would be nothing but a smoking, radiating ruin."[74]

Although the Soviets also pursued an offensive nuclear capability during this period, there is retrospective consensus among analysts that their emphasis was on active defense.[75] Until 1954, the only potential threat to U.S. territory was the TU-4, a propeller-driven medium-range bomber (with a maximum radius of 1,500 miles) capable of reaching the United States on a one-way "suicide" mission. (Some Western experts have maintained that Soviet nuclear weapons of this period were too large to be carried by the TU-4.)[76] According to one recent analysis, the TU-4 "represented a perceived need on the part of Soviet military planners to target NATO's air and military bases, rather than an attempt to achieve an intercontinental capability against the United States."[77] Assuming the TU-4 was nuclear capable, the crucial limiting factor on the Soviet Union's offensive strength was the size of its nuclear stockpile. In 1953 the United States estimated the stockpile at 120 bombs (with yields from thirty to one hundred kilotons, and a total of six megatons).[78]

---

in a simulated surprise attack, the Air Defense Command was able to achieve only two interceptions. "Memorandum Op-36C/jm, 18 March 1954," reprinted as "Document One" in *International Security* 6 (Winter 1981–82), pp. 24–25. For a review of these and other estimates of U.S. air defense capabilities, see Betts (n. 62), pp. 147–59. For a review of the succession of U.S. plans to address inadequacies in air defense during 1952–53, see n. 148.

73. Thomas B. Cochran, William M. Arkin, and Milton M. Hoenig, *Nuclear Weapons Databook* (Cambridge, Mass.: Ballinger, 1984), p. 15.

74. "Document One" (n. 72), pp. 19–22.

75. For an extensive look at this issue drawing on both U.S. and Soviet sources, see Evangelista (n. 64), pp. 451–79.

76. Robert P. Berman and John C. Baker, *Soviet Strategic Forces: Requirements and Responses* (Washington, D.C.: Brookings Institution, 1982).

77. Evangelista (n. 64), pp. 468–69.

78. "Report of the Special Evaluation Subcommittee of the National Security Council," n.d., *FRUS*, pt. 1, p. 332; "Statement of Policy by the National Security Council," September 25, 1953, *FRUS*, pt. 1, p. 479. See also summaries of National Intelligence Estimates in *FRUS*, pt. 1, p. 725.

In 1954 two dramatic developments promised to rapidly increase U.S. vulnerability. First, the Soviets began producing H-bombs (with maximum estimated yields of one megaton). Combined with an expanding stockpile (estimated to reach three hundred sometime during 1955), estimates of the total yield of Soviet nuclear bombs rose to twenty-four megatons in 1954.[79] Although still possessing only a small fraction of the U.S. arsenal, the Soviets were now clearly within reach of the ability to destroy the United States.[80]

The second development in 1954 was the Soviets' deployment of their first intercontinental-range bomber (the Bear), which was also capable of carrying thermonuclear weapons, followed within a year by the jet-powered Bison.[81] Although the existence of an operational Soviet strategic capability was now beyond doubt, by the end of the decade the Soviets had deployed only about thirty-five Bisons and one hundred Bears.[82] (They first tested an intercontinental-range missile in 1957, setting the stage for the massive strategic buildup of the mid-1960s.)

Given the U.S. commitment to offensive force expansion, it is hard to understand the intensity and persistence of the Soviet emphasis on defense. Western analysts have suggested wide-ranging partial explanations: the Soviet (and Russian) historical experience, in which national survival had repeatedly required a costly (but ultimately successful) effort at homeland defense; bureaucratic impediments to "cost-effective" military planning; technical problems besetting several generations of long-range bombers; and a perceptive recognition that the future of the offense lay with development of the long-range missile.

Whatever the roots of their behavior, Soviet policymakers clearly did not share Truman's belief that "there wasn't very much in prospect except a vigorous offense." In effect, Truman's assumption—since it represented the prevailing U.S. view—became a self-fulfilling prophecy. It did so by rationalizing both the neglect of U.S. defenses and the mounting of a massive retaliation threat against the Soviets. In the face of that U.S. offensive buildup, the Soviet policy of defense emphasis proved untenable and indeed provided a concrete demonstration of the technological imbalance between offense and defense in the nuclear age. Once defense was thus proved

79. "Report of the Special Evaluation Subcommittee" (n. 78).

80. For a review of estimates of potential damage from a Soviet attack during this period, see Betts (n. 62), pp. 147–59.

81. Berman (n. 67), p. 110.

82. Ibid., p. 25.

"impossible," the Soviets were left no deterrent option other than to create their own assured destruction capability.

It is noteworthy that had the United States instead imitated Soviet deployment policy through the mid-1950s, both sides would have approached a credible defense-oriented deterrent posture. (For the United States, of course, this would have required a deliberate decision not to exploit its initial offensive advantage.) Such a strategic environment might have been close to Oppenheimer's vision of the conditions necessary for successful disarmament negotiations, where "steps of evasion will be either too vast to conceal or far too small to have, in view of existing measures of defense, a decisive strategic effect."

Serious exploration of that possibility, of course, would have depended on Soviet interest in offensive nuclear disarmament. The standard historical assessment of negotiations during this period is that the Soviets sabotaged the effort by refusing to consider measures for inspection. Two explanations are given for that purportedly crucial obstacle to meaningful negotiations. The first is that sweeping Soviet nuclear disarmament proposals were merely propaganda. The second is that the full magnitude of the Soviets' offensive inferiority would be exposed by a breach of secrecy, so that a forthright exchange of information could endanger their survival. The latter explanation was given credence by Nikita Khrushchev's denunciation of the 1955 U.S. "Open Skies" proposal as a "bald espionage plot." Yet if the Soviets were understandably unwilling to give the United States a detailed blueprint of their capabilities in the absence of a demonstrable U.S. commitment to disarmament, their proposals that same year reflected a dramatic reversal of their previous reluctance to deal concretely with the issue of inspection. Indeed, the Soviet proposals for verification offered in May 1955 at Geneva fully matched those of the West, calling for an international staff to have "unimpeded access at all times to all objects of control . . . on a continuing basis."[83]

83. "Soviet Proposal Introduced in the Disarmament Subcommittee: Reduction of Armaments, the Prohibition of Atomic Weapons, and the Elimination of the Threat of a New War, May 19, 1955," in *Documents on Disarmament, 1945–1959*, vol. 1, *1945–1956*, ed. Department of State (Washington, D.C.: U.S. Government Printing Office, 1960), pp. 456–72 (quotation from p. 467). This proposal envisioned a two-stage disarmament process. The first stage aimed at preventing surprise attack by positioning inspectors at communications centers, ports, airfields, major highways, etc. The implementation of the first stage would "create the necessary atmosphere of trust . . . for the extension of the functions of the international control organ" (p. 466). The

Initially, Western negotiators reacted with great enthusiasm. The British delegate stated that "we have made an advance that I never dreamed possible." Western persistence, he noted, had "now achieved this welcome dividend, and . . . the proposals [of the West] have now been largely, and in some cases entirely, adopted

---

basic argument was that the Soviets would not agree to the radically intrusive inspection necessary for the destruction of nuclear arsenals without such a confidence-building initial stage. Thus the proposal both suggested the level of inspection that would be necessary to verify nuclear disarmament (e.g., admission to military production plants) and withheld acceptance of such measures until "an atmosphere of trust has been created" (pp. 463–65). Although welcoming the Soviet proposal, a U.S. representative would reasonably observe the next day that "it is not clear that the control organ's inspectors can go everywhere and see everything necessary to make sure that . . . nuclear weapons are not being secreted. It will require some time before we will know what is the true Soviet position on this crucial question of controls." "Statement by the Deputy United States Representative on the Disarmament Subcommitte (Wadsworth) regarding the New Soviet Proposal, May 11, 1955," in *Documents on Disarmament*, p. 473. A week later, however, the U.S. delegation was instructed to halt discussions and withdraw from the conference. Subsequently, U.S. references to the Soviet proposal stressed that no system of inspection had been devised that would be sufficient to reliably implement the second stage of the Soviet plan, invoking the Soviets' own acknowledgment of the difficulties of achieving ironclad inspection. No explanation was ever offered for rejecting the first stage of the Soviet proposal, though it in fact appeared to offer an effective hedge against surprise attack and certainly against conventional surprise attack—which should have been the paramount Western concern during this period of massive U.S. nuclear superiority.

The U.S. "Open Skies" plan of July 1955 was in effect a counterproposal to the Soviet plan for inspection teams. The Soviets offered good reasons for rejecting the U.S. plan. Thus Soviet foreign minister Molotov accepted the inclusion of aerial reconaissance, but only in conjunction with the implementation of an arms reduction agreement. Otherwise, he pointed out, "each party which has given information concerning its armed forces and has also permitted the other side to photograph its territory, would be under a constant threat that the other party which has the proper information at its disposal may utilize it for a surprise attack and for aggression." "Statement by the Soviet Foreign Minister (Molotov) at the Geneva Meeting of Foreign Ministers, November 10, 1955," in *Documents on Disarmament*, pp. 544–45. Later another Soviet official invoked public statements by U.S. military officials on the need for better aerial reconaissance in planning strategy for a successful nuclear war, adding: "In light of such statements, I would ask this: How are we expected to treat the proposal on the exchange of military blueprints and on aerial photography, without the reduction of armaments and the prohibition of atomic weapons? The implementation of that proposal, unless it were connected with the cessation of the armaments race, could undoubtedly be utilized by aggressive military circles which cherish plans for preparing and unleashing a new world war." "Statement by the Soviet Representative (Kuznetsov) to the First Committee of the General Assembly, December 7, 1955," in *Documents on Disarmament*, pp. 572–73. Khrushchev's depiction of "Open Skies" as a "bald espionage plot" was reported by Dwight D. Eisenhower in *Mandate for Change* (New York: Doubleday, 1963), p. 521.

by the Soviet Union and made into its own proposals."[84] The reaction of the chief U.S. negotiator was almost identical.[85]

At a higher level of government, however, Soviet responsiveness on inspection quickly prompted the United States to radically reverse its official position on disarmament. After calling for a recess in the negotiations, the United States announced that it "does now place a reservation upon all of its pre-Geneva substantive positions."[86] In 1957, when Harold Stassen (President Eisenhower's special assistant on disarmament) finally announced the new U.S. position, it was explained that the United States now rejected its previous support for "a very extreme form of control and inspection" and explicitly renounced nuclear disarmament as an objective.[87]

84. Quoted in Philip Noel-Baker, *The Arms Race: A Programme for World Disarmament* (London: Atlantic Books, 1958), p. 22.

85. Ibid. See *Documents on Disarmament* (n. 83), pp. 473–74, for similar statements by a U.S. representative—that the Soviets now appeared to have accepted the proposals of the Western powers.

86. The U.S. representative added: "In placing this reservation . . . , may I make it perfectly clear that we are not withdrawing any of these positions, we are not disavowing any of them. But we are indicating clearly that we do not now reaffirm them." "Statement by the Deputy United States Representative (Stassen) to the Disarmament Subcommittee, September 6, 1955," in *Documents on Disarmament* (n. 83), p. 513. The new U.S. position seized on the Soviet admission that no ironclad inspection system had yet been devised, without noting the irrelevance of that point to the Soviet (and earlier U.S.) proposals for a partial inspection system for detecting surprise attack preparations and building confidence for more intrusive measures.

87. From the same speech: "It is our view that if an effort is made to reduce armaments, armed forces, and military expenditures to a level that is too low . . . it would not be conducive to stability in the world. . . . It is our view that if armaments . . . are brought down to too low a level, then . . . the danger of war is increased." This April 11, 1957, statement by the U.S. special assistant on disarmament, Harold Stassen, is quoted in Noel-Baker (n. 84), p. 29.

The formal U.S. repudiation of nuclear disarmament as an objective had occurred in March 1957. In announcing that the United States no longer believed a reliable inspection system was possible, Stassen added: "Is it not clear, then, that no nation could agree that all nuclear weapons should be removed from the face of the earth if it meant that in the ten years ahead . . . some nation might suddenly have and exercise a tremendous, overpowering military force against all other nations solely by reason of having within its hands a clandestinely developed and secretively maintained storehouse of multi-megaton bombs?" "Statement by the United States Representative (Stassen) to the Disarmament Subcommittee: Nuclear Weapons and Testing, March 20, 1957," in *Documents on Disarmament, 1945–1959*, vol. 2, *1957–1959* (Washington, D.C.: Government Printing Office, 1960), p. 763.

That speech, albeit vaguely, endorsed a stable balance of terror as the goal of arms control. Equally vaguely, the United States proposed in the same speech that the alternative to working out a stable balance of terror arrangement would be for both sides to develop an effective defense against nuclear attack. Although it would be stretching the point to describe this as the first official U.S. proposal for mutual de-

Why did a perception of genuine Soviet interest in nuclear disarmament arouse concern in the West? In a 1955 speech before the House of Commons, Winston Churchill provided a succinct answer: "It is easy, of course, for the Communists to say now, 'let us ban all nuclear weapons.' Communist ascendency in conventional weapons would then become overwhelming. That might bring peace, but only peace in the form of subjugation of the Free World to the Communist system."[88]

If President Eisenhower had fully shared that fear, then the U.S. refusal to seriously explore strategic offensive limitations would at least be understandable. Yet the record of Eisenhower's exchanges with his own top officials reveals that he consistently (at least in private) rejected arguments that reflected Churchill's position. To dispel the myth of "justifiable fatalism" regarding the race toward MAD capabilities, let us examine Eisenhower's views on the relation between the Soviet threat to Europe and the common danger posed by strategic nuclear weapons.

Strategic Airpower and the Defense of Europe

From the earliest days of the massive retaliation doctrine, Eisenhower privately expressed a belief that a war-fighting nuclear strategy was unsustainable and dangerous. The following is from the minutes of an NSC meeting in May 1954, discussing whether the United States should agree to an "international moratorium on future tests of atomic weapons":

> The President reiterated the view he had expressed at previous meetings of the Council, that he could perceive no final answer to the prob-

fense emphasis, it is worth repeating Stassen's remarks: "If such an arrangement is not worked out . . . the United States will carry forward with thoroughness research and development concerning the means by which nuclear explosions might intercept and defend against nuclear attack, particularly as regards nuclear devices which themselves do not involve the extensive projection of radioactive particles into the atmosphere or over the surrounding ground. . . . It is in this area of research and development that we foresee one of the more favourable possibilities, namely, that if no agreement results from our work here a defence may be established which would stop and destroy nuclear bombs from any aggressor before they arrived at their targets in the United States or in any other nation which was under attack. I believe that my associates will immediately see the importance of this kind of research and development, particularly if we think of ten years ahead and visualize the possibility of no agreement being reached on the matters we are deliberating" (pp. 768–69).

88. *Winston S. Churchill: His Complete Speeches*, vol. 8, *1959–1963* (London: Chelsea House, 1974), p. 8625.

lem of nuclear warfare if both sides simply went ahead making bigger and better nuclear weapons. . . . It was . . . a matter of despair to look ahead to a future which contained nothing but more and more bombs. . . . We must try to find some positive answer, and to do so would require more imaginative thinking than was going on at present in this Government. Soon, said the President, even little countries will have a stockpile of these bombs, and then we *will* be in a mess.[89]

When Eisenhower made those observations, Treasury Secretary George Humphrey responded with the standard argument against nuclear arms control, stating that "he simply couldn't see how this country could jeopardize the one great advantage that it now possesses over the Soviet Union. . . . It was unthinkable that we should take any measures to retard our progress in this field. We must keep all the edge we now have."[90]

Many high officials in the Eisenhower admininstration shared that view. At a subsequent NSC meeting, Secretary of State John Foster Dulles reiterated his belief that no nuclear arms control agreements (and specifically no test ban) should be pursued as long as the Soviets possessed a conventional advantage in Europe.[91] Eisenhower's response and his subsequent exchange with Dulles reflect an apparently decisive rejection of that view:

The President stated with great emphasis that . . . he would strongly challenge . . . [Dulles's assumption] that the United States continues to oppose abolition except as part of a general disarmament program. . . . He explained that he was certain that with its great resources the United States would surely be able to whip the Soviet Union in any kind of war . . . [other] than an atomic war. . . . The matter of the morality of the use of these weapons was of no significance. The real thing was that the advantage of surprise almost seemed the decisive factor in an atomic war, and we should do anything we could to remove this factor.

Secretary Dulles said that the President's comments were profoundly important and had a great bearing on our national strategy. . . . He thought that the USSR might agree to cease activity in the nuclear area, where they know the United States now has superiority, and go back to an area of conventional armaments where they have superiority. The President interjected that the Secretary meant where they have *initial*

89. "Memorandum of Discussion at the 199th Meeting of the National Security Council, Thursday, May 27, 1954," in *FRUS*, pt. 2, p. 1455.

90. Ibid.

91. "Memorandum of Discussion at the 203d Meeting of the National Security Council, Wednesday, June 23, 1954," *FRUS*, pt. 2, p. 1468.

> superiority. Secretary Dulles agreed with the correction, and went on to point out how much the abolition of atomic weapons would help us in our problems with our allies and in the United Nations. Secretary Dulles stated his agreement that there ought to be a reappraisal of the basic situation with respect to disarmament. . . . The President restated his position that there was no way in which the United States could be licked by any enemy in a protracted war of exhaustion unless we were the victims of surprise atomic attack.[92]

This was not the first time President Eisenhower had expressed this opinion. Indeed, at a high-level meeting four months earlier (which Eisenhower did not attend), Dulles clearly indicated the president's rejection of the argument that nuclear disarmament favored the Soviet Union:

> Secretary Dulles stated that the President feels if a way could be found which would eliminate atomic . . . weapons . . . he would be prepared to accept it even if it left the USSR with a numerical predominance in ground forces. Secretary Dulles said the President indicated he would be willing to do this because he is convinced that the U.S. industrial potential and capability for rapid mobilization would still constitute an effective deterrent to Soviet aggression and that if such aggression should occur, the U.S. industrial capability, when harnessed into a war effort, would ultimately defeat them.[93]

Eisenhower's insight was compelling. Given the Soviets' clear (and widely recognized)[94] inferiority in the overall "correlation of forces" that would be brought to bear in a protracted war with the United States, a decision to invade Europe would have been an act of supreme irrationality. Moreover, although Eisenhower expressed varied sentiments regarding other containment-related issues, he consistently showed confidence in the basic rationality of the Soviet

92. Ibid., pp. 1469–70.

93. "Memorandum of Conversation: Summary of Meeting with the Secretary of State on Implementation of the President's December 8th Speech, 6 January 1954," *FRUS*, pt. 2, pp. 1325–26.

94. See Evangelista (n. 65), pp. 110–38. This article provides persuasive evidence that U.S. policymakers overstated the Soviet conventional threat and ignored information that contradicted their claims. Eisenhower's private evaluation of the Soviet threat echoed, for example, a 1948 Central Intelligence Agency report that offered the following as one reason why the Soviets would not invade Europe: "The resulting global conflict would place the entire Soviet system at stake in a war to the finish at a time when the USSR is inferior to the West in potential military power" (p. 134, n. 76).

leader.[95] The president's sound conclusion that only a Soviet strategic buildup could neutralize underlying U.S. superiority should indeed have resulted in the "reappraisal of the basic situation with respect to disarmament" called for by Dulles.

Yet even if "extended deterrence" already existed without a U.S. nuclear buildup, one could still argue that a massive retaliation threat was critical for bolstering European resolve, given the terrifying capacity of the Red Army to overrun Europe in the initial phase of a war. In fact, declassified documents from this period show that claims of a decisive Soviet conventional advantage were based on blatant misrepresentions of Soviet capabilities.[96] Why did that occur? As the author of a comprehensive review of U.S. intelligence estimates concluded, "Elements of the U.S. military, particularly the proponents of strategic air power . . . , found it desirable to exaggerate the Soviet conventional threat, because this left American atomic weapons as the only alternative to Soviet ground forces." By effectively depicting the situation as hopeless, "the U.S. military gave the American people no incentive to favor improving conventional forces for Europe's defense during the 1940s and 1950s."[97] The airpower lobby's strategy thus involved persuading the public that efforts at homeland defense and at European defense would both be futile. Their success in these two complementary campaigns helped create a self-fulfilling prophecy.

A less alarmist portrayal of the Soviet conventional threat would no doubt have helped allay European concerns in the early 1950s. So too would have a public avowal by the president of his privately expressed confidence in America's overwhelming industrial strength for deterring a third world war over Europe. Yet fear in Western Europe was particularly intense during this period,[98] and reassurance seemed to demand some sort of military response.

95. In documenting the president's belief in the rationality of Soviet leaders, McGeorge Bundy cites the following from a television address by Eisenhower on April 5, 1954: "The very fact that those men . . . are in the Kremlin, means that they love power. They want to be there. Whenever they start a war, they are taking the great risk of losing that power. They study history pretty well. . . . When dictators over-reach themselves and challenge the whole world, they are very likely to end up in any place except a dictatorial position. And those men in the politburo know that." Bundy (n. 3), p. 259.

96. Evangelista (n. 65), pp. 110–38.

97. Ibid., p. 136.

98. George Kennan refers to Western Europe's "mania of invasion" in the late 1940s. See George Kennan, *The Nuclear Delusion: Soviet-American Relations in the Atomic Age* (New York: Pantheon, 1983), pp. 59–60.

Here the Panel of Consultants on Disarmament had offered a viewpoint that lay between the extremes of President Eisenhower's actual policy (which implied that massive retaliation threats were essential for Europe's protection) and his private conjecture (implying that Europe should not fear an environment of complete nuclear disarmament and Soviet conventional preponderance).

What the panel had maintained was that their strategic arms control approach should be accompanied by either conventional arms control or a Western conventional buildup:

> A . . . general proposition about arms regulation is that it should not increase other dangers while it attempts to eliminate the threat of a sudden knockout. . . . The American atomic weapon is now being used not only as a balance to the Soviet atom but also as a counterweight to the massive Soviet armies; if it were abandoned, those armies would have to be considerably trimmed. (But this last requirement might be modified insofar as non-Soviet "conventional" armed strength can become a counterweight to the Soviet armies.)[99]

In contrast to Eisenhower, the panel did not propose to divorce nuclear and conventional issues. It suggested instead that decreased reliance on nuclear threats could be coupled to expanded local defense in Europe. Indeed, it seems likely that the overall deterrent effect of combining a better conventional defense with a secure mobilization base would have equaled the combination of massive retaliation threats and growing vulnerability to retaliation that the United States in fact chose as its policy. Under the panel's proposed environment of mutual defense emphasis, moreover, the Soviets would still have had to fear whatever U.S. strategic offenses were retained by agreement, as well as the near certainty that wartime mobilization would include a rapid U.S. nuclear buildup.

In a more general sense, it is important to consider that the Panel of Consultants was proposing to explore how far an arms control approach could supplant unilateral efforts at defense. It cannot be excluded that the Soviets might have proved willing to redress the conventional imbalance in Europe in return for achieving real protection of their homeland against nuclear attack. In light of its enormous nuclear advantage in the early 1950s, the United States would have had great bargaining leverage in pressing for such an arrangement. A willingness to use that leverage in serious negotiations, however, would have required it to confront the fact that its advantage was, in fact, a "wasting asset."

99. "Report by the Panel of Consultants" (n. 14), p. 1090.

It is clear that reliance on massive retaliation was not driven by any conviction that the Soviets would reject genuine efforts to reduce the nuclear danger. Instead, we see such important figures as Churchill and John Foster Dulles—hardly known for their benign views of the Soviet Union—acknowledging possible Soviet interest in nuclear disarmament. Moreover, we see a U.S. president who at times seems convinced that such a prospect would enhance U.S. security by removing the danger of surprise attack without jeopardizing Western Europe.

The Eisenhower administration never acted on those beliefs. Instead, following the president's apparently decisive rejection of the argument that nuclear and conventional disarmament must be linked, Dulles authorized the U.S. rejection of the proposed test moratorium, based "on the assumption . . . that the United States continues to oppose a total abolition of atomic weapons except as part of an effective general disarmament program."[100]

One can retrospectively construct various explanations for the gap between Eisenhower's private declarations and the actual U.S. refusal to seriously explore measures to restrain or reverse the nuclear arms competition. An adherent of the now fashionable "hidden hand" theory of the Eisenhower presidency[101] might argue that for some extraordinarily subtle reason Eisenhower wanted his entire administration (with the exception of Dulles) to believe—erroneously—that he privately favored nuclear disarmament. The more likely explanation is that Eisenhower, like his predecessor, was hopelessly ambivalent and vacillating about the need to address the long-term dangers of relying on nuclear superiority. By 1960, ambivalence had yielded to deep pessimism about the legacy of his war-fighting approach to nuclear policy, as Eisenhower concluded that the Strategic Air Command had become dangerously obsessed with a strategy that would devastate the Soviet Union and its allies without protecting the United States.[102]

As in the Truman administration, the most glaring weakness of nuclear policy during the Eisenhower years was the president's in-

100. "Memorandum by the Secretary of State to the Executive Secretary of the National Security Council (Lay)," June 23, 1954, *FRUS*, pt. 2, pp. 1466–67.

101. The phrase comes from Fred I. Greenstein, *The Hidden-Hand Presidency: Eisenhower as Leader* (New York: Basic Books, 1982). Declassified Eisenhower administration documents have revealed a dramatic contrast between the knowledgeable, articulate private Eisenhower and his often deliberately bumbling public persona. The mere fact that Eisenhower was aware, involved, and politically competent seems to have inspired in some revisionists an almost unqualified admiration for his policies and leadership.

102. See Rosenberg (n. 31), p. 8.

ability to seriously consider some sort of middle ground (arms control) between complete disarmament and usable superiority. If, as Eisenhower believed, the major obstacle to nuclear disarmament was the difficulty of devising an ironclad inspection scheme, why didn't he explore the alternative approach proposed by such eminent government advisers as Oppenheimer, Vannevar Bush, and Allen Dulles? To answer that question, we must examine how far defense policy options were constrained by a variety of domestic political factors.

Strategic Offense Dominance and Domestic Politics

Economic Conservatism

To a large extent, the appeal of strategic airpower was rooted, however irrationally, in the fiscal conservatism of the Eisenhower administration. As one author described it, "In stating the problem of national security in terms of the military forces that could be maintained without bankrupting the country, fiscal considerations were implicitly given precedence over all others in determining the operational character of the New Look."[103] Dulles put it this way in his January 1954 "massive retaliation" speech:

> We need allies and collective security. Our purpose is to make these relations more effective, less costly. This can be done by placing more reliance on deterrent power and less dependence on local defensive power. . . .
>
> The basic decision was to depend primarily upon a great capacity to retaliate, instantly, by means and at places of our choosing. . . . That permits a selection of military means instead of a multiplication of means. As a result, it is now possible to get, and share, more basic security at less cost.[104]

There is no question that the president and some of his top advisers were drawn toward nuclear weapons out of a preoccupation with limiting the budget. This was particularly the case with Treasury Secretary Humphrey, who believed that relying on strategic airpower was the only way "to frustrate Stalin's design of destroying

103. Edward A. Kolodziej, *The Uncommon Defense and Congress, 1945–1963* (Columbus: Ohio State University Press, 1966), p. 199

104. John Foster Dulles, "The Evolution of Foreign Policy," *Department of State Bulletin* 30 (January 20, 1954): 35.

the power of the United States without war through the sapping of its economic health."[105]

Like other rationales for the strategic buildup, however, the economic rationale also foundered on the fact that the "atomic bomb works both ways." In the race to cover new Soviet targets required by the mission of counterforce "blunting," the preservation of offensive strategic superiority amounted to a commitment to an open-ended arms acquisition program. As a result, by the late 1950s the annual nuclear-dominated Eisenhower defense budgets proved nearly as costly as the more balanced defense programs of the Kennedy and Johnson years (excluding the cost of the Vietnam War).[106] There is no "technological" explanation why it took the United States until the mid-1960s to realize that no amount of spending on a nuclear war-fighting strategy would ever be enough. Notwithstanding the short-term fiscal appeal of massive retaliation, there was never any sound basis for believing that nuclear weapons could actually provide more security at less cost. Moreover, the economic justification for massive retaliation cannot fully account for U.S. policy. The nuclear debate occurred within a broader context of domestic political and military culture, in which numerous factors pointed toward an ultimate preference for offense over defense.

Advocates of continental defense were not alone in arguing against reliance on strategic airpower in the early 1950s. Because of the threat SAC posed to their wartime missions, the Army and Navy also mounted attacks on the bomber buildup, for example, questioning its credibility for deterring limited wars, its utility for waging war, and the morality of targeting cities. Yet only the advocates of defense emphasis arms control offered a possible means for addressing the prospect of a Soviet strategic buildup.

There was another key difference betweeen advocacy of defense emphasis and the promotion of other alternatives to airpower. Although the Army and Navy positions suffered temporary setbacks during the decade of SAC's dominance in policy-making, the defense emphasis position was not merely rejected but denounced as indicating questionable loyalty. It is interesting that such intense hostility was never directed at those (both inside and outside government) who were sincerely promoting complete nuclear disarmament and international control.

105. "Memorandum of Discussion at the 134th Meeting of the National Security Council, Wednesday, February 25, 1953," *FRUS*, pt. 2, p. 1111.

106. See Kahan (n. 2), p. 64.

To understand why defense emphasis was a singularly "unthinkable" option for the United States during the bomber age, one must look at the interlinked factors that undercut decision makers' capacity to assess all available options with an open mind. These include U.S. military tradition, the growing anti-Communist hysteria that began with the "fall" of China in 1949, the appeal of an "ultimate weapon" as a symbol of U.S. omnipotence, and the psychological difficulty of coming to terms with the prospect of "defenselessness" against enemy attack.

Cumulatively, the explanation for a U.S. policy that could only end either in preemptive war or in a world of mutual assured destruction can be described in terms of a prevailing "cult of the offensive."[107] The word "cult" here refers to an almost mystical association of strategic airpower with patriotism and righteous wrath against America's enemies. For its members (led by the Air Force and the most anti-Communist extreme of the political spectrum), the rhetoric of disarmament hardly constituted a danger, since its actual achievement was so remote and since its promotion might have propaganda value. Arms control coupled to a bilateral emphasis on defense, by contrast, was seen as a dangerously appealing potential alternative to an airpower buildup. Although neither Truman nor Eisenhower embraced the airpower cult with any real enthusiasm, its proponents successfully narrowed the bounds of acceptable discourse on nuclear policy.

U.S. Military Tradition

Beyond the particular interest of the Air Force in opposing a major program in continental defense (until massive retaliation guaranteed the primacy of SAC), Samuel Huntington has suggested an underlying explanation for the lack of support among the services for continental defense: "Not since the War of 1812 had the continental United States been the probable target of foreign attack. The doctrines of all three services were based on the assumption that the

107. The phrase "cult of the offensive" was used by Stephen Van Evera in describing the causes of World War I. Van Evera describes such a cult as a phenomenon wherein "militaries glorified the offensive and adopted offensive military doctrines, while civilian elites and publics assumed that . . . offensive solutions to security problems were the most effective." Stephen Van Evera, "The Cult of the Offensive and the Origins of the First World War," *International Security* 9 (Summer 1984): 59. See also Jack Snyder, *The Ideology of the Offensive: Military Decision Making and the Disasters of 1914* (Ithaca: Cornell University Press, 1984).

best defense is the offense."[108] Clark Murdock has supplemented that point by noting the obstacles to radical changes in military doctrine: "Changes in doctrine are inhibited, in general, because the necessity of employing weapons already possessed restrains flexibility in strategy and tactics. Thus, doctrinal changes tend to be incremental improvements of present capabilities—for example a nuclear as opposed to a conventional carrier—rather than the introduction of whole new concepts like continental defense."[109]

Although theories of nuclear strategy often originated from nonmilitary sources, their promotion within the government is strongly linked to the institutional interests of the various services. Thus the development of Polaris in 1957 (with its inaccurate missiles) generated a sophisticated Navy argument for what would later be called MAD. The Air Force, recognizing that submarines alone could accomplish that mission, responded by arguing for counterforce emphasis and circulated studies advocating a "no-cities" doctrine. This represented a striking reversal of positions taken during the B-36 controversy only eight years earlier, when the Navy (then with no strategic mission) questioned the morality of strategic bombing while the Air Force (then capable of little besides city bombardment) insisted that the "greater immorality would be for the U.S. to discard its strongest weapon."[110]

Had the United States (as the Soviets did in 1948) created an independent branch of the armed forces dedicated solely to strategic defense, it is likely that the American civilian leadership and public would have become far more aware of the case for defense emphasis. Indeed, once the Army acquired a major role in strategic defense (in 1955), officers associated with that program (for developing a ballistic missile defense system) were quick to proclaim that defense should replace strategic airpower as the "chief deterrent factor."[111] Yet even then strategic defense was not a priority for the Army as a whole. That, combined with the Army's legacy as the outsider in the struggle over nuclear doctrine, meant that it would never become a top priority for any of the armed services.

The weakness of bureaucratic support for continental defense can be illustrated by comparing the emergence and influence of two bureaucratic entities: the Strategic Air Command and the Continental

108. Huntington (n. 37), p. 328.

109. Clark Murdock, *Defense Policy Formation* (Albany: State University of New York Press, 1974), p. 22.

110. Rosenberg (n. 31), pp. 57–59.

111. *New York Times*, May 2, 1955, p. 1.

Defense Command. SAC was created in 1948 as a semiautonomous branch of the Air Force, moved rapidly to the forefront of nuclear planning, and remained the principal architect of operational nuclear policy throughout the 1950s. By contrast, as Samuel Huntington noted, "interservice rivalry delayed the establishment of an autonomous command devoted exclusively to continental defense."[112] The Continental Defense Command was not established until 1954, and it remained for two years under the auspices of the Air Force's Air Defense Command. Following Army complaints about its "subordinate" position, continental defense was finally separated from Air Force control two years later. Even then, as Huntington observed, the leaders of the Continental Air Defense Command (CONAD) were unable "to dramatize their function and to exert the personal prestige and influence which General Lemay had done with SAC."[113] The transformation of CONAD into the North American Air Defense Command (NORAD) in 1957 effectively ended its potential as a bureaucratic counterweight to SAC, as its role shifted to the integration of U.S. and Canadian forces. The latter half of the 1950s was characterized by bitter rivalry between the Air Force and the Army for control of the emergent ballistic missile defense effort, with each service predictably denigrating the technological promise of the other's programs.[114]

In short, the lack of bureaucratic support for continental defense at the onset of the nuclear age was largely self-sustaining. The absence of a traditional role for homeland defense slowed the formation of any bureaucratic entity dedicated to its promotion. By the time the air defense mission was wrested from the control of the Air Force, strategic airpower was already deeply entrenched as the foundation of U.S. defense policy.

Yet even though military tradition gave the Air Force and SAC a bureaucratic head start in shaping policy in the nuclear age (since strategic bombing appeared to be the ultimate manifestation of offensive power), airpower proponents had good reason to regard support for continental defense and arms control by leading independent advisers in terms of a "life and death struggle." In partial compensation for their lack of bureaucratic clout, defense proponents had, after all, a powerful argument: the United States was heading for a historically unprecedented vulnerability to attack (in-

112. Huntington (n. 37), p. 340.
113. Ibid., p. 341.
114. Murdock (n. 109), pp. 35–43.

deed, to complete devastation), a condition that was virtually ensured by an unconstrained strategic arms buildup.

The political agenda for warding off the potential impact of that argument had three facets. The first was to change the terms of the debate: challenging the loyalty of supporters of defense was seen as a viable alternative to seriously disputing their claims. Second, the Air Force formed an alliance with the political Right, which was highly receptive to the idea of threatening the Soviet Union with massive nuclear devastation, while at the same time limiting the budget. Finally, supporters of strategic airpower, having won the bureaucratic struggle within the executive branch, tried to prevent the debate from spilling over into a broader arena. Keeping the public (and members of Congress) in the dark about the anticipated expansion of Soviet nuclear strength was seen as the key to complacent domestic acceptance of the buildup toward "overkill."

This three-pronged approach in the early years of the nuclear age provided the principal means by which the airpower cult sustained its grip on policy, even though offensive superiority was clearly a "wasting asset." Unfortunately, many historians of the nuclear age have confused the absence of public debate on the issue of offense versus defense with the presence of such obscure causal factors as "technological necessity" and "justifiable fatalism." Instead, it represents the airpower lobby's success in suppressing informed discussion regarding the value of continental defense and arms control.

The Cult of the Offensive

In his 1954 proposal to "ban H-bomb tests and favor the defense," David Inglis noted that "influential extremists have gone so far as to proclaim that any diversion from our offensive effort to defensive preparation is tantamout to treason."[115] What Inglis could not have known at the time was the actual reaction of Defense Secretary Robert Lovett when informed of the Panel of Consultants' recommendation for a "no-first-test" proposal of the H-bomb:

> Mr. Lovett responded most energetically to the matter that had been raised. He felt that any such idea should be immediately put out of mind and that any papers that might exist on the subject should be destroyed. He was deeply troubled that this was the kind of thing that

115. Inglis (n. 33), p. 54.

might very well be traced back to fellows like Dr. Oppenheimer whose motivations in these matters were suspect.[116]

President Eisenhower was hardly immune to this kind of sentiment. On hearing a summary of the report of the Panel of Consultants on Disarmament, his first response was that "it seemed to him strange that two eminent scientists had been put on the Panel and that they had immediately moved out of the scientific realm into the realms of policy and psychology. Their recommendations plainly went beyond the law."[117]

These reactions by Lovett and Eisenhower were hardly harmless asides. As I have already described, the Air Force later conceded that they tried to suppress the evaluation of air defense technologies undertaken by the Lincoln Summer Study in 1952. As for Lovett's call for destroying all evidence that government advisers had recommended consideration of a no-first-test proposal for the H-bomb, there is some evidence that circulation of the panel's initial proposal for offensive arms control was in fact prevented.[118]

Perhaps the most dramatic illustration of success for those who wished to brand supporters of defense emphasis as traitors is the explanation General Gordon Gray offered for depriving Oppenheimer of his security clearance in 1954. Henceforth the standard for fitness to advise the government, stated Gray in announcing the board's decision, would be demonstration of "a genuine conviction that this country cannot in the interests of security have less than the strongest possible offensive capabilities."[119]

Until the U.S. nuclear monopoly ended in 1949, it could be plausibly argued that a sustained airpower buildup might permit the United States to coerce (or defeat) the Soviet Union with little or no risk. Even before separation from the Army in 1947, Air Force offi-

116. "Memorandum for the Files by R. Gordon Arneson, Special Assistant to the Secretary of State for Atomic Energy Affairs: Meeting of the Special Committee of the National Security Council Held in the Office of the Secretary of State, Thursday, October 9, 1952, 4 p.m.," *FRUS*, pt. 2, p. 1035.

117. "Memorandum of Discussion" (n. 105), p. 1110.

118. One historian's recent effort to trace the fate of the no-first-test proposal did identify a few private discussions involving such sympathetic scientist-advisers as Charles Lauritsen and I. I. Rabi, but it cites no official documents that directly addressed the concept of a bilateral test-ban agreement. Despite the prominence of its proponents, the proposal was apparently never brought to Truman's attention. See Bernstein (n. 4), pp. 148–52. The Office of the Historian of the Department of State noted that it was unable to find records to establish the distribution of the no-first-test proposal. *FRUS*, pt. 2, p. 994.

119. *In the Matter of J. Robert Oppenheimer* (n. 34), p. 1016.

cials undertook a concerted effort to persuade Congress that strategic bombing not only had become the essence of modern warfare, but represented the one area where the United States could achieve a decisive advantage over the Soviet Union.[120]

On the other side of the public debate were a large number of scientists, primarily physicists, many of whom had helped to develop the atomic bomb. Just as forcefully, they maintained that the U.S. advantage was short-lived. Their arguments graphically depicted the horrors of a nuclear attack against America's cities and conveyed a belief that, without disarmament, an utterly devastating nuclear war was all but inevitable.

Initially, the impassioned and simultaneous depiction of the same weaponry as representing either the complete salvation of the United States or the total doom of humankind produced an almost schizophrenic responsiveness to both positions, as the United States coupled its presentation of the Baruch Plan for complete nuclear disarmament with the incorporation of nuclear weapons into military planning. That initial debate was, in effect, resolved by the deepening intensity of the Cold War. The perception of a real danger to U.S. security supplanted what remained a hypothetical argument identifying atomic weapons as a transcendent danger confronting the entire world.

In principle, the first Soviet A-bomb test in August 1949 might have shifted concern back to the dangers of a nuclear arms race. After all, real and imminent Soviet advances in offensive power were now dramatically confirming the bleak predictions that had inspired the Baruch Plan. Simultaneous events (particularly the Communist victory in China), however, were providing a far greater impetus for the original rationale for an atomic buildup: that is, that the Soviets were actively seeking total victory over the West. Given that widespread perception, the initial debate over whether a meaningful nuclear advantage could be sustained yielded to the assumption that it *must* be sustained. Thus, congressional debates over the defense budget between 1949 and the mid-1950s (with the exception of the Korean War years) were largely preoccupied with arguments over what level of strategic bombing represented the margin of victory over the Soviet Union.

The Korean War (i.e., the desire to avoid future Koreas), moreover, greatly reinforced the appeal of a nuclear solution to global containment. In reality, the limited applicability of nuclear threats to

120. Kolodziej (n. 103), pp. 38–41.

the problem of Communist expansion in the Third World was demonstrated within months of Dulles's January 1954 "massive retaliation" speech. In Vietnam, Western influence was threatened by an indigenous leftist insurgency, to which massive retaliation threats against the Soviet Union were clearly irrelevant. Moreover, the prospective immediate local use of nuclear weapons to rescue the French at Dien Bien Phu (in April 1954) helped impress on President Eisenhower the prohibitive moral constraints that would prove to be an enduring legacy of Hiroshima and Nagasaki.[121] Perhaps most important, contemplation of even a very limited nuclear attack in the Third World dramatized that the overall strategic and political consequences of such use were dauntingly uncertain.[122]

During the critical period in the forging of postwar security policy culminating in the massive retaliation doctrine, however, faith in the Air Force supplanted any reasoned weighing of the presumed benefits of nuclear reliance against the costs and risks of a U.S.–Soviet strategic arms race. An early example of the hysteria underlying congressional support occurred during the debate over the 1949 defense budget, when one congressman provided the following reaction to the Air Force's request for a large budget increase: "This movement to increase our Air Force is to me the most encouraging step that has yet been taken on this floor. We have reached the time when our Air Force is the first line of defense. The next war will be an atomic conflict. It will be fought with airplanes and atomic bombs. It may mark the end of our civilization. I shall vote for the top amount offered here."[123]

Two years later, in a call to produce nuclear weapons "by the thousands and tens of thousands," then congressman (and later senator from Washington) Henry Jackson would make a similar appeal: "How can we conceivably not want to make every possible atomic weapon we can? . . . I cannot . . . imagine any member of this House going before his constituents and saying that he is not in favor of making every single atomic weapon it is within our power to produce."[124]

121. Eisenhower later reported responding to advice to use the bomb by saying: "You boys must be crazy. We can't use those awful things against Asians for the second time in less than ten years. My God." Stephen E. Ambrose, *Eisenhower*, vol. 2 (New York: Simon and Schuster, 1984), p. 184.

122. See Bundy (n. 3), pp. 260–70.

123. Kolodziej (n. 103), p. 81.

124. Jackson was "struck by the irony of having to advance complicated and detailed arguments in support of an all-out atomic program," since he believed "that

During Eisenhower's first year in office, he temporarily moved to scale back the Air Force expansion that President Truman had projected. Air Force chief of staff Hoyt S. Vandenberg, in leading the attack on the proposed budget cut, testified that "an Air Force of no less than 143 wings . . . was the minimum force which can assure the ability of this nation to resist successfully an all-out Communist attack."[125] Whether 143 wings (or Eisenhower's proposed 120 wings) were sufficient for this purpose became the central focus of the ensuing debate. No one in Congress appeared to recognize that the thousands of bombers called for in both proposals would be largely irrelevant for "resisting an all-out Communist attack" unless the United States was willing and able to strike first at the Soviet Union. Here is one historian's account of the 1954 congressional debate:

> Much of the emotional zeal and salvational fervor that had animated the pre-Korean War movement for more air power was revived and directed at the new target goal. . . . Controversy in Congress . . . spilled over into the press, radio, and television and swelled into a national debate over the nation's air power strength. (Arthur Godfrey even used his early morning TV program to press for a larger air force.) . . . Dispute in Congress centered exclusively on the comparative adequacy of the Truman and Eisenhower air force estimates. . . . There was no questioning during the long hearing and floor discussions in Congress of the strategic posture itself. No one publicly questioned the nation's increasing dependence on nuclear weapons that was already sharply outlined in the FY 1954 budget. The debate suffered, too, from its superficial analysis of a nuclear strategy. Ignored were the multiple and interrelated psychological and political dimensions of nuclear planning and diplomacy, including such questions as . . . the credibility of a nuclear deterrent in the face of the developing Soviet atomic capacity, . . . and the effect of an expansion of nuclear arms on the buildup of conventional forces within a contracting budgetary framework. . . . The defense of Europe and, indeed, the remainder of United States interests around the world were capsulized in Congress in a debate over the physical capacity of the nation's nuclear deterrent.[126]

Supporters of continental defense and offensive arms control were well aware that the public debate on nuclear policy was not grap-

---

reasonable men can differ only on the degree of expansion that is now physically possible." *Congressional Record—House*, Proceedings and Debates of the 82d Cong., 1st sess., vol. 97, pt. 10 (October 3–20, 1951), p. 12868.

125. Kolodziej (n. 103), p. 173.

126. Ibid., pp. 172–73.

pling with these essential questions. In his one published article on the subject (which appeared as the congressional debate was taking place), Oppenheimer coupled his appeal for defense emphasis arms control with the following:

> The political vitality of our country largely derives from two sources: One is the interplay of opinion and debate in the diverse and complex legislative and executive agencies which contribute to the making of policy. The other is a public opinion which is based on confidence that it knows the truth.
>
> Today, public opinion cannot exist in this field.[127]

Behind the scenes, several members of the Panel of Consultants on Disarmament tried personally to persuade President Eisenhower to undertake a policy of "candor" to the American people. The failure of their effort illustrates the internal decision-making process that doomed the prospects for informed public debate over the relative merits of defense emphasis and offense dominance.

Candor and Continental Defense

In its first recommendation, the report of the Panel of Consultants on Disarmament appealed for "candor to the American Government and People." The crucial data they wanted divulged were estimates of anticipated Soviet atomic strength; that is, that "within the time span of current planning the Soviet Union may have many hundred atomic bombs; within ten or fifteen years she could have several thousand."[128]

127. Oppenheimer (n. 25), p. 193. Promoters of civil defense were natural allies in the unsuccessful struggle for candor. Two months after Oppenheimer's article, the head of the Federal Civil Defense Administration stated: "I would say this—that, as far as I am concerned, I think the American people should be told everything possible that we could tell them about atomic bombs and about enemy capabilities and weapons. And, in general, I believe that in a democracy, where the affairs of government are the business of all the people, I believe that the people can be depended upon to make the proper decision—if they have the facts. I don't believe that any other position is defensible in a democracy." "Interview with Governor Val Peterson" (n. 45), p. 239. That same month, a participant in the Project East River civil defense study complained of public ignorance of growing U.S. vulnerability, adding: "At the root of many of our civil defense problems—whether they concern public apathy, congressional reluctance to appropriate funds, or the organization and operation of a civil defense system—lies a lack of authoritative information, which can be corrected . . . by lifting the veil of secrecy." McLean (n. 41), p. 288.

128. "Report by the Panel of Consultants" (n. 14), p. 1079.

But to the panel, candor meant more than a mere sharing of basic information:

> In addition to providing the facts and figures, the United States government should direct public attention to the fact that the atomic bomb works both ways. . . .
>
> There is altogether insufficient emphasis upon . . . the fact that no matter how many bombs we may be making, the Soviet Union may fairly soon have enough to threaten the destruction of our whole society. In these matters, there is no substitute for authoritative official warnings. . . .
>
> In the end, it is the province of the nation to make its own foreign policy, and we are not among those who believe that we are necessarily wiser than the people and government of the United States, *when they are truly informed*. (Emphasis in the original)[129]

The panel did not disguise its hope that a policy of candor would improve the prospects for adoption of its preferred approach. Indeed, candor about growing Soviet capabilities, an increased effort at continental defense, and serious U.S. pursuit of arms control were all mutually reinforcing:

> The very act of increasing our attention to continental defense is bound to help in developing a healthy sense of the dangers of the atom. . . .
>
> . . . both as it improves our defensive capacity and as it sharpens our awareness of danger, a continental defense effort will help the United States government take a posture in which it can face the possibility of serious negotiations on the regulation of armaments. In thinking about such negotiations it is important to raise the ceiling of our danger and to be clearly aware that the ceiling is there; both these purposes are served by an intensified effort to protect ourselves.[130]

The hopes the panel invested in combining candor and continental defense corresponded to the worst fears of the airpower cult. Thus, the same month that the panel submitted its report, a request Paul Nitze drafted for approval of a distant early warning line (as a minimal first step toward defense) met with the following response from the Joint Chiefs of Staff:

> A statement of policy related to this one aspect of national security would focus undue attention on defensive measures as opposed to of-

129. Ibid., pp. 1079–81.
130. Ibid., p. 1084.

> fensive measures. A chain reaction . . . might be set off which would result in so much effort being expended on home defense that the ultimate result would be the loss of any future war through failure to provide adequately for U.S. offensive capability.[131]

One important consequence of the policy of government secrecy was to prevent an informed public debate over the recommendations of the Lincoln Summer Study. The only substantive public description of U.S. strategic defense powers and prospects appeared in the November 1953 issue of *Fortune*. It was written by the same author whose anonymous article six months earlier had implicated the scientific supporters of continental defense in a "ZORC" conspiracy against the Strategic Air Command. The November article provided a detailed description of existing U.S. defenses, ongoing research, and future possibilities. Although still scornful of the "widely ballyhooed, self-constituted Lincoln Summer Study," the author now agreed that radical improvements (even a 90 percent interception rate) were attainable. The main criticism was that buying such a "superdefense system" (for a prospective cost of $100 billion) would come at the expense of weakening U.S. retaliatory power.[132]

The shift to emphasizing the cost of defense rather than its infeasibility reflected the basic endorsement of the Summer Study findings by subsequent government reviews. Inside the Eisenhower administration, opponents of a major effort were also falling back on the argument that an effective defense would either break the budget or force reductions in other programs.[133] The article also suggested that the pro-defense scientists were unduly optimistic about

131. Jockel (n. 36), p. 185.

132. C. J. Murphy, "The U.S. as a Bombing Target," *Fortune* 9 (November 1953): 118–20, 219–28.

133. Once the Kelly Committee had reported in July that major improvements in continental defense were possible and essential, airpower supporters stopped arguing that nothing could be done about the problem. Moreover, the shock of the Soviet H-bomb test on August 12 further altered the tone of government discussions of continental defense; U.S. vulnerability would henceforth be acknowledged as a critical problem. Debate now focused on two equally unpalatable options for improving continental defense: increasing the overall budget or cutting other programs. The emergence of the cost issue as the principal argument against a major effort at defense is reflected in the August 27 NSC meeting, e.g., in the comment by General Matthew Ridgeway (the new Army chief of staff) that "the United States could not, at one and the same time, assure adequate defense of the continental United States and an adequate defense posture overseas." "Memorandum of Discussion at the 160th Meeting of the National Security Council, Thursday, August 27, 1953," *FRUS*, pt. 1, p. 452.

the rapid achievement of critical innovations, especially in data processing. As the only available assessment of active defense, it was summarized at length in a subsequent issue of the *Bulletin of the Atomic Scientists*, under the heading "Fortune's Own 'Operation Candor.'" Noting that *Fortune*'s source was "obviously well-informed," the *Bulletin*'s report concluded: "It is inevitable that such 'education through leaks' acquires partisan collaboration and that some facts or relationships become distorted. . . . Since the . . . authorities have so far considered it unadvisable to reveal this information officially, the scientists . . . to whom the *Bulletin* would have naturally turned for authoritative interpretation, are unable to discuss these matters in public."[134]

Had the scientists been able to respond, they could have pointed out, for example, that the Air Force's leaked projections of the costs for an integrated air defense system were gross exaggerations of classified estimates.[135] Those misrepresentations prompted MIT pres-

134. "Fortune's Own 'Operation Candor,'" *Bulletin of the Atomic Scientists* 9 (December 1953): 374, 382. One egregious case of the use of leaks to manipulate debate occurred in the April 13, 1953, issue of *Aviation Week*, in an article titled "New Air Power Plan Would Scuttle SAC." The Pentagon was in an "uproar," this article claimed, because new defense secretary Charles E. Wilson, under the influence of the Project Lincoln air defense study, "would like to slash jet bomber production heavily and concentrate on fighters and defensive missiles to bolster air defense of North America against threat of Russian atomic attacks. USAF is bitterly resisting what it terms a 'Maginot Line' concept of Air Defense and warns that neglect of its jet bomber striking force would be courting national disaster." Air Force officials had purportedly resisted "threats of courts martial" in order to disclose the danger. Wilson in fact never advanced the view ascribed to him, though he was more supportive of continental defense than other high-level Eisenhower administration officials. This article typified the airpower supporters' reaction to any sign of pro-defense sympathies. *Aviation Week* 58 (April 13, 1953): 13–14.

135. In July 1953 *Fortune* reported that the early warning line proposed by the Lincoln Summer Study would cost "at the very least $20 billion." "Air Defense: Kelly vs. 'Summer Study' Group," *Fortune* 48 (July 1953): 40. Killian and Hill noted that "this group estimated no such figure," which "bears no recognizable relationship to any informed estimate which has yet been made, and . . . has misled many people in their appraisal of air defense possibilities" (n. 44), p. 39. The classified estimate by the Lincoln Summer Study was $1.1 billion. "Statement by the Chairman, National Security Resources Board on Possibility of an Improved Continental Early Warning System," September 22, 1952, Attachment to "Memorandum for the National Security Council," S. Everett Gleason, October 13, 1952, *Declassified Documents Quarterly Catalog*, 1985, document no. 1235. In November, *Fortune* revealed that the most recent estimate for an overall defense presented to the NSC was between $18 billion and $27 billion for 1955–60, with the higher figure representing a "military optimum." In contrast to that classified estimate, the author simply asserted that a highly effective

ident James Killian and Lincoln Laboratory director A. G. Hill to denounce the political tactics of the antidefense lobby. Killian complained in the *Atlantic* of SAC's "evangelical zeal," denounced public characterizations of the classified Lincoln Summer Study findings with terms ranging from "misleading" to "rubbish," and claimed that such tactics were impeding consideration of continental defense both outside and inside the military establishment.[136]

In effect, the Panel of Consultants on Disarmament was asking President Truman (and soon President Eisenhower) to take the lead in undercutting the Air Force leaders and their political supporters. As the consultants soon learned, however, both these presidents and their closest advisers opposed a policy of "candor" for the very reason the panel supported it: a concern that a nation authoritatively informed that the atomic bomb works both ways would reject visions of massive retaliation in favor of an effort to defend the nation and to limit the arms race. In its conclusion, the report noted that "in one form or another, proposals like these have been made before and have met different kinds of opposition which prevented their acceptance. All of them will meet opposition of some sort now. It is not the province of a Panel of Consultants to decide whether it is practical now to try to overcome this opposition; that is a tactical decision and it is not our business."[137]

The accounts of the panel members' meetings with Eisenhower and his advisers, however, revealed that they were ill prepared for the degree of incomprehension and disparagement they initially received. The panel may have been completely wrong about whether a policy of candor would change the direction of American nuclear policy in the early 1950s. Right or wrong, however, the supporters of the emergent policy of massive retaliation feared that the panel's predictions were accurate. Over time, the panel members' appeals did have a major impact on the debate within the executive branch over nuclear policy. Their arguments helped lay the groundwork for the continental defense program finally approved in October 1953, and their rationales for informing Congress and the public of the nuclear danger acquired significant support.

In the end, though, President Eisenhower accepted the reasoning

---

defense would in fact cost up to $100 billion. Murphy (n. 132), pp. 120, 219–20. All of these figures, of course, missed the key point made by supporters of defense and arms control: that any amount spent on continental defense would ultimately be wasted if the superpowers pursued an offensive arms race.

136. Killian and Hill (n. 44), pp. 37–41.

137. "Report by the Panel of Consultants" (n. 14), p. 1086.

of the airpower supporters that a frank public acknowledgment of growing U.S. vulnerability could derail domestic support for the airpower buildup. In effect, the debate ended with rejection of candor in favor of misleading assurances to the American public, and ultimately with John Foster Dulles's "massive retaliation" speech in January 1954.

From beginning to end, there was an almost surreal quality to the interaction between President Eisenhower and members of the Panel of Consultants on Disarmament. During the February 1953 NSC meeting at which he was first briefed on the panel's report, the president's obscure remark that its recommendations "clearly went beyond the law" was followed by the realization that one of the panel members—Allen Dulles—was attending the meeting in his new capacity as director of the Central Intelligence Agency. It was thus left to Dulles to undertake the initial defense of the panel's recommendations. He began by explaining the American public's ignorance of the "enoughness" problem; that is, that the Soviets would be able to severely damage the United States "regardless of the fact that the United States might itself possess a much larger stockpile of weapons." When Eisenhower indicated his opposition to sharing this information, Secretary of Defense Charles E. Wilson added that "it seemed foolish to scare our people to death if we don't need to and can't really do anything about the problem."[138]

When Allen Dulles pointed out that the object was not "scaring our people" but "giving them a realistic picture of the dilemma in which they would find themselves," Treasury Secretary George Humphrey responded (irrelevantly) that "there was no use whatever in blowing hot and cold with the public on the atomic situation, frightening them one day and reassuring them the next."

When Atomic Energy Commission chairman Gordon Dean expressed his fear that candor might jeopardize the impending congressional vote on the "atomic preparedness program" (the proposed rapid expansion of the atomic stockpile), Eisenhower concurred that "it would make us look very silly if at this stage we reversed the field and called off the expansion program which had been approved." When the president later interjected his belief that the American people already had "the information which the members of the Panel were so anxious to give [them]," administrative assistant Robert Cutler attempted to explain what the panel was talking about:

138. "Memorandum of Discussion" (n. 105), p. 1111.

> Mr. Cutler broke in to say that according to his understanding the Panel was making a strong recommendation that the people of the United States be informed about what was called the "enoughness" problem and its significance for them. "I read in this report," continued Mr. Cutler, "that the people of the United States are mature and should be informed in so far as compatible with security."
>
> The President agreed with Mr. Cutler's statement as to the maturity of the American people, but remained unconvinced of the desirability of the . . . recommendation.[139]

Subsequent debate over the panel's proposal for candor led to two rather tragicomic outcomes, the first relatively minor and the second of great long-term impact. On May 27, 1953 (three months after the meeting described above), Oppenheimer (along with Vannevar Bush) finally received an opportunity to make the panel's case to the president and the National Security Council. The two panel members argued for both candor and continental defense, with Oppenheimer concluding that "to explain to the people the nature of their dilemma it was necessary for the highest voice in the land to speak. Only a wise and informed people could be expected to act wisely."

The president, in response to this impassioned appeal, "said he had another thought on this subject which he wanted to try on Dr. Oppenheimer. If he was to go to talk to 160 million people on this tremendous subject, he thought it was unwise to make any distinction between fission and fusion weapons. Indeed, he thought we should suppress in all future official statements any reference to the term 'thermonuclear.'"[140] Whether or not the ridicule of Oppenheimer's appeal was deliberate, Eisenhower's "thought on this subject" immediately became policy. The official record of the meeting shows that the council "noted the President's desire that reference in official statements to 'thermonuclear' weapons be discontinued for security reasons, and that such weapons be included within the term 'atomic' weapons."[141]

Over the following months, however, the appeals of the panel had a more consequential impact. As its report circulated inside the government, a spirited (though classified) debate over candor ensued. Moreover, pro-defense elements (notably the Policy Planning

139. Ibid., p. 1112.

140. "Memorandum of Discussion at the 146th Meeting of the National Security Council, Wednesday, May 27, 1953," *FRUS*, pt. 2, p. 1171.

141. Ibid., p. 1174.

Staff) enthusiastically endorsed most of the report's rationales for continental defense, the notable exception being a scathing denunciation of coupling it to offensive arms control.[142]

Finally, the unfolding debate over candor and continental defense became linked to a third issue. During the first NSC meeting concerned with the panel's recommendations, Allen Dulles's appeal for a forthright presentation of the implications of the arms race had elicited another new idea from the president: the possibility of one day diverting part of the U.S. atomic energy program toward peaceful uses. Eisenhower later made it clear that if he was to make a grim portrayal of the dangers of the arms race, he wanted to counterbalance the mood with such an optimistic promotion of "Atoms for Peace."[143]

Eisenhower moved forward with plans for a major public address on the nuclear danger by authorizing a series of "candor breakfasts" led by presidential special assistant C. D. Jackson. As late as October 1953, the main thrust of these breakfasts was to develop a "frank speech on the atomic age and Continental Defense."[144]

At this point it almost appeared that the case made by the Panel of Consultants on Disarmament could become the basis of a new U.S. policy. The key intervening event had been the Soviet hydrogen bomb test on August 12 of that year, which, as Samuel Huntington

142. Thus one Policy Planning Staff document argued: "The principal objection to the . . . new proposal is that such a reduction in atomic stocks might leave the United States and the U.S.S.R. in relatively less danger from each other, but it would expose our European and British Allies to mortal peril." The author's concerns were not allayed by the panel's point that there would have to be a "considerable reduction in conventional weapons to balance any limitation on the instruments of mass atomic attack." Thus, "There are dangers in linking a reduction of atomic stockpiles to a reduction in conventional weapons and land armies. It would be much easier for the Soviet Union to remobilize any elements disbanded under such a scheme than it would for us to try to recover the atomic stockpiles which have been 'reduced.'" In other words, even assuming the Soviets were amenable to a verifiable agreement eliminating any capability either to destroy the U.S. or to attack Europe, it would still be against U.S. interests to pursue arms control! "Memorandum by Edmund A. Gullion, Member of the Policy Planning Staff, Subject: Consultants' Report on Disarmament," March 4, 1953, *FRUS*, pt. 2, pp. 1114–21. As special assistant to the under secretary of state for atomic energy matters in 1947 and 1948, Gullion had been the ranking official concerned with the department's day-to-day atomic energy policy (see footnote on p. 1114 in *FRUS*, pt. 2).

143. For a discussion of how the disarmament panel's proposal for candor was transformed into the Atoms for Peace proposal, see Robert Donovan, *Eisenhower, the Inside Story* (New York: Harper's, 1956), pp. 184–86.

144. "Memorandum to the President by the Special Assistant to the President (Jackson); Subject: Briefing Memo for Saturday's 'Candor' Breakfast," October 2, 1953, *FRUS*, pt. 2, p. 1224.

noted, "broke the back of resistance to air defense within the Administration."[145] On September 25, NSC 159 both approved the recommendations of the Lincoln Summer Study and stated that continental defense must become a priority goal of U.S. national security policy.[146]

For supporters of defense emphasis arms control, the role of the Soviet H-bomb test in radically changing the debate over continental defense was ironic. It represented a radical potential expansion in the offensive threat they had hoped to avoid by arms control and rendered the prospects for a meaningful population defense far more problematic. Moreover, although the Soviet H-bomb test demolished the Air Force's effort to minimize the need for a population defense, it failed to inspire the fundamental change of policy for which the panel had argued.

Between October and December, Eisenhower was pressured to drop the notion of a major address on "the bomb and continental defense,"[147] on the grounds that he risked unleashing political forces that could force a fundamental reshaping of nuclear policy. Thus an NSC committee assigned to study the panel's candor proposal ex-

145. Huntington (n. 37), p. 333.

146. The first NSC policy statement focusing on continental defense had been Truman's authorization for development of an early warning system (NSC 139, December 31, 1952). On June 10, 1953, NSC 153 called for "development of a continental defense system . . . adequate to prevent disaster and to make secure the mobilization base necessary to achieve U.S. victory in the event of general war." On June 4, the Continental Defense Committee of the NSC Planning Board was created, and their report (NSC 159, submitted on July 22) became the basis for an unprecedented period of high-level attention to establishing a comprehensive program (see *FRUS*, pt. 1, p. 465, n. 2). The Soviet H-bomb test on August 12 (though the bomb was not a "true thermonuclear weapon") increased estimates of the maximum potential yield of Soviet bombs from one hundred kilotons to one megaton and made it clear that even larger bombs were a near-term possibility. The final version of NSC 159 highlighted these recent developments in proclaiming the inadequacy of existing programs and concluded that a "reasonably effective defense system can and must be attained." This document was the first to prescribe a detailed program for early warning, active defense, and civil defense, "to be developed to a high state of readiness over the next two years." "Continental Defense: Statement of Policy by the National Security Council," September 25, 1953, *FRUS*, pt. 1, pp. 477–90.

147. Although he failed to specify what he had in mind, the president's special assistant recommended to Eisenhower that the speech on "the bomb and continental defense" incorporate "new and fresh proposals which could be acceptable to the Russians if they possess a shred of co-existential reasonableness or desire." Thus, "This can not only be the most important pronouncement ever made by any President of the United States, it could also save mankind." "Memorandum to the President by the Special Assistant to the President (Jackson)," October 2, 1953, *FRUS*, pt. 2, pp. 1224–26.

pressed great alarm over its possible consequences. For one thing, the members argued, authoritative confirmation of the "enoughness" problem might arouse public concern over reliance on nuclear threats. Moreover, a collapse of public confidence in "the deterrent effect of our ability to project our power abroad might result in excessive preoccupation with defense at home."[148] In particular, it was seen as vital that Europe be kept unaware of the extent of America's anticipated vulnerability: "Unless the U.S. power base is regarded as secure, a public exposure of the dangers in the atomic arms race would have serious adverse effects in Europe. Such adverse effects would be compounded if there were created a fear on the part of the Europeans that the vulnerability of our population centers might even make us unwilling to use our atomic strength in the event of war."[149]

But it was the budgetary conservatives who made the greatest impression. Treasury Secretary Humphrey and Bureau of the Budget director Joseph Dodge argued that proposed increases in spending on continental defense were simply incompatible with a balanced budget. Indeed, if candor resulted in the erosion of support for reliance on strategic airpower, their whole fiscal strategy (based on avoiding both continental defense and a conventional buildup) could be undermined.[150]

148. "Report to the National Security Council by the NSC Planning Board," May 8, 1953, *FRUS*, pt. 2, p. 1154.

149. Ibid., p. 1155. Although this analysis was correct in predicting that a growing perception of U.S. vulnerability would erode European confidence in extended nuclear deterrence, it is amazing that anyone thought U.S. defenselessness could be kept secret indefinitely. Ironically, another argument simultaneously used against continental defense was that awareness of U.S. defenselessness was essential for *preserving* Europe's faith in the American guarantee. Thus Secretary of State Dulles argued: "A U.S. shift in emphasis, reflected by new military dispositions and changed budgetary approaches in favor of increased continental defense . . . would probably be interpreted abroad as final proof of an isolationist trend and the adoption of the 'Fortress America' concept." "Memorandum by the Secretary of State," September 6, 1953, *FRUS*, pt. 1, p. 458.

150. Humphrey had first expressed his belief that a policy of "candor" could jeopardize pursuit of a "normal economy" during the first NSC discussion of the Panel of Consultants' report (n. 105) in February 1953. In the aftermath of the Soviet H-bomb test in August, however, Humphrey could find little support for his defense policy agenda: further troop withdrawals in Europe, opposition to continental defense, and a firm administration decision to rely principally on the offensive nuclear threat. Thus, at an NSC meeting in October, Humphrey and Dodge found little sympathy for their claim that the economy, the nation's security, and the fate of the Republican party hinged, as Humphrey awkwardly put it, on "the use of atomic weapons . . . on a broad scale." Defense Secretary Wilson's reply illustrated the administration's shift

By November, Eisenhower had retreated from his brief flirtation with candor. Instead, he returned to his original inclination to deflect the prospect of growing public concern over the nuclear danger with a reassuring, upbeat speech focusing on the benefits of nuclear power. The candor breakfasts, now designated "Operation Wheaties," turned to preparing the president's Atoms for Peace proposal.[151] Under this plan, the United States and the Soviet Union would donate a portion of their stockpile of fissionable materials to an international atomic energy agency. Promoting the global spread of nuclear power plants would then be billed a "new imaginative approach" to nuclear disarmament. The "Atoms for Peace" speech was delivered to the United Nations General Assembly on December 8. After touching on the dangers of nuclear weapons, Eisenhower announced that he had a plan to "hasten the day when the fear of the atom will begin to disappear from the minds of people."[152] In a sense this speech represented the final unintended outcome of the work of the Panel of Consultants on Disarmament.

One historian of this period noted the inadvertent consequences of transforming the panel's proposal for candor, which was originally aimed at creating a national constituency for arms control, into Atoms for Peace: "This literal conversion of 'swords into plowshares' would symbolize the great benefits to man of international cooperation in the atomic field. . . . Ironically, the main effect of the Atoms for Peace Plan . . . may be to accelerate the capability of many nations to produce their own nuclear weapons."[153]

Atoms for Peace represents a striking example of how the desire to foster complacent public acceptance of massive retaliation undercut the nation's capacity to rationally consider the long-term dangers

---

in attitude: "It was vital and costly to improve continental defense. We also now knew that the Russians could make H-bombs. Whatever Secretary Humphrey thought, we have got to be able to tell the American people that we are doing something to confront the threat posed by these developments to their security." See "Memorandum of Discussion at the 166th Meeting of the National Security Council, Tuesday, October 13, 1953," *FRUS*, pt. 1, pp. 534–49 (quotation from p. 547).

151. The reluctance to follow through with an address based on the Panel of Consultants' "candor to the American people" recommendation was reflected in C. D. Jackson's impression of an actual effort to produce such a speech: "New draft, including Russian potential for injuring the U.S. This was closer to what was wanted, but it had the basic defect that all it really contained was mortal Soviet attack followed by mortal U.S. counterattack—in other words, bang-bang, no hope, no way out at the end." "Memorandum for the Files: Chronology—'Atoms for Peace' Project," September 30, 1954, *FRUS*, pp. 1526–27.

152. Eisenhower (n. 83), p. 253.

153. Gilpin (n. 26), p. 128.

of the nuclear age. In a revealing encounter with Soviet foreign minister Vyacheslav Molotov shortly after Eisenhower's speech, John Foster Dulles attempted to explain that U.S. and Soviet donations to an international agency (for the purposes of supplying reactors around the world) would actually *decrease* the amount of fissionable material available for weapons. It was left for Molotov to explain that reactors could potentially be used to "increase the production of material needed to produce atomic bombs." Upon hearing this, Secretary Dulles asked his assistant for mutual security affairs "if this made any sense, to which the latter replied that it didn't to him and that it was an angle which he had never heard of. . . . Mr. Molotov replied carefully that he believed men of science have the necessary data to substantiate this angle."[154]

Months later, in the face of mounting administration concern over the danger of diverting fissionable material from atomic reactors around the world, Dulles revealed that "he had been completely puzzled by Molotov's reference to it during the Geneva conversations."[155] In effect, the United States had undertaken a major commitment to the global dissemination of nuclear energy with no prior effort by the administration to acquire even a rudimentary understanding of its risks. A call for candor, continental defense emphasis, and arms control had ultimately been reduced to an irrelevant and misleading effort to establish in the public consciousness a comforting association of growing nuclear stockpiles with disarmament and global prosperity.

Just as the panel's recommendation for candor brought wholly unintended consequences, its arguments for continental defense and arms control provided inadvertent support for a somewhat more balanced nuclear war-fighting strategy. Yet despite the panel members' failure to redirect American nuclear policy, they had displayed unique insights in identifying the consequences of the policy they were challenging and in recognizing that meaningful bilateral efforts to address the nuclear danger would require mutual deterrence and arms control rather than complete disarmament and international controls. Yet the cogency of their critique of U.S. policy in the early 1950s does not establish that their preferred approach constituted a viable alternative.

154. "Memorandum of Conversation, by the Assistant Secretary of State for European Affairs (Merchant)," May 1, 1954, *FRUS*, pt. 2, p. 1415.

155. "Memorandum for the File, by the Consultant to the Secretary of State for Atomic Energy Affairs (Smith)," December 2, 1954, *FRUS*, pt. 2, p. 1578.

The Feasibility of Defense Emphasis in the Bomber Age

That the scientists who studied air defense were optimistic about its feasibility does not mean they were right. For one thing, there is no way to assess the accuracy of Air Force charges that the technological assessments by "ZORC" were biased by a political commitment to arms control. Many of the scientists participating in the Lincoln Summer Study *were* explicitly fearful that an offensive buildup would increase "the danger of a catastrophic resort to atomic weapons on both sides." There may even be some truth to the claim, noted by MIT president James Killian in a defense of the Summer Study, that some "scientists have a guilt complex for having developed the atomic bomb and that this guilt complex leads them to denounce . . . offensive concepts and to take refuge in the Maginot Line complex of an idealized defensive system."[156]

As Philip Stern wrote in his commentary on the Oppenheimer security trial,

> How does the non-expert layman who receives such [technical] advice distinguish a scientist-advisor's "technical views" from his political, moral or philosophical predelictions? For example, when such an advisor gives counsel as to the "technical" feasibility of a new weapon, might not his judgment be clouded—however unconsciously—by his view that the weapon is, say, morally repugnant, or, on the contrary, absolutely essential to the survival of the nation?[157]

The lesson that emerges from the fate of the Lincoln Summer Study, however, has little to do with the feasibility of its recommendations. What is significant is the basic irrelevance of technical assessments to the decisions of the Truman and Eisenhower administrations to pursue offense-dominant nuclear force postures. Thus Truman, without scientific evidence to counter the findings of the Summer Study, simply rejected its conclusions out of a personal conviction that "the only defense . . . was a vigorous offense."

Eisenhower, by contrast, could no longer simply ignore the emergent Soviet offensive strength. Once it became clear that a continued reliance on strategic airpower could no longer be rationalized without a corresponding effort to protect the American homeland, the new administration found it convenient to fully accept the Lincoln Summer Study recommendations.

156. Killian and Hill (n. 44), p. 39.
157. Stern (n. 37), p. 496.

So too did the Air Force. By late 1953 it was clear that resisting a greater effort at defense was futile. It was also reassuringly evident that the Eisenhower administration had no interest in exchanging SAC's preeminence for defense emphasis. Consequently, assertions of the near-term infeasibility and prohibitive cost of an effective early warning line were dropped before the end of 1953, as was the entire public campaign to rebut claims of rapid technological advances in air defense. In general, Air Force supporters' emphasis on the inherent ineffectiveness of defense shifted to calls for a balanced mix of offense and defense, that is, making the case for a complete war-fighting capability. Air defense funding increased fourfold between 1953 and 1957, when it approached the amount spent on strategic offense.[158]

Despite impressive technological advances (including the design of a computerized battle management system called SAGE),[159] however, even a far larger investment in defense would have been doomed to failure. The reasons had been spelled out clearly in advance by the Panel of Consultants on Disarmament, earning them the president's rebuke that they had "immediately moved out of the scientific realm into the realms of policy and psychology." The consultants' unpalatable message was that arms control cooperation with the Soviet Union was a "necessary complement" to any effort to preclude societal devastation in a nuclear war.

Would the mutual defense emphasis approach they recommended have created unacceptable dangers? Earlier, I noted that had the United States mimicked Soviet deployment policy up to the dawn of the missile age, the outcome would have approximated a strategic environment of mutual defense emphasis. Would that situation have created an unacceptable risk of nuclear war? The refined principles of deterrence stability that emerged with the onset of the missile age suggest that such force postures were incompatible with a stable balance. But nuclear deterrence theory was itself inextricably linked to the reality of overwhelming offense dominance, which in turn had been the direct consequence of the U.S. commitment to the

158. For continental defense expenditures for fiscal year 1953–55, see "Draft Statement of Policy Proposed by the National Security Council," February 11, 1954, *FRUS*, pt. 1, p. 616. For estimated spending on air defense from 1950 to 1975, see Herbert F. York, "Strategic Defense from World War II to the Present," in *Strategic Defense and the Western Alliance*, ed. Sanford Lakoff and Randy Willoughby (Lexington, Mass.: Lexington Books, 1987), p. 22.

159. Jockel (n. 36), p. 173. Installation of SAGE (Semi-automatic Ground Environment) was abandoned in 1960, when it was concluded that Soviet ICBMs would make its computer centers hopelessly vulnerable to attack. York (n. 158), p. 21.

massive retaliation doctrine. The following chapter includes a detailed inquiry into mainstream deterrence theory's claim that population defenses are destabilizing. Even without detailed critical scrutiny of those long-prevalent assumptions, however, a commonsense assessment of the hypothetical environment outlined above reveals no obvious temptations for one side to strike first.

Since it is assumed that both superpowers would have possessed the strategic forces the Soviets in fact constructed, any incentives to launch a surprise nuclear attack would have been identical for both sides. Thus, a potential aggressor would have had to contemplate the outcome of launching fewer than 150 strategic bombers through several lines of radar stations and against thousands of fighter interceptors, antiaircraft artillery installations, and surface-to-air missiles.[160]

To conclude that the benefits of such an attack outweighed prospective costs and risks, the aggressor would need enormous confidence in a series of highly uncertain outcomes. First, enough of the defender's bombers must be destroyed on the ground to justify the depletion of the aggressor's strategic offense. (Even if most of the attacking bombers were able to evade the defense, an effective performance by the defender's early warning system could allow the entire retaliatory force to be launched.) Since a potential aggressor would be unable to preclude a full retaliatory strike, a decision to attack would also require discounting the possibility that its own defense would largely fail. In short, one would need supreme confidence that the defender's defenses would prove largely ineffectual, combined with equal faith that one's own defenses could cope with whatever retaliatory forces survived the attack. Even with such confidence, an attacker could not assume it had sufficient surplus striking power to divert many of its bombers to attacks on population centers (which were themselves defended). Thus, even if this version of mutual defense emphasis in the bomber age failed to avert war, it almost certainly would have provided meaningful protection for the defender's population.

160. The number "fewer than 150" refers to the upper range of estimates for the total of Soviet Bear and Bison bombers by the end of the 1950s. Although the United States feared that Soviet medium-range TU-4 bombers might reach the United States on one-way missions, retrospective Western assessments disagree on whether this would have been possible (see nn. 76, 77). We now know that Khrushchev at least did not regard these Soviet bombers as capable of attacking the United States. See Strobe Talbot, ed., *Khrushchev Remembers: The Last Testament* (New York: Little, Brown, 1974), p. 516. Khrushchev also considered the Bison (regarded by the United States as an intercontinental bomber) capable only of a one-way mission, a prospect he ridiculed (p. 39).

Nevertheless, although such a strategic environment would have deterred any rational decision maker from launching a surprise attack, it would have represented a situation of far greater fear and uncertainty than the United States actually faced in the mid-1950s. Here I should note that the Lincoln Summer Study's optimism over defense took too little account of the rapidity and unpredictability of change in the technological environment of the 1950s. The critical innovation looming on the horizon was the intercontinental-range missile. Although the United States' massive retaliatory bomber threat provided a secure hedge against a decisive Soviet breakthrough in ICBMs, this new factor could have been radically destabilizing in an environment of mutual defense emphasis.

Although an ICBM potential was achieved almost simultaneously by the superpowers, there was no way that outcome could have been anticipated with any confidence by either side. Thus any merely tacit arms control understanding to emphasize the defense in the bomber age would almost certainly have foundered in the face of an impending decisive innovation in the strategic offense.

That does not mean, however, that the proposals of the Consultants on Disarmament were inherently unrealistic. They were, after all, maintaining that the purpose of an initial emphasis on defense (which did not entail complete offensive disarmament) was to enhance America's freedom to establish a negotiated, durable arms control regime. Whether technological change would have inescapably disrupted that process is an unanswerable question: we cannot know what sort of political and technological environment might have emerged had the United States attempted to initiate, at the dawn of the nuclear age, a policy based on a "mutual forswearing of strategic air warfare."

Actually, the imminent development of the long-range missile was not wholly ignored in arms control discussions during the bomber age. At the very first meeting of the disarmament panel in April 1952, Oppenheimer raised the possibility of a ban on missiles,[161] and in March 1957 the Soviets proposed that "international control shall be instituted over guided rockets in order to insure that all types of such rockets which are suitable for use as atomic or hydrogen weapons shall be used exclusively for peaceful purposes."[162]

161. "Minutes of Meeting with the Panel of Consultants on Disarmament at the Department of State, April 28, 1952," *FRUS*, pt. 2, p. 903.

162. "Soviet Proposal Introduced in the Disarmament Subcommittee: Reduction of

At the same time, the United States (noncommittally) outlined a plausible concept for dealing with the impending missile age, as it called for a "technical committee to study the design of an inspection system which would make it possible to assure that the sending of objects through outer space will be exclusively for peaceful purposes."[163]

Earlier I noted that the Policy Planning Staff, while endorsing the panel's call for far greater emphasis on continental defense, had attacked the proposed link to offensive arms control. In part its attack was based on a rejection of the panel's claim that future arms control agreements could be based on broad safeguards against big violations.

In retrospect we know that the disarmament panel had identified the general principle on which future arms control negotiations would be based. Yet it is also true that Oppenheimer's belief that a combination of large-scale defenses and limited inspection could resolve fears of cheating was questionable at that time; in the 1950s it is hard to imagine how broad safeguards could have ruled out Soviet concealment of substantial offensive forces. The means for addressing that problem did not arrive until the end of the decade, when the missile-launched satellite revolutionized the prospects for verifying an arms control agreement, even as it represented the emergence of a weapon against which defense was then literally impossible.

Considering whether the strategic missile could have been incorporated into an MDE arms control regime in the 1950s takes us to the outer reaches of historical conjecture. A serious U.S. commitment to arms control might have radically transformed the context in which technological innovations emerged, or it might have foundered either on Soviet rejection or on insurmountable technical obstacles regarding implementation. In the face of these incalculable factors bearing on the actual prospects for constructing a meaningful defense in the bomber age, it is clear that the favorable technical estimates of defense in the early 1950s were unavoidably enmeshed in a web of "variables which fall outside the traditional natural sci-

---

Armaments and Armed Forces and the Prohibition of Atomic and Hydrogen Weapons, March 18, 1957," ed. Department of State, in *Documents on Disarmament, 1945–1959*, vol. 2, *1957–1959* (Washington, D.C.: U.S. Government Printing Office, 1960), p. 755.

163. Cited in Noel-Baker (n. 84), p. 26.

ence disciplines."[164] A belief in the need for arms control undoubtably helped generate enthusiasm for air defense among the "finite containment" scientists and may well have contributed to evaluations that were unwarrantedly optimistic.

Given the political and technological environment of the early 1950s, the pessimism of the continental defense supporters regarding the short-term prospects for arms control was certainly appropriate. In an era of rapid, revolutionary changes in military technology, even a serious superpower dialogue on arms control might have been unable to establish a framework that could inspire confidence on both sides. Moreover, the Soviets may well have lacked the will or capacity, during Joseph Stalin's last years and the prolonged power struggle that followed his death, to move decisively toward a nuclear accommodation with the West.[165] Finally, even assuming a U.S. leadership convinced of the futility and danger of pursuing nuclear superiority, appeals that a state surrender a powerful military advantage (however short-lived) over an intimidating adversary may have been unrealistic.

On the other hand, the repudiation of defense emphasis was also driven by political factors unrelated to a rational pursuit of U.S. national security interests, since a preference for offense was embedded both in military tradition and in the bureaucratic structure of the defense establishment. Those factors, moreover, were reinforced by the political climate at the inception of the Cold War, in which nuclear weapons and airpower seemed almost a providential solution to the seemingly incompatible needs of stopping Communist expansionism and of cutting the budget.

In a sense, the struggle between the airpower advocates and MDE supporters was a battle to focus attention on different fears. Those who wanted to direct national anxieties toward the specter of Soviet expansionism could point to the reality of greatly expanded Communist influence or control and could bolster terrifying portrayals of internal subversion and betrayal with some actual cases of Communist penetration and espionage.

From there it was not too large a step to declare Oppenheimer

164. The quotation is taken from Albert Wohlstetter's argument that technological assessments must be made within an overall political, military, and strategic context. Albert Wohlstetter, "Scientists, Seers and Strategy," *Foreign Affairs* 41 (April 1963): 468. For full citation, see chapter 3.

165. Stalin died on March 5, 1953. For speculation that both Stalin and the subsequent Soviet leadership might have been receptive to a serious U.S. arms control proposal, see Bundy (n. 3), pp. 227–28, and Bernstein (n. 4), pp. 152–53.

unfit as a government adviser simply because, as the Gray Board noted, "his convictions were . . . not necessarily related to the protection of the strongest offensive military interests of the country."[166] The Gray Board, after all, was only restating a more restrained version of the sentiment Senator Joseph McCarthy had directed toward Oppenheimer one week before its hearings began. In an appearance on national television, McCarthy had asked: "If there were no Communists in our government, why did we delay for eighteen months, delay our research on the hydrogen bomb. . . . And may I say to America tonight that our nation may well die, our nation may well die because of that eighteen-month deliberate delay. And I ask you, who caused it? Was it loyal Americans or was it traitors in our government?"[167]

Supporters of arms control and defense emphasis were trying to evoke a far less tangible fear, especially since initially the nuclear danger was primarily something for the Soviets to worry about. The effort by MDE supporters to overcome that fact yielded a political strategy that was extraordinarily convoluted. Whether "candor" and a national mobilization toward homeland defense would have created a climate favorable to arms control was questionable in itself. That these policies required the active collaboration of their political antagonists inside the executive branch made the whole enterprise seem almost self-evidently hopeless.[168]

That the 1950s did not generate any active promotion, or even meaningful inquiry, into mutual strategic defense emphasis had nothing to do with the relative merits of offense-dominant or defense emphasis mutual deterrence systems. The explanation lies in the fact that arms control itself was denied serious consideration. Thus Secretary of State Dulles would write in 1957: "Past efforts have usually proceeded from the assumption that it is possible to establish and maintain certain defined levels of military strength, and to equate these dependably as between the nations. Actually, military potentials are so imponderable that this has always been and always will be a futile pursuit."[169]

If MDE supporters were engaged in a somewhat quixotic effort to

166. *In the Matter of J. Robert Oppenheimer* (n. 34), pp. 19–20.

167. Shepley and Blair (n. 46), p. 218.

168. As Barton J. Bernstein noted, "The consultants' useful allies were few, and seldom in high places." For his depiction of high-level hostility to the Panel of Consultants on Disarmament, see Bernstein (n. 4), pp. 147–58.

169. John Foster Dulles, "Challenge and Response in U.S. Policy," *Foreign Affairs* 36 (October 1957): 34.

concentrate public and official attention on the nuclear danger, one might consider whether the architects of massive retaliation were guilty of a far more dangerous lack of realism. Indeed, that the decade passed without a nuclear war should not inspire undue confidence that some hidden hand was safely orchestrating nuclear policy. Instead, prolonged presidential inattentiveness allowed SAC to develop a war plan whose execution would have gone beyond the "overkill" of Eastern Europe, China, and the Soviet Union to endanger most (if not all) of the Northern Hemisphere.[170] For most of the Eisenhower years, execution of war plans fell into the hands of a SAC commander (and later Air Force chief of staff) whose obsession with nuclear use included repeated boasts that he intended to launch the strategic arsenal without presidential authorization (in a variety of circumstances, including his belief that the Soviets were preparing to attack).[171]

Finally, when a range of crises (two of which focused on strategically marginal islands off the coast of China) attracted high-level attention, the president's private conception of the nuclear arms race as "a matter of despair" yielded to flirtations with rapidly improvised nuclear threats. Here we should remember that the same powerful secretary of state who introduced the phrase "massive retaliation" also confided his belief that "the ability to get to the verge without getting into the war is the necessary art."[172]

Given the political factors that propelled U.S. policy, Oppenheimer was almost certainly right when he told the president that any hope of redirecting U.S. policy would require "the highest

170. The first Single Integrated Operational Plan (SIOP), produced in November 1960, called for launching the entire U.S. strategic arsenal of 3,500 weapons, delivering a total megatonnage (approximately 6,000 equivalent megatons delivered) more than four times greater than that contained in the current U.S. arsenal. Long before the advent of sophisticated "nuclear winter" studies, U.S. military officials were expressing concern over whether America's European and Asian allies would survive the fallout from such an attack. See Rosenberg (n. 31), pp. 6–7. The number of equivalent megatons in the U.S. arsenal peaked at 6,627 in 1965 and then began to drop rapidly (about 40 percent over the following three years). See Graham T. Allison and Frederic A. Morris, "Armaments and Arms Control: Exploring the Determinants of Military Weapons," *Daedalus* 104 (Summer 1975): 109.

171. For accounts of SAC commander (and later Air Force chief of staff) Curtis LeMay's "enthusiasm for a first strike," see Betts (n. 62), p. 162. In an interview conducted in 1984, LeMay maintained that he was not "going to sit there fat, dumb and happy" during a wartime situation in which the "president was out of action or something else turned up." Richard H. Kohn and Joseph P. Harahan, eds., "U.S. Strategic Air Power, 1948–1962," *International Security* 12 (Spring 1988): 84.

172. *Life* magazine interview, January 11, 1956. Cited in Louis J. Halle, *The Cold War as History* (New York: Harper and Row, 1967), p. 282.

voice in the land to speak." Oddly enough, at that point of origin of the policy that would carry the nation through the bomber age, Eisenhower found himself choosing between diametrically opposed viewpoints coming from two brothers, each of them within the inner circle of presidential advisers. The older brother, John Foster Dulles, was trying to persuade him that arms control either was futile or would yield a Soviet advantage, that American defense policy should be built on the greatest possible expansion of offensive nuclear power, and that any challenges to American security interests could be resolved by an artful use of nuclear brinksmanship. Allen Dulles, by contrast, was trying to explain that even if neither side became too tempted by a real or imagined first-strike advantage, pursuit of nuclear superiority would instead yield a "MAD" world, in which U.S. survival would depend on the endless restraint and rationality of leaders. Both sides should therefore agree to expand their defensive capabilities while reducing their offenses below any capability "to strike each other direct and crippling blows."

In analyzing the role of scientific assessments and advice in shaping foreign policy, Warner Schilling wrote that "the contributions that science and technology will bring to international politics will largely turn . . . on the purposes of statesmen and the theories they have about the political world in which they live."[173] No despairing technical estimates of continental defense stood in the way of the president's directing further exploration of the political approach offered by Allen Dulles and his fellow panel members. No one offered a critique of their assumption that deterrence could be preserved in the context of mutual defense emphasis. Nor did anyone venture the opinion that Soviet antipathy to the idea was so obvious that there was no point in seeking a private dialogue on the subject.

In sum, defense emphasis was not considered because its supporters were burdened by a politically unpalatable theory of arms control, one based on the assumption that the atomic bomb works both ways. In an environment of Cold War fears and fiscal conservatism, offense offered a far more attractive theory about the political world, one based on the premise of "more security at less cost." The assumption of the supporters of defense emphasis proved correct, but that fact had very little impact on the original political choice between offense and defense.

173. Warner R. Schilling, "Scientists, Foreign Policy and Politics," in *Scientists and National Policy-Making*, ed. Robert Gilpin and Christopher Wright (New York: Columbia University Press, 1964), p. 173.

[5]

The Origins and Influence of Offense-Only Arms Control Theory (1960–1972)

In 1980 McGeorge Bundy wrote that "so far the weapons of thermonuclear assault [had] outpaced efforts to defend against them, and the Anti-Ballistic Missile Treaty [had] made a virtue of what most experts thought a technological necessity."[1] Commenting on the 1953 recommendations of the Panel of Consultants on Disarmament, in 1982 he argued that its case for defense-oriented deterrence and arms control had "largely been overtaken by the missile age."[2] Bundy's contention is supported in that the development of both thermonuclear weapons and long-range ballistic missiles had had at least as great an impact on the technological balance between offense and defense as had the creation of the atomic bomb. The case for radical measures to improve attrition rates against enemy bombers had already been strained by the introduction of fusion bombs whose explosive yield was theoretically almost limitless. The onset of the missile age meant that for the first time the superpowers could deploy delivery systems against which, at least initially, prospects for defense were nonexistent. Finally, even as those two developments seemed to demonstrate that the gap between offense and defense was not likely to be narrowed, the launching of Sputnik in 1957 shattered confidence that the United States could rely on maintaining a technological advantage over the Soviets.

1. McGeorge Bundy, "Strategic Deterrence Thirty Years Later: What Has Changed?" in *The Future of Strategic Deterrence, Part I*, Adelphi Paper no. 160 (London: International Institute for Strategic Studies, 1980), p. 6.

2. McGeorge Bundy, "Early Thoughts on Controlling the Nuclear Arms Race," *International Security* 7 (Fall 1982): 4.

These events produced an intense and divided reaction among those who sought to shape U.S. nuclear policy. Although technology continued to evolve in ways unforeseen by analysts in the 1950s, the basic doctrinal arguments that emerged at the dawn of the missile age remained fundamentally unaltered by subsequent events. Proponents of a nuclear war-fighting doctrine were forced to abandon assumptions rooted in the period of the U.S. atomic monopoly or near monopoly. It was no longer tenable that a simple accumulation of nuclear weapons and delivery vehicles could counter military threats against the United States and its allies. In terms of strategic nuclear policy, Soviet progress dictated more sophisticated analysis of the offensive and defensive requirements for deterrence and war-fighting. Broadly speaking, the defensive mission had three components: protection of strategic forces, damage limitation by counterforce, and strategic defense of the U.S. economic base and population.

Recognition of the minimal defensive requirement—the need to protect U.S. strategic offensive forces—grew out of the RAND basing studies conducted in the early 1950s. Although the "second-strike theory" would later be espoused by arms control advocates as the critical element of a stable deterrence-only arms control regime, its implications were viewed very differently by the designers of operational nuclear policy. As Albert Wohlstetter (the principal author of the RAND basing studies) has written, "Popularizations of the second-strike theory and some recent academic accounts distort history to make it seem essential deliberately to threaten innocents rather than military forces in order to deter. They frequently identify a second-strike with attacks on civilians. In its origins the second-strike theory assumed no such identity."[3]

Early attention to preserving a second-strike capability did not signal acceptance of an assured-destruction-only strategy (let alone acquiescence in MAD). Instead, it represented the inception of the view that damage limitation, rather than city bombardment, would be the critical mission of offensive strategic forces. Although the possibility of using offensive forces exclusively for "defensive" purposes would not be officially endorsed until McNamara's tenure as defense secretary (under the label of a "no cities" doctrine), application of the second-strike theory to U.S. forces in the 1950s was only one aspect of a new U.S. doctrine that enshrined damage limitation

3. Albert Wohlstetter, "Bishops, Statesmen and Other Strategists," *Commentary*, June 1983, p. 20.

as the primary strategic mission.[4] "The basing studies," Laurence Martin has observed, "were the dawn of counterforce."[5]

The emergence of a Soviet strategic threat in the 1950s launched an era of ongoing military preoccupation with the dual tasks of protecting U.S. strategic weapons and targeting Soviet ones. It also raised the intractable problem of population defense. The Air Force–led arguments against continental defense had collapsed (intellectually and politically) in the wake of Soviet development of the H-bomb and long-range bombers. Yet as the United States moved toward establishing an integrated air defense system in the mid-1950s, obstacles to a survival-oriented strategy were compounded by the impending Soviet ICBM capability.

The problem facing advocates of a major effort to defend the United States was that arguments drawing attention to the gravity of the Soviet missile threat could not help but dramatize the enormous technological gap between offense and defense. Even the case for a civil defense effort, which received increasing attention in the late 1950s, faced the formidable criticism that the absence of active defense against missiles cast doubt on the efficacy of all defensive efforts.

During the six years between the beginning of an active research program in antiballistic missles and the first successful test interception of an ICBM (1955–61), war-fighters were unable to invoke the optimistic technological evaluations later offered in support of a succession of proposed ABM systems. As late as 1962 the strongest argument that could be made for ABM deployment was the entreaty by Army chief of staff Maxwell Taylor that "we would be learning by doing."[6]

If nothing else, the continued political and theoretical support for a victory doctrine during this period shows that commitment to a nuclear war-fighting strategy may precede, and largely be immune to, the technological realities of the moment. With no ABM system to praise, war-fighting proponents simply invoked the axiom that

4. Although "blunting" (i.e., counterforce) had been the priority mission of offensive strategic forces since August 1950, it was not until 1954 that U.S. planners envisioned—as SAC commander Curtis LeMay put it—"a comprehensive plan for the defeat of Communist air power." David Allan Rosenberg, "The Origins of Overkill," *International Security* 7 (Spring 1983): 35.

5. Laurence Martin, "The Determinants of Change: Deterrence and Technology," in *The Future of Strategic Deterrence, Part II*, Adelphi Paper no. 161 (London: International Institute for Strategic Studies, 1980), p. 11.

6. Ernest J. Yanarella, *The Missile Defense Controversy: Strategy, Technology and Politics, 1955–1972* (Lexington: University Press of Kentucky, 1977), p. 93.

"every decisive new means of attack inevitably leads to a new means of defense."[7] Although faith in that proposition could sustain dedicated war-fighters, supporters of arms control recognized that the obvious dimming of prospects for a meaningful defense could spur the search for an agreement with the Soviet Union. Thus, Jerome Wiesner wrote in 1960: "Ballistic missiles and thermonuclear weapons taken together create a situation in which it is unlikely that any nation can achieve, in the foreseeable future, an overwhelming military position. There has been an increasing acceptance of the idea that the continued arms race will result in less . . . security for everyone."[8]

These new developments could be expected to increase the constituency for arms control, but theorists could hardly agree on such fundamental issues as whether arms control should wholly replace or merely modify unilateral policy (the pursuit of comprehensive vs. limited agreements) and, in the case of the former, over the structure of such an arms control regime. As I described in chapter 3, Soviet arms control doctrine moved toward adopting the defensive umbrella concept first developed by Oppenheimer and the disarmament panel, favoring ABM (and other forms of strategic defense) while calling for very low offensive force levels as an interim step toward their complete elimination.

In presenting his own argument for MDE in 1979, Freeman Dyson raised the question of why the United States, at that early stage in the transition to emphasis on missiles, had proved wholly unsympathetic to the Soviet perspective:

> The defensive strategy that I am advocating is not far removed from the strategy that I found recorded in the Soviet literature at the Arms Control and Disarmament Agency in 1962. . . . We had a chance then to offer Khrushchev a bilateral limitation of offensive forces to small numbers, leaving free the deployment of defensive systems which would in time have become adequate to nullify the limited offensive forces on both sides. Khrushchev, being at that moment ahead in de-

7. Although that citation comes from a Soviet source (Nikolai Talensky, "Antimissile Systems and Disarmament," *International Affairs* [Moscow], October 1964, p. 15), it is also repeatedly invoked by U.S. war-fighters. For example: "All of recorded history has shown swings in the pendulum of technical advantage between offense and defense." Keith Payne and Colin Gray, "Nuclear Policy and the Defensive Transition," *Foreign Affairs* 62 (Spring 1984): 826.

8. Jerome B. Wiesner, "Comprehensive Arms-Limitation Systems," published in *Daedalus* 89 (Fall 1960) and reprinted in Wiesner, *Where Science and Politics Meet* (New York: McGraw-Hill, 1965), p. 215.

> fensive and behind in offensive weapons, would probably have accepted such an offer. At least, we could have tried.[9]

To explain why the United States did not explore such an approach in 1962, it is probably sufficient to note that the goal of substantive strategic arms control (aside from the related issue of the test ban) was not yet under serious consideration by U.S. political leaders. Instead, the Kennedy administration was attempting to widen a "missile gap" that had turned out to favor the United States, even as Secretary of Defense McNamara entertained a "no cities" doctrine predicated on a growing counterforce capability.

U.S. antipathy toward the Soviet position was due to more than a lack of commitment to substantive arms control, however. The basic tenets of the U.S. arms control approach that would emerge five years later in the discussions preceding SALT were already well formulated by 1962. A common assumption uniting the arguments offered by U.S. arms control theorists at the dawn of the missile age was that the superpowers should forgo efforts to defend their populations against nuclear attack.

The simplest explanation for the dismissal of a mutual defense emphasis approach would be the arms control community's skepticism that ABM technology could prove feasible even against an offense limited by agreement. But in that case one would think that the dramatic strides in ABM development between 1962 and 1966 would have prompted a reassessment of that potential linkage.

Yet the plea for a reassessment by such MDE advocates as Donald Brennan and Johan Holst elicited little sympathy from the mainstream arms control community. In fact, opposition to strategic defense in the missile age was founded less on pessimism over prospects for significant progress in ABM than on a concern that such progress would erode support for arms control. In 1960 Jerome Wiesner had in mind not a useless ABM system but a workable one, when he wrote that "a missile deterrent system would be unbalanced by the development of a highly effective anti-missile missile and if it appears possible to develop one, the agreements should explicitly prohibit the development and deployment of such systems."[10]

In light of that statement, it is not unwarranted to be skeptical of Wiesner's position in the public debate in 1969 that ABM deploy-

9. Freeman Dyson, *Disturbing the Universe* (New York: Harper and Row, 1981), p. 145.

10. Wiesner (n. 8), p. 227.

ment should merely be postponed, since "deploying Sentinel/Safeguard . . . would not make a start for developing a deterrent defense with the characteristics required for effectiveness. Rather, it would raise political and economic obstacles to the design of an effective system, which would have to proceed almost from scratch."[11]

Clearly, for opponents no less than advocates, the effectiveness of particular systems was at best of secondary importance in judging whether ABM could contribute to security in the nuclear age. For Wiesner and others prominent in the arms control field, defense would be considered bad whether or not particular pieces of defensive hardware looked impressive. The reasons they preferred offense over defense can be found in the lessons they derived from the technological environment at the beginning of the missile age.

The first comprehensive government-sponsored effort to assess the prospects for sustaining a war-winning strategy in the missile age was the Gaither Study, commissioned by President Eisenhower in 1957 to consider "measures to protect the civil population in case of nuclear attack."[12] More than earlier documents, the Gaither Report—submitted one month after the launching of Sputnik—reflects the sense that fears about U.S. vulnerability to total destruction were finally approaching realization. In that sense it represents the origins of the debate over the proper U.S. response to an environment of MAD.

In one sense, the report can be viewed as a classic statement of war-fighting doctrine, with strategic defense seen as essential even while highest priority is assigned to an offensive buildup. The report stated: "As long as the U.S. population is wide open to Soviet attack, both the Russians and our allies may believe that we shall feel increasing reluctance to employ SAC in any circumstances other than when the United States is directly attacked."[13] The political objective of the report's most active authors was to overcome the Eisenhower administration's reluctance, in the face of growing Soviet capabilities, to undertake the effort necessary to reacquire meaningful nuclear superiority. Thus the report condemned existing programs in active and passive defense as hopelessly inadequate even

11. Abram Chayes, Jerome B. Wiesner, George W. Rathjens, and Steven Weinberg, "An Overview," in *ABM: An Evaluation of the Decision to Deploy an Antiballistic Missile System*, ed. Abram Chayes and Jerome B. Wiesner (New York: New American Library, 1969), p. 48.

12. "The Gaither Committee Report," published in Morton Halperin, *National Security Policy-Making* (Lexington, Mass.: D. C. Heath, 1975), p. 78.

13. Ibid., p. 83.

as it extolled the United States' political, economic, and technological capacity to address those shortcomings. Four years before any demonstration that missiles could be intercepted even under test conditions, the report recommended simply that "the importance of providing active defense of cities or other critical areas demands the development and installation of the basic elements of a system at an early date."[14] "If deterrence should fail," the report concluded, "and nuclear war comes through miscalculation or design, the programs outlined above would, in our opinion, go far to ensure our survival as a nation."[15]

Yet although the Gaither Report, unsurprisingly, claimed that the United States would be gravely imperiled by a failure to pursue its recommendations, it also contained (in its appendix) a strangely anomalous passage drawing the opposite conclusion: that war-fighting doctrine was no longer viable and that a continuation of the arms race would most likely *increase* the vulnerability of the United States. That passage, partially reproduced below, presages a conception of the future of the arms race that would undergird much of the subsequent opposition to strategic defense.

First, it predicts an unending offense-defense arms race between the superpowers:

> 1. U.S. and USSR both will continue to produce large amounts of fissionable material and long-range ballistic missiles. . . .
>
> 3. Both U.S. and USSR will develop improved means for detecting and defending against missile attacks.
>
> 4. The missiles will in turn be made more sophisticated to avoid destruction; and there will be a continuing race between the offense and the defense. Neither side can afford to lag or fail to match the other's efforts. There will be no end to the technical moves and countermoves.

Next, we learn of the probable futility of defense and, even worse, of the possible impact of one side's achieving a defensive advantage:

> 1. The net megaton attack which each side could deliver through the other's defenses might destroy approaching 100 percent of the urban population even if in blast shelters. . . .
>
> 2. This could be a period of extremely unstable equilibrium.
>
> 3. A temporary technical advance (such as a high-certainty missile defense against ballistic missiles) could give either nation the ability to come near to annihilating the other.

14. Ibid., p. 104.
15. Ibid., p. 89.

These projections demonstrated "the great importance of a continuing attempt to arrive at a dependable agreement on the limitation of armaments and the strengthening of other measures for the preservation of peace.[16]

One Gaither Study participant who identified with that perspective was Jerome Wiesner. Wiesner, who four years later would become science adviser to President Kennnedy (and a leading proponent of arms control in that administration), reacted as follows to his experience as staff director of the Gaither Study:

> The conclusions of this study convinced me that it was not really feasible to protect the American people if a global nuclear war occurred. . . .
> . . . at best, if we did all the things we could think of—if we built blast shelters, worked very much harder than we are now doing on air and missile defense, even if we committed twice the resources we now have to defense—we could not prevent a major nuclear war, history's greatest catastrophe. I became convinced that the job we had to do was to assure that such a war did not take place.
> It was with this very sobering background that . . . I began to work on technical problems related to arms limitation and control.[17]

Wiesner's comments, coupled with the vision of the future contained in the Gaither Report appendix, reflect a formative stage of the reasoning subsequently directed against ballistic missile defense. Beyond the fact that the assumptions regarding the future balance between offense and defense pointed decisively to the need for substantive arms control, strategic defense would come under particular criticism for several reasons. Of least significance is the complaint that strategic defense "could not prevent a major nuclear war." Clearly, as long as there was no basis for fearing that defensive measures would increase the likelihood of war, they would still be valuable to the extent that they could reduce wartime damage.

Of far greater importance is the suggestion that a "temporary technical advance" in ABM could give one side a meaningful advantage. Even worse, the potentially ephemeral nature of that advantage could provide an incentive to strike during a fleeting opportunity to defeat the adversary. That argument indeed provides a rationale for seeking an arms control agreement specifically directed at ABM. With no defenses, technical advances in offensive systems

16. Ibid., p. 92.

17. Jerome B. Wiesner, "The Relationship of Military Technology, Strategy and Arms Control." This 1960 address is published in Wiesner, *Where Science and Politics Meet* (n. 8).

would be unlikely ever to provide a decisive first-strike capability. A defensive breakthrough could therefore be uniquely destabilizing, and no one could reliably predict which side might acquire a defensive advantage or how significant or lasting such an advantage would be. Each side, therefore, should be willing to forgo a technological race in defensive weapons in exchange for eliminating the risks that could stem from falling behind.

In the wake of Sputnik, with its implications of an uncertain outcome in the technological race between the superpowers, that argument was widely adopted by proponents of arms control. Their reasoning was expressed as follows (in 1961) by Thomas Schelling and Morton Halperin: "*Either* we *or* the Russians may be the victim or beneficiary of technological break-through. . . . Each of us may well be willing to relinquish capabilities in future contingencies on condition that the other side do likewise. (If a flip of a coin might give either of us the capability for successful attack it could look like a bad bet to both of us.)"[18]

That perspective, if viewed as an explanatory hypothesis for subsequent ABM decision making, offers an interesting alternative (or supplement) to McGeorge Bundy's assertion of technological necessity as the driving force behind the ABM Treaty. Applied to the Soviets' behavior, it suggests that their agreement in 1972 to forsake substantial ABM deployments may have had nothing to do with despair over the possibility of strategic defense in the missile age. Instead, the Soviets might have concluded that in the anticipated technological environment of the 1970s, a race for a defensive capability would not necessarily favor their side and might even give the United States a meaningful strategic advantage. (That, they certainly noted, was the explicit objective of most U.S. ABM proponents.) In light of subsequent Soviet pursuit of a range of ways to limit damage (including modernization of the Moscow ABM system), that type of hindsight explanation has gained support in recent years.

The Schelling-Halperin "flip of a coin" model of arms control incentives (a better gambling analogy might be that of two enemies contemplating a round of Russian roulette) can also be applied to U.S. thinking. The Gaither Report's apprehension that an ABM breakthrough could work to either side's advantage was later reflected in the intense anxiety U.S. policymakers felt over early Soviet ABM efforts. (As Freeman Dyson noted in 1964, "the fear of Soviet

18. Thomas C. Schelling and Morton H. Halperin, *Strategy and Arms Control* (New York: Twentieth Century Fund, 1961), p. 13.

ABM . . . seems to be more deeply felt than the fear of Soviet offensive forces.)[19] Had critics' assertions of manifest ABM infeasibility been wholly convincing, the United States should have welcomed such a useless diversion of Soviet technical and economic resources (as Dyson himself recommended at the time).[20] Instead, even those who loudly proclaimed the near-total uselessness of missile defense systems developed in the 1960s were generally wont to add—as Jerome Wiesner did in 1969—that "expansion and improvement by one side might, at some point, call into question the ability of the other's ICBMs to get through in a retaliatory strike."[21]

Partisans in a heated political debate may be excused for advancing two somewhat contradictory arguments: that ABM is bad because it cannot possibly work and that is is bad because it might. Yet differing perceptions of the technological potential of defensive systems have profound implications for the desirability of banning defenses in favor of an offense-only arms control regime. One might think that if it appeared possible to both sides to build even a moderately effective defense, U.S. arms control theorists would be quick to consider, as the Soviets did, an arms control framework that could augment defensive capabilities while constraining or eliminating offenses.

Clearly, during the interim of total defenseless against the missile, a process of reappraisal had gone on within the expert community of U.S. arms control supporters. After all, they not only were ignoring Soviet expressions of preference for strategic defense but were also abandoning the mutual defense emphasis approach of U.S. arms control advocates during the bomber age. One might imagine that they would have done so with great reluctance. From the dawn of the nuclear age, the arms control effort had been inspired by a belief that a nuclear arms race would expose whole populations to the threat of annihilation. In that sense, defense emphasis advocacy in the early 1950s belonged to the same tradition as the earlier appeal for nuclear disarmament and international control. The chief differences lay in the MDE advocates' belief that the total disarmament approach was utopian—both because of the U.S.–Soviet adversarial relationship and because the destructive power of nuclear weapons made the prospect of even small-scale cheating an insur-

19. Freeman Dyson, "Defense against Ballistic Missiles," published in the *Bulletin of the Atomic Scientists*, June 1964, and reprinted in Henry A. Kissinger, ed., *Problems of National Strategy* (New York: Praeger, 1965), p. 161.

20. Ibid.

21. Chayes et al. (n. 11), pp. 54–55.

mountable barrier to an agreement. In its place they offered a version of what in the 1930s had been called "qualitative disarmament" —a system of mutual security based on distinguishing between offensive and defensive weapons and force structures.

If arms control theorists at the dawn of the missile age were deciding to abandon that traditional goal of limiting offensive capabilities, they must have believed they had compelling reasons to do so. Drawing on the now familiar logic of "mutual assured destruction," one can speculate that two related beliefs could have dictated abandonment of mutual defense emphasis. First, that any framework that could reduce damage from a nuclear attack would simultaneously weaken deterrence. Second, that even if one could conceptualize a stable regime incorporating bilateral defenses, any attempt to reach that goal would be thwarted by the inability to design a manageable transition.

The fact is, however, that neither of those beliefs entered into the thinking of arms control theorists in the early 1960s. Indeed, they made no effort to assess such potential drawbacks to MDE until 1969, and the limited attention the approach then received from opponents of strategic defense failed to identify any insurmountable technical obstacles. At the origin of efforts to apply deterrence theory to arms control, MDE was not overlooked because it was deemed unachievable or dangerous. Rather, theorists believed they had discerned an alternative path toward safety, founded exclusively on offensive weapons. Thus, although McNamara and a few others (after the success of SALT I, many others) found themselves harping on the unwelcome message that mutual vulnerability to total destruction was inevitable and permanent, most of the early architects of what later evolved into the SALT I framework rejected that proposition. Indeed, the later claim that MAD-based arms control was an end in itself represents a dramatic distortion of the objectives of most early proponents of an offense-only arms control regime.

Instead, it was widely believed that an important purpose of a mutual deterrence system was to limit wartime damage. Some even held that its promise as a confidence-building measure would draw the superpowers toward complete nuclear disarmament. As Wiesner wrote in 1960,

> Nuclear deterrence, using aircraft and missile-delivery systems, provides the basis of military security for both the United States and the Soviet Union, so that one could contend we are just proposing to en-

> dorse the present situation. However, the proposal for a stable deterrent system is an attempt first to end the nuclear arms race by imposing a limit upon the size of the legal deterrent, and then to carry out extensive disarmament under the security umbrella which it provides.[22]

This was the positive side of the anti-ABM argument. Defense was bad not because it "could not prevent a major nuclear war," nor because it necessarily represented an ill-considered gamble on victory in the technological arms race, but because it would disrupt the envisioned process of substantive offensive arms reduction.

Arms control did not become an important focus of research and analysis in the United States until the late 1950s. As interest in the subject rose, it attracted attention from two groups: those whose past work had placed them in the mainstream of U.S. strategic thought and those, particularly atomic scientists, who had previously been associated with the international control approach to disarmament. Whereas the former group tended to advocate limited arms control measures, the latter envisioned a comprehensive agreement to reverse the arms race.[23] A typical example comes from a 1961 book titled *The Nation's Safety and Arms Control*: "This 1000-missile proposal [does not] represent the ultimate goal. . . . Rather, such a stable deterrence system appears the best method of providing at least a few years in which to work out further solutions."[24]

As Robert Gilpin characterized the scientists' approach, "All arms control measures seemed to them to be temporary expedients which could do no more than stabilize the balance of terror and thus give the nations time in which to seek elimination of nuclear weapons. Moreover, the suggestion that permanent peace be based on a 'balance of terror' was anathema to these scientists. In the long-run, they argued, it would not work."[25]

22. Wiesner (n. 8), p. 230.

23. The best collection representing arms control views at the dawn of the missile age is *Daedalus* 89 (Fall 1960), later expanded and reprinted as Donald Brennan, ed., *Arms Control, Disarmament, and National Security* (New York: George Braziller, 1961). See also the reprints from the *Bulletin of the Atomic Scientists* contained in Morton Grodzins and Eugene Rabinowitch, eds., *The Atomic Age: Scientists in National and World Affairs* (New York: Simon and Schuster, 1963), pp. 188–285.

24. Arthur T. Hadley, *The Nation's Safety and Arms Control* (New York: Viking Press, 1961), p. 108.

25. Robert Gilpin, *American Scientists and Nuclear Weapons Policy* (Princeton: Princeton University Press, 1962), p. 165. Wiesner clearly shared this view: "While it is clearly true that a smaller force can do less damage, I . . . regard a system of stable

The most influential of those scientists was Jerome Wiesner, who, after serving as science adviser to Presidents Kennedy and Johnson, would become a leader in the anti-ABM lobby at the end of the 1960s. In 1967 McNamara publicly credited Wiesner with contributing to his belief that ABM was unwise. An analyst on McNamara's staff less sympathetic to Wiesner's approach assessed his influence as follows: "Only Wiesner could write memos to JFK without staffing them, without exposing them to anyone else. He sent a couple of memos to JFK that were wildly wrong on technical and arms-race questions. These arguments have set the tone of debate ever since: . . . cost exchange ratios, arms race implications, inherent advantage of defense [*sic*], and the idea that technology has reached a plateau."[26]

Wiesner, of course, was hardly the sole architect of U.S. arms control doctrine. Yet among the promoters of comprehensive strategic arms control, he uniquely served a dual role as theorist and high-level government adviser. He was thus either a source or an important conduit for the types of arguments alluded to in the quotation above. In the following discussion I use Wiesner as a focal point for examining the belief that technology had reached a plateau, dramatically enhancing prospects for a particular type of arms control.

Earlier I noted that the Gaither Report appendix predicted a strategic environment where the "attack which each side could deliver through the other's defenses might destroy approaching 100 percent of the urban population." That perception prompted a flurry of proposals to avert the state of "saturation parity" (to use Leo Szilard's term) through an arms control agreement on a bilateral "minimal deterrent." Although the envisioned size of such a force varied widely (Szilard sugested as few as "twelve rockets and bombs of one to three megatons each"),[27] the proposals had a common objective. As one contributor to a 1961 collection of offense-only arms control plans noted, "One of the particularly appealing features of most sta-

---

mutual deterrence only as a means of making the transition from the present situation to a state of comprehensive disarmament." Wiesner (n. 8), p. 236.

26. Clark Murdock, *Defense Policy Formation* (Albany: State University of New York Press, 1974), p. 121. Herbert York traced the onset of government consideration of a ban on ABM to Wiesner. Herbert York, *Making Weapons, Talking Peace: A Physicist's Odyssey from Hiroshima to Geneva* (New York: Basic Books, 1987).

27. Leo Szilard, "'Minimal Deterrent' vs. Saturation Parity," in Kissinger (n. 19), pp. 376–91.

deterrence schemes is that they envision nuclear forces reduced to the point where "annihilation" of one or both sides is impossible even if, through accident or miscalcuation, stabilized deterrence fails."[28]

That damage limitation was seen as a goal of arms control rather than as an obstacle meant that advocates of comprehensive arms control saw offensive weapons precisely as Oppenheimer a decade earlier had looked at defensive weapons: not as a means of securing saturation parity but as a technical instrument for addressing the danger of hidden weapons. The following statement by Wiesner is only a paraphrase of Oppenheimer's argument: "The importance of a stable deterrent system used as a component of an arms-limitation arrangement is that it provides a means of reducing the danger from clandestine nuclear weapons and long-range delivery vehicles. It may be used in conjunction with any of the comprehensive disarmament systems."[29]

There is, however, an irresolvable dilemma inherent in the Wiesner model of a security umbrella designed to promote disarmament. In the defensive umbrella envisioned by Oppenheimer and the disarmament panel, the very act of limiting damage (through bilaterally augmenting defenses while reducing offenses) would also reduce the consequences of cheating on a disarmament agreement. In the Wiesner model, the two objectives stand opposed: limiting damage requires lowering the (offensive) deterrent umbrella, which at some point has the undesirable effect of increasing the danger of cheating. Wiesner, then, found himself in the difficult position of trying to reconcile two incompatible purposes for his deterrent umbrella. On one hand, the need for high-confidence deterrence pointed toward large offensive forces: "The permissible number of weapons would have to be large enough . . . to insure that stability could not be upset by the illegal weapons which might escape detection."[30]

On the other hand, the fear that deterrence might nevertheless fail argued for a very low level of offense: "There are valid reasons for making the deterrent force as small as possible in spite of the greater stability and ease of inspection of substantial deterrent forces. They

28. John B. Philps, "On the Role of Stabilized Deterrence," in *Arms Reduction Programs and Issues*, ed. David H. Frisch (New York: Twentieth Century Fund, 1961), p. 84.

29. Wiesner (n. 8), p. 230.

30. Jerome B. Wiesner, "A Report on the 1958 Conference Convened to Study Means of Preventing Surprise Attack." This 1959 report was published in Wiesner, *Where Science and Politics Meet* (n. 8), pp. 181–208 (quotation from p. 191).

relate to the dangers of accidental war."[31] Wiesner's own resolution of the quandary is instructive: "One might start with a substantial deterrent force (200–500 missiles) in order to require little or no inspection at the beginning and after experience is gained with the system, confidence is achieved, and inspection built up, the deterrent force could be reduced to a very small size or even eliminated completely."[32]

Wiesner made these suggestions at a Pugwash meeting in Moscow in November 1960. In retrospect, the proposal appears startling: at a time when missiles were first being deployed, he was proposing—as a confidence-building measure—a buildup to as many as five hundred missiles. This bilateral buildup presumably was to be motivated (and constrained) by the "enormous interest" it generated "in the ultimate objective" of comprehensive disarmament![33]

Two related factors explain the faith U.S. comprehensive arms control theorists placed in that apparently paradoxical approach to arms reduction. The first has to do with the specific characteristics that were erroneously attributed to the long-range ballistic missile; the second lies in a more general misperception of the role of technology in influencing policy. The chief virtue discerned in the missile was that it would lead "naturally" to a highly stable nuclear balance:

> It should be noted that a condition of stable deterrents can be reached without explicit agreements between nations; if the deterrent forces on each side are made secure enough, this situation would arise naturally. This is actually the direction in which the development of missiles is going. It is conceivable that as many as five missiles might be required to eliminate a single hardened missile.[34]

Growing recognition that "improvements in missiles would tend to make them more secure" (i.e., through hardening of silos)[35] would eventually eliminate the search for technological solutions to damage limitation. This applied to active population defense: "As missiles become the principal weapon for surprise attack, air defense

31. Wiesner (n. 8), p. 230.

32. Ibid.

33. Describing his call for an agreement to bilaterally deploy up to five hundred missiles in order to later dismantle them, Wiesner wrote that the "enormous interest in the ultimate objective" would mean that "individual steps would not have to be as finely balanced." Wiesner (n. 8), p. 212.

34. Wiesner (n. 30), p. 191.

35. Ibid., p. 198.

becomes of limited value in actually protecting the country."[36] Equally important, such "natural" developments would mean that "there will be no opportunity and therefore no incentive for either [side] to build up a so-called counter-force capability."[37]

The search for safety, in short, would be forced by a technological imperative into an arms control regime founded on missiles. With all alternatives sealed off, the superpowers might finally embrace one of the proposals—repeatedly rejected during the first decade of the nuclear era—for overcoming the "clandestine weapon" obstacle to disarmament:

> We still face the question of clandestine . . . nuclear weapons and ballistic missiles, but a solution of this problem appears to be possible if both sides really want it. Among the various means of minimizing the danger . . . are the creation of an international security force sufficiently strong and dispersed to be a true counterthreat to any likely clandestine force, the creation of a sufficiently effective inspection system to make the retention or creation of this force extremely difficult, and the maintenance of nuclear weapons depots under international surpervision to be available to their owners in the event of the sudden appearance of such weapons in the hands of any other nation.[38]

Writing two decades later, Laurence Martin described the implications of subsequent events for the theory of the "technological plateau": "On the technological side, the optimistic hopes . . . were destroyed by the collapse of their basic assumptions. Anti-ballistic missile defences, if not yet adequate to afford economical protection for populations, at least revealed that defence was not beyond aspiration. Increasing missile accuracy and the multiple warhead opened up renewed possibilities of defence by offensive action."[39] Thus, contrary to Wiesner's analysis, technology did not evolve "naturally" toward eliminating incentives to pursue damage limitation by military means. In light of the considerable subsequent influence of that approach, let us consider the nature of Wiesner's misperception of what Martin has aptly described as "a passing technological moment."[40]

One important mistake was overestimating the extent to which offensive missiles (however invulnerable and inaccurate) would be

36. Wiesner (n. 8), p. 221.
37. Ibid., p. 226.
38. Ibid., p. 241.
39. Martin (n. 5), p. 12.
40. Ibid.

regarded as reassuring. Advocates of missile-based arms control systems believed that states would wish to encourage their adversary to exchange its bomber force for a weapon that allowed for no defense and that could deliver an annihilating attack within minutes. One might think that simple common sense would have prompted those who wished to reverse the arms race to consider how to reduce bomber forces while *avoiding* a missile buildup. Thus, no attention was paid to such factors as the inability to recall missiles in flight, with its implications for the risk of accidental or unauthorized attack, or the consequences of reduced early warning owing to the missile's far greater speed.

Nevertheless, had the missile actually embodied the benign qualities ascribed to it, there might have been some basis for hoping that "technological necessity" would have driven the superpowers toward a plan such as Wiesner's. In overestimating the appeal of their approach, however, arms control theorists correspondingly paid too little attention to the corrosive forces at work on what they saw as a technological plateau.

Even in 1960 it was not impossible to discern that missiles could in fact serve (as readily as ABMs) the purposes of those who wished to shape them as war-fighting instruments. Greater recognition of the possibility of technological change might have alerted them that the properties they celebrated in missiles could also be viewed as technically manageable deficiencies in a promising counterforce weapon.

More important, alertness to technological change would have directed greater attention to the forces underlying weapons-system evolution. In scrutinizing the notion that missiles were naturally developing toward fulfilling the technical requirements of "minimal deterrence" arms control, Wiesner might have considered that "blunting" (counterforce damage limitation) had been the priority mission of U.S. offensive forces since 1950. (Indeed, the problem of accurately locating the appropriate targets made counterforce as problematic in the early bomber age as it was at the beginning of the missile age.)[41] Given that history, it would not have been far-fetched to conclude that, like the bomber, the missile would be perceived by defense-minded strategic planners as a "naturally" dual-purpose weapon.

Had the goal of "assured vulnerability" arms control proved politi-

41. Four decades of uninterrupted counterforce emphasis in operational planning began in August 1950 when the Joint Chiefs of Staff formally assigned "first priority" to "the destruction of known targets affecting the Soviet capability to deliver atomic bombs." Rosenberg (n. 4), p. 17.

cally attractive to both superpowers, the "technological plateau" theory might have gained apparent plausibility over time, as both sides joined in a political decision to halt technology at the stage of secure and inaccurate missiles. That did not happen, however, and the technological plateau theorists found themselves confronted with a very different technological environment than they had anticipated.

By remaining loyal to the theory (and more important, to the arms control regime the theory prescribed), the proponents of comprehensive arms control tended to react to events in three arguably unfortunate ways. The first was to selectively perceive how the strategic environment was evolving. The second was to engage in what might be called the politics of technological assessment: an attempt to dramatize the thesis that defense was "impossible" by depicting actual ABM technology in black-and-white terms of manifest infeasibility and prohibitive cost. These reactions were accompanied by a third effort (which continues to the present) to intervene politically, reshaping technology to match the environment that gave rise to the theory.

In the early years of the missile age, probably the most significant impact of the U.S. arms control mind-set was that it led to passivity in the face of the rapid U.S. missile buildup. Those who had argued in the name of arms control for reliance on the missile proved little disposed toward active opposition to actual deployments, even when the extent of the proposed Minuteman ICBM force and Polaris SLBM force far exceeded the size envisioned for a mutual deterrence arms control system.

Although Wiesner later testified that McNamara's ICBM deployment recommendation was due to intense Air Force and congressional pressure (950 Minuteman missiles "was the smallest number Congress would settle for"),[42] his report at the same hearing that

42. U.S. Congress, Senate, Subcommittee on Arms Control, *International Law and Organization*, 91st Cong., 2d sess., 1970, p. 360. The major study of the factors influencing the ICBM buildup in the early 1960s is Desmond Ball, *Politics and Force Levels* (Berkeley and Los Angeles: University of California Press, 1980). Ball questions the claims of Wiesner and McNamara regarding irresistible Air Force and congressional pressure, noting that the Air Force was still principally interested in bombers and that Congress had opposed efforts to expand the Polaris program (see p. 248). He also documents McNamara's considerable political skill in achieving his preferred deployment outcome (see especially pp. 223–24). Overall, Ball depicts a host of reinforcing factors that created the "climate of opinion" in favor of a major buildup, including "strategic ideologies" based on the pursuit of superiority, bureaucratic politics, and fear of the Soviet Union. He gives most emphasis to the impact of candidate John Kennedy's accusation of a "missile gap" during the 1960 election campaign. Despite

"we had come into office under the most fantastic pressure to put the Nike-Zeus, the first ABM system, into operation"[43] indicated that it was not wholly inconceivable to resist such pressures. Five years later, McNamara's reaction to the imminence of ABM deployment was to solicit presidential approval for proposing a joint limitation agreement with the Soviets,[44] a strategem no one thought to employ against domestic "war-fighters" at the onset of the massive U.S. missile program.

Clearly, U.S. arms control advocates in the early 1960s considered the missile buildup a minor issue. Rather than seeking a bilateral limit on a revolutionary new offensive weapon, they were already arguing against active and passive defense, even while largely preoccupied with the peripheral issue of a nuclear test ban. (In part, support for a test ban was generated by fears that further testing would contribute to ABM development.)

That lack of concern with the (initially one-sided) arms competition in strategic missiles was accompanied by inattentiveness about where missile development was headed. One might think that MIRV development would have inspired at least as much alarm as ABM, especially since MIRV's utility for limiting damage required striking first (before the adversary could launch its strategic forces). Instead, the arms control community was predisposed to accept McNamara's misleading depiction of MIRV as a retaliatory "countervalue" weapon.[45]

From that perspective, one could regard MIRV as useful for convincing the superpowers that damage limitation was hopeless. Placing multiple warheads on offensive missiles could saturate a population defense, and MIRV development could be invoked, as Herbert York characterized McNamara's view, as "the final clincher in the argument against ABM."[46] It followed that actual deployment of

---

President Kennedy's early recognition that the Soviets had in fact deployed few ICBMs, the campaign had created a political climate for a major ICBM buildup, which the administration allowed to shape policy. As a result, Ball concludes that the magnitude of the buildup was driven by "unnecessarily political" considerations (see pp. 174–98, 269–74).

43. U.S. Congress (n. 42), p. 408.

44. See Halperin (n. 12), pp. 129–31.

45. For sources documenting the role of a counterforce strategy in MIRV development, see chapter 3, note 8. Herbert York's account mentions several arms control supporters who (unlike most of their colleagues) were alert to the dangers of MIRV. But even in their case "the short-term considerations" of stopping ABM "overrode the long-term ones." York (n. 26), p. 224.

46. York (n. 26), p. 224.

MIRVs would be averted by a ban on ABM. As George Rathjens testified in 1969, "Incentives for either side to expand its offensive missile force or to put MIRVs on them would be much reduced, since . . . each side could be confident that it had an adequate deterrent."[47]

Had advocates of comprehensive arms control denounced both MIRV and ABM with equal fervor, the nuclear policy debates of the late 1960s might at least have been informed by a coherent presentation of the requirements for an "offense-only" mutual deterrence system. But since stopping ABM alone was misperceived as tantamount to restoring the "technological plateau" of the early 1960s, efforts to promote a general theory of arms control yielded to a narrow campaign directed against a particular weapons system. For that purpose it seemed unnecessary—even counterproductive—to base opposition to ABM on claims that it was desirable to keep populations exposed to nuclear attack. Instead, proponents of that view sought to highlight the shortcomings of the ABM system developed in the 1960s, a line of argument that implied they might in fact support a more technically impressive (and less costly) means to protect the nation against nuclear attack.

Probably the most useful technological criticism of ABM was that only a near flawless defense should be considered. That helped shift attention from a claim that had clearly become invalid (that ballistic missile defense was impossible) to one whose validity was beyond dispute: that an ABM system could never approach 100 percent reliability. Whatever the usefulness of that argument in dampening enthusiasm for strategic defense, it provided a poor substitute for inquiry into the potential utility of an ABM system.

Although "leakage" in a defensive screen would be both inevitable and catastrophic should a large-scale nuclear attack occur, the magnitude of the disaster would depend largely on the relative size and quality of the competing offensive and defensive systems. In that context it was significant that McNamara, despite his opposition to missile defense, estimated that a large-scale defensive deployment in the mid-1970s would save 100 million lives (in a Soviet first strike "against military and city targets")—provided the Soviets did not augment their offensive forces.[48]

47. George Rathjens, "A Breakthrough in Arms Control," *Bulletin of the Atomic Scientists* 25 (January 1969): 5.

48. The "Posture B" deployment, which McNamara claimed would reduce U.S. fatalities by approximately 100 million in the absence of Soviet offensive offsets, was

Table 1. Number of Fatalities in an All-Out Strategic Exchange, Mid-1970s (in millions)

		Soviets strike first against military and city targets, United States retaliates against cities		United States strikes first at military targets, Soviets retaliate against U.S. cities, United States retaliates against Soviet cities	
U.S. response	Soviet response	U.S. fatalities	Soviet fatalities	U.S. fatalities	Soviet fatalities
No ABM	None	120	120	120	120
Sentinel	None	100	120	90	80
	Pen-aids[a]	120	120	110	80
Posture A	None	40	120	10	80
	MIRV, pen-aids	110	120	60	80
	Plus 550 mobile ICBMs	110	120	90	80
Posture B	None	20	120	10	80
	MIRV, pen-aids	110	120	40	80
	Plus 550 mobile ICBMs	100	120	90	80

Note: At fatality levels approximating 100 million or more, differences of 10 to 20 million in the calculated results are less than the margin of error in the estimates.
Source: Defense Posture Statement of Secretary of Defense Robert S. McNamara, prepared January 22, 1968.
[a] Penetration aids.

Studies by the Office of the Secretary of Defense (OSD) also undermined a second line of technological criticism against ABM: that even if one conceded the value of ABM against a constrained offensive threat, the cost-effectiveness gap between offense and defense would drive both sides toward the option of overcoming the adversary's defense. Although skepticism regarding anyone's particular assessment of the cost and effectiveness of ABM was certainly justi-

based on a defense of the fifty largest U.S. cities by a combination of area and terminal defenses. "Statement of Secretary of Defense Robert S. McNamara before a Joint Session of the Senate Armed Services Committee and the Senate Subcommittee on Department of Defense Appropriations on the Fiscal Year 1968–72 Defense Program and 1968 Defense Budget," January 23, 1967, p. 52.

fied (Aaron Wildavsky appropriately characterized starkly opposed findings as "a clash of rival intuitions"),[49] it was nevertheless of interest that by McNamara's own estimates it would cost more to nullify a large-scale ABM system than to build one.

That conclusion did not imply that defense had now attained a technological advantage over ballistic missiles. The assessment was presented in terms of "cost-exchange ratios," that is, the cost of U.S. defenses compared with the Soviet cost of overcoming the defense. Department of Defense studies showed that in an arms race between U.S. defenses and expanded Soviet offenses, the cost-exchange ratio favored the defense if the Soviets were determined to restore more than 90 percent of the fatalities they could inflict against an undefended United States. By contrast, if the Soviets sought to restore a more limited retaliatory capability (e.g., raising prospective American fatalities from 20 to 60 million), the exchange ratio continued to favor the offense, though decreasingly so as the stipulated number of American deaths was raised.[50] In short, it was not viewed as cheap or easy for the Soviets to counter an American population defense against missiles.

In 1969 Freeman Dyson described the equilibrium point that would be reached if the both sides chose to base deployment decisions purely on the cost-exchange ratio. His assessment was consistent with McNamara's while allowing for the wide range of uncertainty inherent in such estimates:

> The economics of attack and defense have this character: the relative cost of defense is extremely high if you try to defend 95 per cent of

49. Aaron Wildavsky, "The Politics of ABM," *Commentary*, November 1969, p. 57.

50. For a discussion of the 1967 and 1968 Posture Statement estimates, see Donald G. Brennan, "The Case for Population Defense," in *Why ABM? Policy Issues in the Missile Defense Controversy*, ed. Johan J. Holst and William Schneider, Jr. (New York: Pergamon Press, 1969), pp. 93–100. Clark Murdock, in analyzing McNamara's change in tactics resulting from improvements in ABM cost-effectiveness, cites the following statement by a member of the Office of Systems Analysis: "McNamara started using some new arguments—principally the arms-race argument. It is a very simple argument—that regardless of the cost-exchange ratio, we feel very strongly about deterrence and so do they. Thus if we deploy anything affecting their deterrence, they will override. . . . These arguments were based on absolutely no analysis at that time. Wiesner had used it fairly casually in 1961–62. This was a very convenient argument for McNamara, for it was not affected by studies showing that the system was much better than they had thought and that it would also cost less. This argument kind of confused the Army and others—they didn't know what kind of appeals to make to the Secretary of Defense for if this argument applies, then even if a perfect defense against the present threat existed, it still would be overcome." Murdock (n. 26), pp. 132–33.

> your people; it is moderate if you try to defend 75 per cent of your people; and it becomes quite low if you try to defend 25 per cent of your people. If the defense is prepared to spend, roughly speaking, up to the point where the cost exchange ratio swings over to being favorable to the offense, then you will arrive at some sort of equilibrium between offense and defense, at a level where you certainly are not saving 95 per cent of your people, but at the same time you are not killing 75 per cent of them. Somewhere in the middle you reach an equilibrium.[51]

Obviously, neither side was compelled to use such an equilibrium point, based on a "unity" exchange ratio, to allocate spending between offense and defense. Opponents of defense could accurately maintain that the United States had more than enough resources to nullify any Soviet expenditure on defense. Dyson, by contrast, argued that both sides should agree to a "preponderantly defensive orientation."[52] Both McNamara and the MDE proponents were maintaining, in effect, that although estimates of cost-effectiveness needed to be considered, choices between offense and defense should not be shaped entirely by such narrow technical factors.

Not only did the OSD findings represent the best available approximation of a thorough empirical study, that they emerged under McNamara's auspices should have removed any doubts that they were biased in favor of ABM. Indeed, their release in January 1967 prompted McNamara himself to drop the cost-effectiveness argument. He based his subsequent opposition on the assertion that mutual assured destruction criteria dictated that each side would overcome the other's defense at any cost.

If true, the claim that the superpowers were irrevocably committed to preserving their existing assured destruction capabilities indeed provided the strongest possible argument against the feasibility of defense. (Estimates at the time of the 1967 presentation of cost-exchange ratios stipulated prospective fatalities from either side's retaliatory strike at more than 100 million, not including "deaths resulting from fire storms, disease, and general disruption of everyday life.")[53] It was not, however, an argument that appealed to those whose arms control goals ranged from minimum deterrence to comprehensive disarmament. After all, to its early advocates, of-

51. Freeman Dyson, "A Case for Missile Defense," *Bulletin of the Atomic Scientists* 25 (April 1969): 32.

52. Ibid., p. 33.

53. Statement of Defense Secretary McNamara (n. 48).

fense-only arms control had been seen as an *alternative* to the saturation parity they predicted would result from an offense-defense arms race.

Thus there were very few instances (before the 1972 ABM Treaty) when arms control experts outside government proclaimed that defense was futile because both sides' security required a capability for assured destruction. Instead, they continued to stress that ABM was hopelessly overmatched by offensive strategic technology. In at least one instance, that attachment to the technical critique of ABM introduced a demonstrable bias into the scientific assessment campaign against ABM, as leaders of the scientific opposition (including Hans Bethe and Richard Garwin) opted in public forums simply to misreport McNamara's finding that cost-effectiveness criteria no longer weighed decisively against ABM. Among those scientists was Wiesner, who commented in *Look* magazine that "Secretary McNamara . . . concedes that an anti-Soviet ABM would not be worth the huge expense, because the Russians could nullify its effectiveness at considerably lower cost to themselves."[54]

The handling of the cost-effectiveness issue in the ABM debates is instructive for two reasons. First, the anti-ABM scientists were highly successful in their polemical effort to create an image of manifest ABM infeasibility. The best evidence of that is how far the distorted version of McNamara's technical evaluation has been routinely incorporated into later reviews of the Sentinel/Safeguard debates.

Thus Morton Halperin's 1975 study declares that "McNamara then proceeded to show that the Russians could offset our ABM deployment at substantially smaller cost, and casualties would return to their previous level."[55] Similarly, John Newhouse's 1973 study of SALT attributes to McNamara the argument that U.S. deployment would "encourage Moscow, and at far less cost, to make a compensatory increase in Soviet offense."[56] In short, McNamara's purported findings regarding cost-exchange ratios have evolved into a widely cited explanation for the ultimate rejection of missile defense.

The anti-ABM experts' claims regarding cost-effectiveness also illustrate how far, by the late 1960s, the earlier hope that technology

54. Jerome B. Wiesner, "The Case against an Antiballistic Missile System," *Look*, November 28, 1967, p. 26. The misstatements regarding McNamara's estimates were documented by Brennan in "The Case for Population Defense" (n. 50), p. 96.

55. Halperin (n. 12), p. 127.

56. John Newhouse, *ColdDawn: The Story of SALT* (New York: Holt, Rinehart and Winston, 1973), p. 79.

had reached a plateau had yielded to an intense political effort to shape perceptions of the technological balance. Misrepresenting the Department of Defense findings was a natural consequence of trying to sustain the technological necessity argument long after it had been weakened by technological change. Technological uncertainty became a minor theme in the political debate; emphasizing that a defensive system should be rejected because it might work was simply too undependable an instrument for promoting acceptance of assured vulnerability. As Jerome Kahan observed, "By emphasizing these technical and economic factors and downplaying the more controversial notion that damage limitation programs were destabilizing, sensitive issues were avoided."[57]

As I argued earlier, technological uncertainty can provide an entirely reasonable basis for "relinquishing capabilities . . . on condition that the other side do likewise." A belief that strategic defense technologies are promising would provide a highly compelling argument for addressing their development through bilateral agreements—unless one side is wholly convinced that it will win the flip of a coin.

By contrast, arguments against ballistic missile defense based on the technological plateau perspective can easily tempt antidefense scientific experts into overstating their case. Basing opposition to strategic defense on the claim that it is technologically impossible places experts in an uncomfortable position: the more promising an ABM system appears, the more energetically must they seek to persuade policymakers that it cannot work.

Indeed, both war-fighters and arms control supporters in the 1960s adopted a strategy of trying to crystallize the inherent uncertainty of ABM capabilities into one of certainty: certainty that defense is feasible (from the war-fighters) versus certainty that defense is impossible (from the arms control community). The latter group may have felt politically compelled to rely on that claim; that is, to the extent that defense is considered "possible," support for any form of arms control might be weakened.

There may have been considerable justification for that fear during the ABM debates at the end of the 1960s. Nevertheless, the polemical benefits of characterizing ABM as manifestly infeasible had two related negative consequences. First, the maturation of ABM technology in the early 1960s made assertions of infeasibility depend in-

57. Jerome Kahan, *Security in the Nuclear Age: Developing U.S. Strategic Arms Policy* (Washington, D.C.: Brookings Institution, 1975), p. 132.

creasingly on a political assumption: that states are compelled in all conceivable circumstances to overwhelm the defenses of potential adversaries. Shorn of that assumption, scientists evaluating ABM feasibility would have been assessing ABM's potential effectiveness against a continuum of possible strategic force postures ranging from high defense/low offense to low defense/high offense. Such conditional assessments, in turn, might have inspired serious inquiry into whether and how bilaterally effective defenses might be achieved by a U.S.–Soviet agreement.

As I describe in the following chapter, when anti-ABM scientists set aside their political assumptions about superpower nuclear policy objectives, they often conceded that both sides' defenses might be made highly effective in the context of an arms control regime. By and large, however, they restricted themselves to depicting bleak scenarios of defensive prospects in an arms race environment. In short, the scientists were preoccupied with bolstering a theory of nuclear-age weapons technology whose acceptance dictated submission to their preferred (offense-only) arms control framework. That polemical strategy undermined the prospects for inquiry into whether significant improvements in defenses by both superpowers were creating new arms control options. It is not surprising that in 1966 one supporter of mutual defense emphasis arms control argued that "one of the most grossly misleading conceptions in recent discussions of arms control issues is the argument that the technology of armaments has arrived at a plateau."[58]

Another negative consequence of characterizing the infeasibility of ABM in stark terms of technological necessity was that it contributed to confusion about subsequent superpower behavior. In particular, it produced a tendency for the anti-ABM lobby to exaggerate how well the ABM Treaty in 1972 reflected acceptance of the enduring validity of the technological plateau thesis: that the manifest technical futility of homeland defense had finally quashed the vestigial (prenuclear age) impulse to protect one's nation against attack. Thus was born the myth of a decisive superpower "convergence" in acceptance of mutual vulnerability.

That lack of appreciation of the continued appeal of damage limitation led to near incomprehension on the part of the arms control community regarding the superpowers' behavior in the early years

58. Richard B. Foster, "The Impact of Ballistic Missile Defense on Arms Control Prospects," in *Arms Control for the Late Sixties*, ed. James E. Dougherty and J. F. Lehman, Jr. (New York: Van Nostrand, 1967), p. 86.

following SALT I. Paul Warnke, for example, would write as follows in a 1975 article titled "Apes on a Treadmill":

> The limitation imposed on anti-ballistic missile systems in SALT I . . . should at least have brought about tacit mutual restraint in the further accumulation of offensive strategic weapons. With no defensive missiles to overcome, a fraction of the existing strategic forces on either side is adequate to wreak devastion on the other's society, and initiation of nuclear war thus means national suicide.
>
> But in defiance of this dread logic, both the Soviet Union and the United States have continued to move ahead. . . . We have proceeded with our MIRVing of the Poseidon fleet and our Minuteman missiles. The Soviet Union has continued to test its own MIRVs and to develop a new family of intercontinental ballistic missiles.[59]

One U.S. arms control supporter who was not surprised by these developments was Hudson Institute analyst Donald Brennan. In the weeks after the signing of SALT I in May 1972, Brennan had argued that the Soviets' interest in damage limitation would now propel them toward redressing the MIRV imbalance within the five-year period of the Interim Agreement.[60] Indeed, not only had he long argued that any durable Soviet commitment to arms control would have to incorporate the traditional Soviet emphasis on defense, but he had similarly argued (three years before the ABM Treaty) that MAD had no real roots in the U.S. defense establishment:

> There is . . . something of a "fashion" in some circles against interfering with the so-called requirements for "Assured Destruction" capabilities on either side, especially when (almost only when) the interference comes from missile defense. . . . "Assured Vulnerability" has characterized the trend of our strategic posture in recent years because of the views of McNamara and a few others, not because of the defense community as a whole, most of which has opposed the trend. Therefore, while the kind of fashion mentioned above has and has had important adherents, it seems unlikely to prove dominant in the U.S. policy process in the future.[61]

Four weeks after the signing of the ABM Treaty, it was Brennan who ensured the durability of the phrase "mutual assured destruc-

59. Paul Warnke, "Apes on a Treadmill," *Foreign Policy* 18 (Spring 1975): 25–26.
60. Donald G. Brennan, "When the SALT Hit the Fan," *National Review*, June 23, 1972, p. 687.
61. Brennan (n. 50), pp. 108–9.

tion" by noting that its acronym was MAD. Here is his explanation of what has evolved into an almost value-neutral depiction of offense-only arms control:

> The concept of mutual assured destruction provides one of the few instances in which the obvious acronym for something yields at once the appropriate description; for it, that is, a Mutual Assured Destruction posture as a goal is, almost literally, mad. MAD. If technology and international politics provided absolutely no alternative, one might reluctantly accept a MAD posture. But to think of it as desirable—for instance, as a clearly preferred goal of our arms-control negotiations . . . —is bizarre.
>
> . . . There are three problems here: The first is that, in spite of our best efforts, a major nuclear war could happen. An institutionalized MAD posture is a way of insuring, now and forever, that the outcome of such a war would be nearly unlimited disaster for everybody. . . .
>
> The second fundamental difficulty is essentially political: We do not have a Department of Defense for the purpose of deliberately making us all hostages to enemy weapons. . . . The Defense Department should be more concerned with assuring live Americans than dead Russians.
>
> The third fundamental difficulty is moral: We should not deliberately create a system in which millions of innocent civilians would be exterminated should the system fail. The system is not *that* reliable. . . . [W]e should be looking for ways out of [MAD], not ways to enshrine it.[62]

The SALT I agreements, Brennan noted, "were a particular disappointment to those of us who have been hoping and working for a strategic arms-control agreement that would make a genuine contribution to American security."[63] The pact Brennan had promoted called for the superpowers to harness defensive technology to a mutual deterrence system that would progressively reduce wartime casualties if deterrence somehow failed. Brennan and his associates, by expanding on the tradition of mutual defense emphasis established by Oppenheimer and the disarmament panel in the 1950s, constructed a theory of MDE that has direct relevance to the current strategic environment.

62. Brennan (n. 60), p. 689.
63. Ibid., p. 685.

[6]

Mutual Defense Emphasis in the 1960s

Study of defense emphasis arms control in the missile age began in the early 1960s at the Hudson Institute, under the direction of then president Donald Brennan, who later summed up his conclusions in this way:

> I do not believe that any of the critics of BMD have even the beginnings of a plausible program for achieving major disarmament of the offensive forces. . . . Many of them seem committed to support forever a strategic posture that appears to favor dead Russians over live Americans. I believe that this position is as bizarre as it appears; we should rather prefer live Americans to dead Russians, and we should not choose deliberately to live forever under a nuclear sword of Damocles.[1]

The long-term project on the issue was called "Arms Control through Defense" (ACD).[2] The Hudson Institute was part of the mainstream "defense establishment," and the ACD project included supporters of the war-fighting approach that had dominated nuclear policy since the late 1940s. The early 1960s mark the beginning of a division among MDE advocates, as some began to advertise MDE in a way that blurred the distinction between the role of defense in a victory doctrine and strategic defense as the foundation of a comprehensive arms control regime. Hudson Institute analyst Herman

1. Donald G. Brennan, "The Case for Population Defense," in *Why ABM? Policy Issues in the Missile Defense Controversy*, ed. Johan J. Holst and William Schneider, Jr. (New York: Pergamon Press, 1969), p. 108

2. Herman Kahn, *Thinking about the Unthinkable in the 1980s* (New York: Simon and Schuster, 1984), p. 51.

Kahn exemplified this doctrinally inconsistent mix of MDE and war-fighting, writing, for example:

> With ACD, arms control (e.g., deep reductions in nuclear forces) can be made to work because the deployment of active and passive defense permits greater trust of controls on strategic forces, and defenses can be made to work better because of the limitations on strategic offensive forces. . . . And if a nuclear war does break out, strategic defenses (along with doctrines and capabilities for controlled war) make it much less likely that the outcome of the conflict would be "mutual homicide."[3]

Kahn's reference to "capabilities for controlled war" may not seem antithetical to arms control, but its association with theories of nuclear victory emerges more clearly in the context of his other work.[4] The pernicious effect of proposing MDE while clinging to war-fighting doctrines would reduce MDE advocacy to near incoherence during the Reagan administration. In 1969 another Hudson Institute analyst, Johan Holst, noted the impact of war-fighting rationales for ballistic missile defense (BMD) on efforts to promote MDE:

> Much of the political support for ballistic missile defense in the U.S. emanates from quarters which are not known to be particularly friendly to arms control. There are exceptions, of course, but analysts . . . who tend to favor some BMD on arms control grounds have good reasons to feel uncomfortable about their "allies" on the subject . . . and we should not be surprised that the Russians are similarly concerned.[5]

The Hudson Institute's ties to the defense establishment helped create a situation where, unlike the 1950s, rationales for MDE would find a degree (albeit very limited) of consideration within the armed services. After a prolonged struggle with the Air Force, in January 1958 the Army had finally acquired the mission of developing an

3. Ibid., p. 138.

4. Kahn's two most notable contributions to the nuclear war-fighting literature are *On Thermonuclear War* (Princeton: Princeton University Press, 1960) and *Thinking about the Unthinkable* (New York: Horizon Press, 1962). In the former, Kahn acknowledges simply, "I am personally sympathetic to the notion that offensive strategies are to be preferred to equally good-looking defensive strategies." Quotation from 2d ed. (New York: Free Press, 1969), p. 335.

5. Johan J. Holst, "Missile Defense, the Soviet Union and the Arms Race," in Holst and Schneider (n. 1), p. 160.

antiballistic missile system.[6] In July 1963, as part of a campaign to buttress the case for ABM, the Army turned to the Hudson Institute to undertake a Threat Analysis Study on the implications of its Nike-X ABM system. (With some modifications it was Nike-X—relabeled as Sentinel and then as Safeguard—that comprised the defensive technologies at issue in the pre–SALT I ABM debates.)

The completed Threat Analysis Study, submitted to Secretary of Defense McNamara in January 1965, claimed that a variety of defensive improvements were resulting in a "unity" cost-exchange ratio between offense and defense. The study also presented strategic rationales for BMD (e.g., its contribution to damage limitation in a war-fighting strategy and its capacity to negate the missile threat of small nuclear powers). In addition, it presented the argument that bilateral ABM deployments could contribute to negotiated reductions in strategic offenses by providing a safeguard against cheating.[7]

Although the Army was little disposed to make the case for MDE the central selling point for Nike-X, the arguments for MDE attracted the attention of Richard Foster, who had served as director of the strategic, economic, and cost studies for the Army's Nike-X Threat Assessment Study. A year later Foster's article "The Impact of Ballistic Missile Defense on Arms Control Prospects," was among the first public arguments for mutual defense emphasis to appear in the missile age.[8]

From 1967 to 1972, however, it was Donald Brennan who occupied Oppenheimer's earlier role as principal advocate of defense emphasis arms control. Although many others supported MDE in articles, speeches, and conference papers during this period,[9] the

6. For discussions of the bureaucratic struggle for control of the ABM mission in the 1950s, see Benson D. Adams, *Ballistic Missile Defense* (New York: American Elsevier, 1971), pp. 22–31; Ernest J. Yanarella, *The Ballistic Missile Defense Controversy: Strategy, Technology and Politics, 1955–1972* (Lexington: University Press of Kentucky, 1977), pp. 26–42; and Clark Murdock, *Defense Policy Formation: A Comparative Analysis of the McNamara Era* (Albany: State University of New York Press, 1974), pp. 30–43.

7. James Trainor, "Nike-X Fate Keyed to DOD Study," *Missiles and Rockets*, May 18, 1964, pp. 14–15.

8. Richard B. Foster, "The Impact of Ballistic Missile Defense on Arms Control Prospects," in *Arms Control for the Late Sixties*, ed. James E. Dougherty and J. F. Lehman, Jr. (New York: Van Nostrand, 1967), pp. 80–92.

9. Sources of arguments in the 1960s for defense-emphasis strategic arms control that are *not* discussed in this chapter include the following: David R. Inglis, "Region-by-Region Disarmament with Anti-ballistic Missiles," in *Implications of Anti-ballistic Missile Systems*, ed. C. F. Barnaby and A. Boserup, Pugwash Monograph 2 (London: Souvenir Press, 1969), pp. 87–92; Alvin M. Weinberg, "Let Us Prepare for Peace," *Bulletin of the Atomic Scientists* 24 (July 1968): 17–20; Raymond D. Gastil, "Mis-

following depiction of their approach will draw primarily on the arguments advanced by Brennan.

Development of an arguably workable ABM system by the mid-1960s had fundamentally changed the technological environment that inspired the original conception of an offense-only arms control regime. By the time McNamara publicly endorsed MAD in 1967, the simple assertion that defense was impossible now served as a shorthand for controversial political and technical assumptions.

If the unalterable preference of the superpowers was to maintain assured destruction capabilities, only unlimited faith in defensive technology could justify unilateral efforts to protect populations, since MIRVing and other offensive innovations could confront a defense with tens of thousands of nuclear weapons (and "penetration aids" designed to fool the defense) delivered by a variety of means. MDE advocates acknowledged that each superpower had the capacity to overwhelm the other's efforts to defend. But they cogently challenged three other claims underlying MAD doctrine: that the Soviets were irrevocably committed to preserving an assured destruction capability; that U.S. security required "AD," and that population defenses were inherently incompatible with stable deterrence and arms control.

The domestic political environment, however, was not conducive to reasoned debated on the merits of MAD versus MDE arms control. Several factors made such a debate unlikely. One was the continuing influence of the war-fighters, whose rationale for ABM undercut dispassionate assessments of the role of defense in an arms control regime. Another was the political activism of an arms control community that had, in effect, come to regard the possibility of unlimited destruction as the solution to the nuclear problem rather than as the source of its danger. Moreover, evolving public perceptions of the nuclear danger had yielded a widespread antipathy toward defensive efforts.

Those attitudes, however, cannot be explained without reference

---

fense and Strategic Doctrine," in Holst and Schneider (n. 1); and Freeman J. Dyson, "A Case for Missile Defense," *Bulletin of the Atomic Scientists* 25 (April 1969): 31–34. In addition to the material discussed in this chapter, Donald G. Brennan wrote the following articles promoting mutual defense emphasis: "New Thoughts on Missile Defense," *Bulletin of the Atomic Scientists* 23 (June 1967): 10–15; "Missile Defense and Arms Control," *Disarmament*, no. 14 (1967): 1–4; "Post Deployment Issues in Ballistic Missile Defence" (with Johan J. Holst), in *Ballistic Missile Defence: Two Views*, Adelphi Paper no. 43 (London: International Institute for Strategic Studies, 1968), pp. 1–23; "A Start on Strategic Stabilization," *Bulletin of the Atomic Scientists* 25 (January 1969): 35–36; and "The Case for Missile Defense," *Foreign Affairs* 43 (April 1969): 433–48.

to the role of the U.S. leadership, whose nuclear policy was dominated by a defense secretary deeply committed to heading off efforts to defend the United States. We need to consider how a leadership that supported both defense and arms control might have changed the context of the domestic debate over nuclear policy. Regardless of MDE's abstract merits, and even with the benefit of a sympathetic defense secretary, however, MDE was precluded for a reason that would have defeated any comprehensive strategic arms control regime during this period: the unwillingness of the United States and its European allies to reconsider the value of extended nuclear deterrence despite impending superpower nuclear parity.

THE MDE CRITIQUE OF MUTUAL ASSURED DESTRUCTION

The intense technical debate over ABM by the mid-1960s, replete with eminent experts divided on the issue, indicated that the gap between offense and defense had narrowed sufficiently to prompt a second look at making unopposed offense the foundation of an arms control agreement. Certainly, that McNamara's own analysis depicted a cost-exchange ratio ranging from 4:1 (in favor of the offense) to below 1:1 ("unity")[10] should have served notice that the technogical offense-defense gap was no longer wide enough to resolve the debate. Donald Brennan observed:

> In the actual world . . . of cost-exchange ratios near unity, perhaps one-half or three but not one-tenth or ten, the attitudes prevailing are not driven by the technology toward either deterrence or defense, but may (and do) go in either direction. It is much more a matter of preference and conscious decision whether we and the Soviets wish to spend our strategic-force budgets chiefly to increase the level of "hostages" on the other side, or to decrease our own. Thus, whether we are to have an offense-defense arms race or not depends . . . on whether Soviet and American attitudes are lined up the same way or not.[11]

10. According to McNamara's estimates, with a deployed U.S. ABM that could reduce U.S. fatalities in a Soviet retaliatory strike to twenty million, preventing a rise in fatalities to forty million would require spending four dollars on additional defense for each Soviet dollar spent on additional offense. That 4:1 ratio dropped to 2:1 at the level of sixty million fatalities and to 1:1 at ninety million. "Statement of Secretary of Defense Robert S. McNamara before a Joint Session of the Senate Armed Services Committee and the Senate Subcommittee on Department of Defense Appropriations on the Fiscal Year 1968–72 Defense Program and 1968 Defense Budget," January 26, 1967, p. 43.

11. Brennan (n. 1), p. 108.

Since Department of Defense studies were not disputing Brennan's estimate of the cost-exchange ratio between offense and defense, McNamara's argument focused on superpower "preferences" as he asserted that Soviet and American attitudes were irreversibly "lined up" in favor of assured destruction:

> It is this interaction . . . which leads us to believe that there is a mutuality of interests in limiting the deployment of anti-missile defense systems. If our assumption that the Soviets are also striving to achieve an Assured Destruction capability is correct, and I am convinced that it is, then in all probability all that we would accomplish by deploying ABM systems against one another would be to increase greatly our defense expenditures, without any gain in real security for either side.[12]
>
> It is the virtual certainty that the Soviets will act to maintain their deterrent which casts such grave doubts on the advisability of our deploying the Nike-X system for the protection of our cities; against the kind of heavy-sophisticated missile attack they could launch in the 1970's.[13]

What was the basis for McNamara's "virtual certainty" that the Soviets were "striving to achieve an Assured Destruction capability"? There were no Department of Defense (DOD) studies challenging the public and private views of Soviet officials that they in fact preferred a defense emphasis approach to arms control.[14] Indeed, the following segment from a 1985 interview with McNamara suggests he gave some credence to that Soviet view. McNamara was recounting his attempt to explain MAD logic to Soviet premier Alexei Kosygin at the June 1967 summit in Glassboro, New Jersey:

> At one point [President] Johnson turned to me and said, "Bob, you explain to Kosygin how we view their anti-ballistic missile deployment."
>
> I said, "Mr. Prime Minister, you must understand that we will maintain a deterrent under any circumstances. And we view a deterrent as a nuclear force so strong that it can absorb your nuclear attack on it and

12. Statement of Secretary of Defense McNamara (n. 10), p. 44.

13. Ibid., p. 53.

14. Based on a series of interviews of DOD officials, Clark Murdock concluded "there was no analysis done on the question of whether the Soviet Union would react or not" (i.e., according to the dictates of McNamara's "action-reaction" hypothesis). Murdock concluded: "The problem McNamara overlooked was that the decision of whether to react was *itself* an arms-control issue—that the Soviet Union might be interested in reducing the absolute level of damage through a limitation on offensive weapons and a mutual build-up of defensive weapons." Murdock (n. 6), pp. 133–34.

> survive with sufficient power to inflict unacceptable damage on you. And, therefore, if you put a defense in place, we're going to have to expand our nuclear offensive forces. You may think, as the Congress apparently does, that a proper response to the Soviet defense is a U.S. defense; but I tell you the proper response—and it will be our response—is to expand our offensive force. . . ."
>
> He absolutely erupted, He became red in the face. He pounded the table. He said, "Defense is moral, offense is immoral." I think that is what he believed. This was not a show; he believed it.[15]

If Soviet views cast doubt on the mutuality of assured destruction criteria, there was also reason to question its status as a fundamental U.S. requirement. MDE advocates claimed that the United States could preserve deterrence while reducing its retaliatory threat to below the level represented by AD, and that MDE provided a technical framework for doing so.

"Assured destruction" was introduced by McNamara in 1965, when it was coupled to "damage limitation" as the two objectives of U.S. strategic forces. The concept then served only to distinguish between the offensive and defensive components of the traditional U.S. war-fighting approach to deterrence. In terms of cost-effective force planning, this division clearly favored counterforce capabilities. These, unlike either inaccurate "countervalue" weapons or active defenses, could be used to perform both missions.

Only in 1967 did McNamara drop the goal of damage limitation in U.S. declaratory policy, explaining that "it is our ability to destroy an attacker . . . that provides the deterrent, not our ability to partially limit damage to ourselves."[16] But what was the precise meaning of McNamara's blunt descriptions of the phrase "assured destruction"—for example, "destroy an attacker," "the certainty of suicide to the aggressor," and "damaging the aggressor to the point that his society would be simply no longer viable in twentieth-century terms"?[17] Originally, McNamara quantified these concepts in terms of the ability—in the wake of a Soviet first strike—to kill 25 to 30 percent of the Soviet population and destroy two-thirds of Soviet

15. Michael Charlton, *The Star Wars History—from Deterrence to Defence: The American Strategic Debate* (London: BBC Publications, 1986), p. 27.

16. "Statement of Secretary of Defense Robert S. McNamara before the House Armed Services Committee on the Fiscal Year 1968–72 Defense Program and 1968 Defense Budget," January 23, 1967, p. 39.

17. Robert S. McNamara, *The Essence of Security* (New York: Harper and Row, 1968), p. 53.

industrial capacity. In 1967 he reconsidered, adjusting the number to 20 to 25 percent of the population and half of Soviet industry. If the lower estimate raises the suspicion that a capacity to kill more than forty million people might not be enough, it should be noted that calculations were based only on the direct effects of a nuclear attack; no effort was made to factor in deaths from starvation, untended wounds, or other war-related causes.[18]

The antidefense arms control community was silent about these numbers, even though they accepted McNamara's misleading implication that U.S. operational policy was designed specifically to carry out such countervalue threats if deterrence failed. The only objection war-fighters offered was that the specified force levels were grossly insufficient, given the implied abandonment of the offenses required for the counterforce mission. During the ABM debates, the only substantive critique of these numbers as being strategically incoherent came from two advocates of MDE, Johan Holst and Donald Brennan. The basis of their argument was that retaliatory capabilities should be determined not by some absolute capacity to destroy the adversary, but by ensuring that a potential nuclear aggressor would expect to wind at least as bad off as its victim. Put another way, the only requirement for deterrence was to ensure that there was no first-strike advantage.

McNamara's error, Brennan argued, was that he "defined the 'Assured Destruction' requirement *without any reference to the nature or scale of the Soviet threat*."[19] There were, he conceded, two arguable advantages to setting one's counterthreat at a constant, absolute level. For one thing, "trying to forget about any linkage between threat and retaliation" greatly simplified force planning, leaving only the question of "how much is enough" to destroy the adversary.

18. The lowered criteria for assured destruction apparently did not change the quantitative yardstick for setting force levels: i.e., a retaliatory capability of four hundred one-megaton-equivalent delivered warheads. That level was in fact deemed capable of killing seventy-four million Russians (30 percent of the total population) and destroying 76 percent of Soviet industry. These numbers, according to two participants in the OSD decision-making process, were "based on a judgment reached by the Secretary of Defense and accepted by the President, by the Congress, and apparently by the general public as well. That judgment was influenced by the fact of strongly diminishing marginal returns" (i.e., further increases in megatonnage yielded a progressively lower increase in deaths and economic damage). Alain C. Enthoven and K. Wayne Smith, *How Much Is Enough? Shaping the Defense Program, 1961–1969* (New York: Harper and Row, 1971), p. 207. For McNamara's explanation of how he ascertained the proper assured destruction level for China, see *Congressional Record—Senate*, 90th Cong., 2d sess., vol. 114, pt. 4, p. 4640 (February 29, 1968).

19. Brennan (n. 1), p. 101.

Second, a state could be marginally more comfortable in confronting even a very weak nuclear adversary with total destruction. Although Brennan used the example of the U.S. capability against the Soviets in the early days of massive retaliation, the same point can be illustrated with McNamara's strategic policy toward China. The assured destruction level set for China—which then had only a *potential* for developing a strategic nuclear capability—was fifty urban centers (more than fifty million deaths and half of China's industry).

It should be noted that AD threats were specifically linked only to deterrence of nuclear attacks. McNamara (and, he has since claimed, the two presidents he served) had already privately disavowed "first use" in response to conventional aggression.[20] Thus, for the relatively small cost in offensive procurements required to put China on the assured destruction list, the United States acquired the luxury of never having to consider how *small* a deterrent threat was sufficient to prevent a Chinese nuclear attack.

The Soviets could not be expected to tolerate such a gross imbalance in strategic capabilities, however. And as the Soviets approached nuclear parity, any marginal benefits of AD criteria would be outweighed by an enormous cost. As Brennan noted, the Soviet motivation to at least match U.S. retaliatory power "tends to force *us* into a posture of 'Assured Vulnerability.'" Once the United States faced unlimited vulnerability, he argued, it became prudent to establish a link between threat and retaliation. Simply put, the United States should have then considered lowering its retaliatory capability in return for a reduction in the Soviet threat. But how could it do so without fearing that the retaliatory level would fall too low to deter? The key, Brennan maintained, was to exchange the concept of absolute damage for one of relative damage. Brennan's formula for this standard may be paraphrased as follows: "Following any plausibly feasible strategic attack by one side, the defender should have the capacity to inflict as much or more total damage as the attacker had inflicted and could still inflict."[21]

In testimony before Congress in 1969, Brennan stated his perspective in terms of two principles:

20. Early in the Kennedy administration, McNamara notes, "we quickly came to the conclusion" that a nuclear attack on the Soviet Union was an irrational response to Soviet conventional aggression in Europe: "The Soviets would attack New York or London or Paris or Washington, and with such destruction that we would never make the first move. It would be committing suicide." Charlton (n. 15), p. 17.

21. See Brennan (n. 1), p. 105.

> The first principle is that . . . we should be able to do at least as badly unto the Soviets as they had done or could do unto us.
>
> The second principle is that we should prefer live Americans to dead Russians. . . . The Soviets may be expected to prefer live Russians to dead Americans, and therein resides the basis for an important common interest; we may both prefer live Americans and live Russians. This formulation may seem so simple as to sound facetious, . . . but it conceals a point that is profoundly important and surprisingly controversial.[22]

Why were these principles controversial? McNamara's unsubstantiated claim of Soviet subscription to AD criteria certainly raised doubts about Brennan's approach and helped deflect attention from Brennan's other assumptions.

Brennan's core contention about the requirements for basic nuclear deterrence paralleled that of the minimum deterrence arms control theorists of the early 1960s, who also argued that MAD could be exchanged for parity in destructive potential at lower force levels. In the abstract, one could certainly imagine situations in which the prospect of suffering equal or even greater damage might be insufficient to deter. Thus, if one of the superpowers had a decisive advantage across the spectrum of nonnuclear dimensions of power (e.g., economic strength, population, and conventional military forces), it might calculate that a nuclear war in which each suffered equal losses would enhance its relative power over the victim.

In reality, though, from the onset of nuclear parity that began in the 1960s until the end of the Cold War, there was never a wide enough gap in the overall nonnuclear "correlation of forces" between the United States and the Soviet Union to make such an option even remotely viable. In two of the critical dimensions of the balance—economic power and conventional strength relevant to a war over Europe—the superpowers had offsetting advantages. Notwithstanding a U.S. declaratory doctrine implying retaliation solely against cities, target selection would always be based on destroying the assets deemed most valuable to the enemy. (Different priorities could be assigned, for example, to targeting weapons plants, conventional forces, energy sources, civilian or military command centers, etc.) Given Brennan's assumption that forces could be structured so that the postattack balance of strategic forces favored the

22. "Diplomatic and Strategic Impact of Multiple Warhead Missiles," Hearings before the Subcommittee on National Security Policy and Scientific Developments of the House Committee on Foreign Affairs, 91st Cong., 1st sess. (1969), p. 109.

victim, an aggressor would have to fear that any nonnuclear advantages it possessed would be narrowed in a nuclear exchange.

Moreover, the belief that one would be worse off for initiating a nuclear war does not require the prospect of suffering at least as much damage as one's victim. When the cost of aggression is measured in terms of how many cities one might lose, the prospect of inflicting more harm on one's victim is unlikely to make an attack seem worthwhile. Brennan's central point was that the objective of limiting damage to oneself is inherently more valuable than that of inflicting damage on an adversary (an assumption consistent with actual U.S. operational planning). With an aggressor's anticipated losses at least equal to those of the victim, neither side would be consoled (let alone inspired) by the possibility that it might still be ahead in some measures of relative power after initiating a nuclear war. Suffering equally would always seem a poor alternative to not suffering at all.

If one accepted Brennan's "controversial" claim that both sides preferred live Russians *and* live Americans, it followed that forces should be structured to reflect that common interest. Although purely offense-based regimes could deter rational adversaries, MDE could also address dangers that no approach based on nuclear parity could avert: third-party attacks, accidental launchings, irrational behavior under the pressure of domestic or international crisis, or psychotic leaders or lower-level commanders.

Yet even if both superpowers had preferred some degree of transition from MAD toward mutual defense emphasis, they still would have faced a search for an arms control framework for incorporating defenses. If Wiesner was right in his 1960 claim that a missile deterrent system would be unbalanced by the introduction of population defenses, then the MDE option would simply have been precluded. MDE advocates challenged that claim, insisting that as offenses were reduced, stability could be *enhanced* by the deployment of defenses (of both remaining offensive forces and populations).

Mutual Defense Emphasis and Deterrence Stability

In 1969 Brennan outlined a simple arms control proposal to show how bilateral damage limitation need not undermine either the primary requirement of deterrence or the reassurance necessary for an arms control regime. First, both sides should ban MIRV (which was being tested by the United States but had not been deployed by either superpower).[23] Second, they should establish a ceiling on offensive delivery vehicles at some agreed-upon level (which, "at least initially," could have remained high enough "to impose no new inspection requirements"). Third, they should take steps to protect strategic offensive forces. Finally, both sides should deploy population defenses.

Brennan believed that the elimination of any first-strike advantage would be sufficiently assured by the first three measures. Consequently there was no apparent need to impose specific constraints on population defenses: "My personal inclination would be to exempt defensive forces from controls altogether, except perhaps for interceptor missiles that were large enough to serve as offensive missiles, but if there were a suitable consensus that some mild limitation was desirable, such as limiting the rate of deployment to (say) one thousand interceptors per year, I should not oppose it."[24] As Brennan pointed out, his approach followed the same stability principles that had guided the minimum deterrence arms control proposals originating at the onset of the missile age. In both cases, a first-strike advantage would be avoided by combining parity in offensive capabilities with protection of retaliatory forces. In part, that protection would be ensured by limiting both sides to single-warhead missiles (thereby preserving the clear-cut second-strike advantage that had led minimum deterrence theorists to prefer missiles as the basis for their envisioned regime). As for protecting deterrent forces, an ABM hard-point defense would simply have reinforced the types of measures (e.g., silo hardening) supported by Wiesner and others.

In 1960 Wiesner had predicted a "natural" evolution toward great stability in the missile balance, based on the hope that "as many as five missiles" would be "required to eliminate a single hardened missile." Accuracy improvements alone had undercut that 5:1 ratio, and even some ABM opponents agreed that point defense of missile sites was an available means of restoring it. Thus the only point of apparent difficulty with Brennan's argument was the belief that population defenses on both sides would invariably increase the temptation to strike first.

During the national ABM debates in the late 1960s, the anti-ABM scientists commonly supplemented their technological critiques of

23. Ibid. For Brennan's testimony before Congress against MIRV (and in favor of ABM), see pp. 105–15.
24. Brennan (n. 1), p. 113.

Sentinel/Safeguard with claims that population defenses were *inherently* destabilizing. One example was MIT physicist Steven Weinberg's contention that "any such [population defense] system, however 'thin,' will raise Soviet doubts about their own ability to retaliate after a U.S. first strike."[25] The repetition of such claims by ABM opponents made it difficult to redirect attention to Brennan's argument that an arms control understanding could address such concerns about population defenses—even though Brennan was relying on the same principles of deterrence that had inspired the mutual deterrence arms control approaches of the early 1960s.

One can visualize the type of balance Brennan was proposing by referring to the simplified "missile deterrent system" model often used by arms control theorists in the early 1960s. Instead of Wiesner's five hundred single-warhead missiles on both sides, one might add, say, one thousand ABM interceptors limited to the defense of ICBM sites and one thousand interceptors defending cities. No matter what degree of effectiveness one assigns to either defensive or offensive missiles in that hypothetical environment (and even if one assumes a considerable gap between the overall operational performance of the two sides' forces), there would have been no rational incentive for either side to strike first.

Thus, even in the extreme case that hard-point defenses were wholly ineffective, the principal effect of an all-out counterforce first strike would be to utterly disarm the attacker. Assuming that two missiles would have to be allocated to each target (in the absence of defenses), the victim could expect that half of its land-based missiles would survive a first strike. One purpose of hard-point defense in such a regime would be to preclude meaningful cheating. Without defenses, five hundred covertly deployed warheads would make a disarming strike theoretically feasible. One thousand interceptor missiles would dramatically raise the required number of hidden (or rapidly deployed) counterforce offenses; and even a defense that seemed vulnerable to countermeasures would introduce great uncertainty into the attacker's calculations.

Brennan was not insisting that ABM was the only means to protect land-based retaliatory forces, though MDE advocates argued that it appeared to be the most attractive option in a regime envisioning deep offensive cuts. He was merely noting that "strategic

25. Steven Weinberg, "What Does Safeguard Safeguard?" in *ABM: An Evaluation of the Decision to Deploy an Antiballistic Missile System*, ed. Abram Chayes and Jerome B. Wiesner (New York: New American Library, 1969), p. 85.

offensive forces must be quite well protected" in any damage-limiting arms control regime. In effect, as a response to fears of covert or "breakout" counterforce deployments by the adversary, adding hard-point defenses would substitute for expanding the size of the retaliatory force.

While lowering offenses was one side of the damage-limitation equation, adding population defenses was the other. Without population defenses, only extremely low offenses could preclude an annihilating attack. Population defenses would make attacks on cities less attractive as an option as well as lowering the total amount of societal damage that could be inflicted. Thus, although an undefended "soft" target might be destroyed by a single warhead, ensuring destruction of a heavily defended target would require a far larger allocation of offensive forces. The overall effect would be to reduce the total number of cities that could be destroyed. To the extent the defenses proved effective, a limited attack against a population center might simply fail.

Opponents of population defense often suggest that in an environment of bilateral population defenses, the attacker's need to cope only with a weakened retaliation gives it an inherent advantage. Since both the aggressor and the victim lose weapons in a counterforce attack, however, both will be weaker in subsequent exchanges. Assuming forces are designed so that the initial exchange ratio favors the victim, the burden on an MDE regime would be to ensure that neither side possessed enough of an advantage in population defenses to compensate for the disadvantage in offensive capabilities left to the initiator of an attack.

In short, although population defenses alone would enhance first-strike incentives, that tendency might be countered by a compensatory increase in the proportion of offensive forces that could survive a counterforce strike. MDE proposals to defend retaliatory forces and to prohibit multiple warheads were consistent with well-established principles for enhancing stability. The greater the progress toward those objectives, the higher the threshold of population defenses that could be tolerated without creating first-strike incentives.

In terms of 1960s defensive technologies, one should remember that the 1972 ABM Treaty provided a concrete framework for regulating the introduction of ground-based defenses: missile site by missile site, city by city. That the agreed number in 1972 was one city and one missile site for each side (with one hundred interceptors per site) resulted from a political decision not to proceed down the path of bilateral damage limitation. Those numbers would have been susceptible to negotiated revision. Similarly, there would have been no reason why protection of other military targets—for example, bomber bases, command, control, and communication (C^3) centers—would have defeated an MDE negotiating framework, or why protection of populations could not have been defined in terms of "areas" as well as cities.

In the hypothetical MDE framework mentioned above, the concept of deterrence by threat of "punishment" has not disappeared. Either side could absorb a first strike and still saturate the defenses of some of the attacker's cities. At some point, lowering offenses and raising defenses would bring the retaliatory capabilities of both sides below McNamara's standards of assured destruction. Yet as long as the balance of postattack forces favored the victim, there would never be a rational incentive to strike first.

As was described in chapter 5, reducing wartime damage by an "offense-only" system faced the inherent obstacle that lowering the deterrent level would increase the consequences of cheating. The first detailed public presentation in the missile age of the need for defense in approaching meaningful disarmament was given by Richard Foster in 1966.[26] Although neither he nor other MDE advocates indicated any awareness of the fact, they were merely resurrecting Oppenheimer's 1953 argument that with large-scale defenses cheating would be "either far too vast to conceal, or far too small to have . . . a decisive strategic effect."[27] The following is Brennan's presentation of that argument in 1969:

> I believe the only possible routes to major reductions in offensive forces—i.e., to a degree that would make a large difference in the scale of possible damage . . . all involve substantial defenses. . . .
>
> At 1969 levels of offensive forces, an uncertainty of say, one hundred missiles . . . would be of relatively little consequence. . . . However, if it were decided to reduce offensive forces by agreement to a level that could not cause more than, say, twenty million fatalities, then the allowed forces themselves would have to be limited to something like one hundred missiles on each side, if there were no defenses. At *this* level of offensive forces, a clandestine stock of one hundred missiles could be of great—indeed, literally overwhelming—significance. . . .
>
> [A] BMD system that would reliably intercept all or almost all of one hundred or two hundred missiles is highly feasible, and, if deployed,

26. Foster (n. 8), p. 86.

27. J. Robert Oppenheimer, "Atomic Weapons and American Policy," in *The Atomic Age: Scientists in National and World Affairs* (New York: Basic Books, 1963), pp. 195–96. This article originally appeared in *Bulletin of the Atomic Scientists*, July 1953.

> would substantially reduce or wholly eliminate the threat a modest clandestine force could constitute. (A large clandestine force probably could be detected by inspection.) Thus, defenses would make possible major disarmament of the offensive forces.[28]

In several ways, the model MDE environment described above overlooks the complexities of the strategic environment of the 1960s. Most obviously, it assumes away strategic weapons other than single-warhead ballistic missiles. States pursuing a comprehensive arms control regime might agree to retain more than one type of delivery system or might choose to base a mutual deterrence system solely (or primarily) on bombers. Here it is sufficient to note that technical analyses of prospective deterrence systems at greatly reduced force levels have demonstrated the feasibility of designing forces (including submarines, bombers, and more recently, cruise missiles) so that the postattack balance favors the victim of a first strike.[29]

As with MDE in a ballistic missile–only regime, regimes that preserved other types of delivery systems would have to establish ceilings on relevant defensive capabilities that precluded a first-strike advantage. Some level of defense would be required even against a banned offensive system, unless verification and other control measures precluded a covert redeployment.

Aside from the added complexity of designing an MDE regime involving more than one type of offensive delivery system, MDE might be threatened by a decisive technological innovation that one side could rapidly exploit. That issue (which Brennan addressed) will be considered shortly. In explaining the U.S. failure to consider MDE in the 1960s, however, the critical point is that opponents of MDE either ignored Brennan's arguments or continued their opposition despite conceding the technical feasibility—and even necessity—of incorporating defenses into any arms control regime aimed at meaningfully reducing offensive capabilities.

The most illuminating response to Brennan's argument came from Jerome Wiesner, whose influence on the development and popularization of "offense-only" arms control I described earlier. Wiesner's 1967 reaction is worth citing at length:

28. Brennan (n. 1), pp. 115–16.

29. For a recent proposal for a "finite deterrence" regime based on two thousand total warheads, see Harold A. Feiveson and Frank N. von Hippel, "Beyond START: How to Make Much Deeper Cuts," *International Security* 15 (Summer 1990), pp. 154–80. Although this proposal is based on preserving MAD capabilities, the exchange ratio that results would dramatically favor the victim of a first strike.

> Another proposal, made possible by even a modest ABM system, is the total elimination of offensive weapons. Such an ABM system would also make a small stable deterrent force . . . even more secure than it would be by itself. Several general and complete disarmament systems considered previously were based upon such minimal deterrence arrangements. But these were not acceptable in the United States because of doubt . . . that one could deal adequately with the threat posed by small numbers of strategic weapons that might be manufactured clandestinely. . . . An antiballistic missile system that could cope with a very few missiles—and I believe that such a system is possible—would eliminate this danger because any clandestine weapons (or even small numbers of weapons developed by a third of fourth power) need not concern either the United States or the Soviet Union.
>
> This possibility opened up by the deployment of an antiballistic missile system . . . should be considered seriously. There are some obvious problems with this idea. For example, there will come a point during the reduction of the missile force at which their effectiveness as a deterrent will be questionable at the same time that the ABM effectiveness will not be clearly established. This is a point of considerable worry, but one which I believe can be overcome.[30]

There is no way of knowing whether the superpowers, in the type of prolonged SALT negotiations that were undertaken a year later, could have overcome the problem Wiesner identified. They may not have wished to, preferring instead to stop well short of completely eliminating their retaliatory power. What is significant is that there was no serious effort to consider the specific requirements of a defensive transition, despite the absence of any compelling demonstration of its infeasibility.

A final argument against the technical feasibility of MDE acknowledged the possibility of designing an initial framework for augmenting defenses while questioning whether such an arrangement could be sufficiently robust to withstand technological change. Thus, Jerome Kahan argued:

> Real or perceived technological advances could easily upset defense emphasis arrangements and result in increased tension, rapid offensive rearmament, or consideration of preemptive first-strike attacks. Agreed verification systems might help but could not substantially alleviate these problems. ABM performance could not be checked in detail, nor

30. Jerome B. Wiesner, "Hope for GCD?" *Bulletin of the Atomic Scientists* 24 (January 1968): 13.

could qualitative improvements in offensive or defensive systems be adequately monitored.[31]

The effort to cope with technological innovation in weaponry has been a central feature of the nuclear era. When the nature of atomic-age deterrence first attracted attention, there were good reasons to fear an imminent loss in the ability to deter. In the absence of realistic efforts to limit the size of strategic forces, qualitative changes in offensive weaponry were occurring with great speed. The A-bomb, the intercontinental-range bomber, and the H-bomb all emerged within a decade, and by its end the missile age was clearly on the horizon.

As each side pursued the next breakthrough, hopes for usable advantages alternated with fears of being almost instantly overtaken. Finally, the inability to determine where one stood technologically was complicated by great uncertainty regarding the actual size and composition of the other side's forces. In that environment, the possibility of suffering a complete defeat had to be seriously considered.

By the end of the 1960s, that situation had changed in three fundamental ways, and each of them greatly enhanced prospects for arms control. First, the deployment of satellites now meant that decisive changes in the strategic balance could not occur without substantial warning. Second, there were no imminent technological breakthroughs remotely comparable to those that occurred between 1945 and 1957. Finally, early predictions that an unregulated competition would inevitably lead to a balance of terror had been fully realized, making it far harder for decision makers to press for unilateral solutions to the nuclear danger.

The last two changes had a special bearing on the prospects for an MDE regime sufficiently robust to cope with technological change. Most important, there was no defensive technology in sight that—given the time available for the other side to react—could deny either superpower the capacity to inflict massive retaliatory damage. Significantly, there was expert consensus on this point, notwithstanding the violent disagreements among scientists over the cost and effectiveness of the defensive systems developed during the 1960s. In all of the congressional testimony on behalf of ABM, no one with any claim to technical expertise denied that either side could overcome the other's defense if it were determined to do so.

31. Jerome H. Kahan, *Security in the Nuclear Age: Developing U.S. Strategic Arms Policy* (Washington, D.C.: Brookings Institution, 1975), p. 258.

Thus, in striking contrast to statements Edward Teller would make fifteen years later (regarding space-based BMD's potential to cope with even an unconstrained offensive threat), the strongest appeal he could offer for the ground-based technologies of the 1960s was that "no one claims today as great an imbalance in cost between offensive and defensive weapons as used to prevail. In case defense has a chance comparable to that of the offense, there are strong reasons of common humanity . . . to place great emphasis on the development of a defensive force."

That even ABM supporters recognized technological supremacy for the defense as a distant dream suggests that an MDE regime need not have foundered on fears of qualitative improvements in defensive systems alone. The more valid concern was that expansion and improvements in both strategic defenses *and* counterforce capabilities could provide one or both sides with a meaningful first strike advantage. Here, however, Kahan's critique simply dismisses a central feature of the regime envisioned by MDE advocates: the imposition of verifiable constraints on offensive forces. Thus, in acknowledging the claim that even a partially effective defense might make a first strike seem feasible, Teller stated:

> I think we can make a big contribution by abstaining from one thing, and that is not to abstain from justified defense, but to abstain from what is called the counterforce, our ability to destroy Russian silos.
>
> . . . I do not believe we ever can destroy all their silos. And if we stop trying to do this impossible thing, then the Russians will indeed not have to fear an American first strike.
>
> Defense should not make them uneasy, but our talk about a counterforce, . . . that indeed may make them uneasy and I would be happy if we abstained from that.[32]

As I noted earlier, Brennan was proposing a ban on MIRV, coupled with a freeze or reduction of offensive forces. An MDE regime would presumably combine such limits on force levels with constraints (e.g., test bans) on development of new methods of penetrating defenses.[33] For example, a ban on developing maneuvering

32. Edward Teller, "Strategic and Foreign Policy Implications of ABM Systems," Hearings before the Subcommittee on International Organization and Disarmament Affairs of the Senate Committee on Foreign Relations, 91st Cong. 1st sess. pt. 1, pp. 504–5.

33. After noting the difficulties of estimating the technical capabilities of offensive and defensive systems, the 1987 OTA study on SDI adds: "At the same time, if the

reentry vehicles (MaRVs)—often invoked by ABM opponents as one reason why defense would prove impossible—would have been an essential concomitant to an MDE regime. Kahan's claim that improvements in offensive or defensive systems could not be "adequately monitored" suggests that the original defense emphasis arrangement he envisioned was designed with no serious provision for limiting future weapons development, testing, and deployment.

Kahan is almost certainly right that one side's defection from an MDE regime would have led to "rapid offensive rearmament." Yet it is hard to see how a breakdown would lead to "consideration of preemptive first-strike attacks." All that any arms control agreement can do is provide time to react to meaningful cheating. The prospect of a breakout leading to a first strike suggests that a vast augmentation of offensive or defensive capabilities, or both, could evade timely detection, giving a defector absolute confidence that it could preclude the destruction of its major cities in a retaliatory strike.

Of course, any definitive judgment about breakout risks would require scrutiny of a treaty that would have represented the culmination of prolonged negotiations. But we can address the basic plausibility of claims that an MDE regime would have been inherently fragile by considering the incentives to comply or defect. Given expert consensus that defensive technology alone could not deny either side an assured destruction capability, the predictable outcome of defecting from MDE would be a return to MAD. Thus a defecting state would have been exchanging a progressively growing capacity to defend its homeland for a repetition of the offensive arms race that produced MAD in the first place. The only rational incentive to defect from MDE, then, would be a near certainty that one could quickly achieve meaningful superiority, coupled with a determination to initiate war before the victim had time to restore its retaliatory force. Given the slim chance that the massive preparations required for such an effort would remain invisible to the adversary, that opportunity would be extremely unlikely to occur.

Although wanting to win a war could prompt a defection from any type of arms control regime, MAD introduces a powerful alternative incentive to break out of an agreement: the basic desire to survive. As Robert Jervis pointed out (shortly before the U.S. nu-

---

Soviets decided, along with the United States, that defenses were desirable, then each side could help make them more effective by agreeing to deep cuts in offensive weapons and to restrictions on countermeasures against defenses." Office of Technology Assessment, *SDI: Technology, Survivability, and Software* (Princeton: Princeton University Press, 1988), p. 44.

clear survival instinct resurfaced in the 1980s): "Both interest and tradition may lead the USSR to view nuclear strategy more in terms of defense than deterrence; to seek the capacity to fight and win wars. . . . (It is important to note, however, that the Russians could seek to take their cities out of hostage even if they desired only increased security and did not intend to use this ability to make new political gains."[34] The 1970s and 1980s indeed witnessed the emergence of technologies that promised arms race instability: first MIRV, and then intensified research on space-based defenses that (as is discussed in the following chapter) seemed designed to provide a first-strike advantage.

As Brennan recognized, the best way to head off the search for a war-fighting advantage was to limit *all* offensive systems. He was the only expert who testified for ABM and against MIRV. (Teller, as I noted above, combined support for ABM with a more general condemnation of counterforce capabilities.) Had the principle underlying those combined recommendations been accepted, the United States might have entered the arms control era with a means to constrain the technological race in offensive damage limitation that characterized the next two decades. As the next chapter shows, MDE would also provide a more compelling repudiation of Star Wars than was offered by MAD proponents.

It was easy for Kahan to discredit his "straw man" MDE regime, which existed as a construct of his mind rather than as a result of actual superpower negotiations. No doubt such negotiations would have been more technically demanding then negotiations based on MAD, since MAD's existence requires no negotiations at all. The same technical problems that beset all efforts to impose real symmetry on the strategic balance would have appeared (e.g., disparities in missile throw weight, the differing distribution of offenses across the triad). There also would have been a need to consider existing differences in ABM technology and to agree on what types of systems design changes could be incorporated in the future. At least partially compensating for added technical complexities would have been the fact that more was at stake than merely ratifying the superpowers' inability to defend their homelands unilaterally.

In this context, it is of interest that many mainstream arms controllers conceded, as Wiesner did, that the technical obstacles to an MDE regime might be dealt with by negotiation. They opposed

34. Robert Jervis, "Deterrence Theory Revisited," *World Politics* 31 (January 1979): 296–97.

ABM nevertheless, for a reason Wiesner expressed in the same speech in which he acknowledged MDE as the only feasible way to move below MAD capabilities: "The danger with proposing it is that it will be added to the list of reasons for building an ABM system *before* anything is done to restrict strategic weapons."[35]

In what amounted to a debate with Brennan before the Senate Foreign Relations Committee in 1969, another leading anti-ABM scientist, Wolfgang Panofsky, was asked by a senator if he wished to rebut Brennan's argument for mutual defense emphasis. Panofsky responded: "Yes. I think that even if one can make a plausible scenario in which having defenses on both sides would be a possible component of an arms limitation agreement, I believe that a unilateral increase of a defense on one side before such negotiations have started will certainly complicate our efforts in reaching an agreement."[36]

That it was the *political context* of ABM deployment rather than its technological shortcomings that motivated the anti-ABM scientists was also reflected in the testimony of physicist Herbert F. York, who as director of defense researh and engineering from 1958 to 1961 had presided over work on the original Nike-Zeus ABM system. In 1969 York expressed his fear that ABM would accelerate the arms race by creating a "false hope" in a "technical solution" to U.S. vulnerability. He then added, "An exception would be in the case of the deployment of an ABM as a carefuly integrated part of a major move in the direction of arms control and disarmament."[37]

When Panofsky raised his concern that defense would proceed "unilaterally" before negotiations were under way, Brennan made the following reply:

> In a sense I agree at least partially with Dr. Panofsky's last remark.
>
> I have advocated myself for several years, in fact, that we should begin serious discussion with the Soviets about suitable mixtures of offensive and defensive forces and I think we could have been carrying on these discussions for some time in the past and have missed some opportunities to do so.[38]

35. Jerome B. Wiesner, *Proceedings of the Seventeenth Pugwash Conference on Science and World Affairs*, Ronneby, Sweden, September 3–8, 1967, p. 134.
36. Hearings (n. 32), p. 365.
37. Ibid. For the cited testimony and York's discussion, see Herbert F. York, *Making Weapons, Talking Peace: A Physicist's Odyssey from Hiroshima to Geneva* (New York: Basic Books, 1987), pp. 237–45.
38. Hearings (n. 32), p. 365.

There is no way of knowing whether serious U.S. participation in such discussions could have paved the way for an MDE arms control regime. We might recall, however, Freeman Dyson's observation that as early as 1962 his review at the Arms Control and Disarmament Agency (ACDA) of the Soviet approach showed a clear preference for defense emphasis arms control. Two years later, in the summer of 1964, the Hudson Institute, under contract by ACDA to study the arms control implications of future military technology, submitted its recommendation that it was in the U.S. interest to explore "arms control through defense."[39] As late as 1967, at the same Pugwash meeting in which Wiesner was voicing his fear that defenses would be built before they could be bilaterally negotiated, Soviet general A. A. Gryzlov was presenting a paper laying out the rationale for a defense-protected disarmament regime.[40]

Thus, for the five years preceding McNamara's strenuous effort to establish a MAD arms control framework, experts had been repeatedly exposed to the argument for MDE. Had a serious superpower dialogue on the relative merits of offensive and defensive strategic weapons been undertaken before 1967, there would have been far less need for arms controllers to fear that imminent ABM deployments would automatically fuel the arms race. BMD might have been considered more calmly, with inquiry based on an open-minded search for whatever version of strategic "symmetry" could most reduce the nuclear danger.

In 1980 Hedley Bull observed that "population defenses [and] ABMs are not inherently stabilizing or destabilizing; their effect depends on their purpose and context."[41] In the United States, the context in which defense was regarded as destabilizing was rooted in a theory of arms control that emerged early in the missile age. "Technology" can indeed explain that theory's appeal in the limited sense that "a passing technological moment" inspired hope that a total absence of defense against a terrifying new weapon might finally induce the superpowers to submit to a comprehensive nuclear arms control regime.

It was a mistake, however, to rely so heavily on the absence of a

39. Ibid., p. 376.

40. A. A. Gryzlov, "The Freezing of Defensive Anti-missile Systems," in *Proceedings* (n. 35), pp. 278–81.

41. Hedley Bull, "Future Conditions of Strategic Deterrence," in *The Future of Strategic Deterrence, Part I*, Adelphi Paper no. 160 (London: International Institute for Strategic Studies, 1980), p. 22. Bull, in agreeing with "what Don Brennan has long argued," applies that observation specifically to population defenses on p. 17.

certain type of damage-limiting weapon at some particular point in the nuclear era. The far more durable meaning of their call for arms control was that traditional war-fighting approaches to deterrence and defense could lead to nothing better than a dangerous stalemate based on "saturation parity." Had the superpowers fully converged on that basic point, subsequent decisions on strategic weapons could have been guided by a common effort to minimize the nuclear danger.

By effectively excluding damage limitation as a goal of arms control, the MAD "fashion" vastly reduced the superpowers' incentives to submit to meaningful bilateral constraints. Instead, hopes for surviving a failure of deterrence were driven outside the arms control process and entrusted to a frantic search for new damage-limiting technologies and strategies. The 1972 ABM Treaty only ensured that the search would primarily be directed into a vast bilateral expansion of offensive counterforce-capable nuclear warheads.

If U.S. arms control thought in 1967 had been "lined up" with that of the Soviets, one can imagine a very different Glassboro summit in 1967. McNamara and Johnson would not have confronted Kosygin with a provocative assertion that the United States was bent on preserving an ability to annihilate the Soviet people. Instead of representing helpless outrage, Kosygin's statement that "defense is moral, offense is immoral" would have been the initial, shared premise of the first real arms control dialogue between the superpowers.

Those who engaged Brennan's arguments conceded that the approach might well be both desirable and feasible. Their belief that MDE was not an option was based in large part on their reading of the domestic context of the nuclear policy debate. Thus, after arguing that unilateral defensive deployments would lead to a costly, futile, and dangerous arms competition, Jerome Kahan added, "Obviously, these reactions would not occur if both sides rejected assured destruction as the *foundation* of their posture. But the United States is unlikely to do so (emphasis in original).[42]

That contention in effect transforms the deterministic claim of "technological necessity" into a claim of "U.S. domestic political necessity" as the explanation of why defense is impossible in the nuclear age. Was MDE impossible in the 1960s because of unalterable features of the political landscape? That question requires a look at the domestic political basis for the concept of assured destruction.

42. Kahan (n. 31), p. 258

Mutual Assured Destruction and Domestic Politics

In chapter 4 I noted that assured destruction had no roots in the origins of the second-strike theory of deterrence. That theory merely acknowledged that a rationally planned first strike would aim at the victim's strategic forces, so that an adequate deterrent force must be calculated based on the survivability of those forces. It made no reference to what level or type of retaliation would be adequate to deter, and the participants in the basing studies that developed the second-strike theory were in fact unsympathetic to directing retaliation against civilian populations.

Similarly, assured destruction was not rooted in the "mutual deterrence arms limitation systems" developed at the dawn of the missile age. That approach aimed to avoid saturation parity by a minimal deterrent that supporters hoped would lead to complete nuclear disarmament.

The real source of "assured destruction only" lay in McNamara's domestic struggle to contain the war-fighters in Congress and the military. Johan Holst observed in 1969:

> The concept of "assured destruction" may . . . have served a useful political function . . . by providing a barrier against *internal* American pressures for greater offensive weapons arsenals. It provided a standard of nuclear sufficiency which was defendable against pressures for "more." However, . . . the concept may have become dysfunctional by suggesting that the necessary response to the *external* pressures from the active defense measures of the adversary involves *offsetting* improvements in the offensive forces so as to restore the assured destruction capacity. . . . Is it not feasible . . . that deterrence requirements be considered in regard to relative expected war outcomes rather than in terms of fixed levels of destruction? . . . Such a shift in outlook might lead in the direction of a Defensive Emphasis posture.[43]

Holst's claim that "assured destruction only" originated as an internal arms control measure was subsequently confirmed by national security adviser McGeorge Bundy. After noting (in 1980) that actual targeting under McNamara had continued to emphasize counterforce, he described the meaning of assured destruction:

> In terms of forces deployed, as well as in terms of what was held to be enough, it was, and was designed to be, much more than so-called "minimum deterrence" and much less than a credible first-strike capa-

43. Holst (n. 5), p. 174.

> bility. And the scale on which the doctrine was applied in the deployments of that decade was defined less by the doctrine itself than by the parallelogram of political forces then at work: budgetary, bureaucratic, Presidential and Congressional.[44]

Assured destruction, then, served as a very specific message directed primarily at the U.S. defense establishment. War-fighters could pursue an operational policy of damage limitation. They would, however, be denied a large enough counterforce to threaten a first strike, and they would be completely denied (if McNamara had his way) the population defense on which a credible first-strike threat ultimately depended.

Although it made sense in the struggle to contain domestic nuclear hawks, this policy became questionable once the United States (largely owing to McNamara's efforts) seriously embraced the concept of an arms control regime with the Soviet Union. In terms of domestic politics, assured destruction had represented a useful *ceiling* on levels of (counterforce) offenses. For the U.S.–Soviet relationship, assured destruction had now been suddenly transformed into a *floor* that both sides' offensive capabilities would not be allowed to drop beneath.

Nevertheless, McNamara had a tempting political rationale for continuing to insist on AD as an indispensable requirement. If he could persuade relevant U.S. political actors that the Soviets "also" subscribed to assured destruction criteria, he could bring a powerful new weapon to bear against U.S. war-fighters. The immediate issue was ABM, and in early 1967 McNamara was clearly losing the domestic battle against a large-scale deployment. If the Soviets were deeply committed to assured destruction, only the most devoted proponents of a victory strategy could believe that a ballistic missile defense could protect the nation. Thus, public pronouncements of the "virtual certainty" of such a Soviet standard were coupled to a private effort to "educate" the Soviets on the merits of the doctrine. The latter effort was supplemented by explicitly warning the Soviets that their efforts at defense would prove futile.

But lost in the apparent logic of this approach was an entirely different possibility. McNamara's central (and very plausible) point was that continued pursuit of war-fighting capabilities offered no hope of averting an environment of MAD, a fact that made a contin-

44. McGeorge Bundy, "Strategic Deterrence Thirty Years Later: What Has Changed?" in *The Future of Strategic Deterrence, Part I*, Adelphi Paper no. 160 (London: International Institute for Strategic Studies, 1980), p. 9.

ued arms race senseless. He might, however, have gone on to argue that the only hope of limiting damage therefore rested on a bilateral agreement with the Soviets.

In effect, MAD would have been depicted as the intolerable price of a continued arms race, with arms control the only viable option for reducing the Soviet offensive nuclear threat. By choosing to explain the existence of saturation parity in terms of a bilateral commitment to threats of assured destruction rather than as the inadvertent outcome of a futile war-fighting policy, McNamara placed an arbitrary limit on what an arms control regime could accomplish.

Even had McNamara been inclined to invoke "bilateral damage limitation" as a goal of arms control, it is not evident that such an approach could have been imposed on the U.S. military establishment. MDE would have constituted a far more fateful assault on operational nuclear policy than did the imposition of a MAD arms control doctrine. Although "assured destruction only" placed a theoretical ceiling on counterforce capabilities, it posed no decisive threat to that aspect of the war-fighting strategy. After all, assured destruction criteria, coupled to "worst-case" estimates of future Soviet (and Chinese) strength, could justify extremely high offensive force levels. Moreover, the "assured destruction" fiction that MIRV had been designed solely to penetrate possible future Soviet city defenses meant that the war-fighters could proceed (with little critical scrutiny from MAD arms controllers) toward tripling the counterforce strength of existing land-based missiles.

A crucial issue, then, for the domestic prospects of a "mutual damage limitation" approach to arms control was the relative political strength of the counterforce and active defense lobbies. The Hudson Institute's "arms control through defense" concept entailed a freeze or reduction of offensive forces and a progressively expanding deployment of active defenses. For that to be politically palatable within the defense establishment, the bureaucratic balance would have had to be markedly different from that of the early 1950s, when the Air Force had regarded just such an approach in terms of a "life and death" struggle over institutional power.

Changes had in fact occurred between 1953 and the mid-1960s. That the Army's strategic mission (BMD) was at stake meant that "continental defense" now had strenuous bureaucratic support. Such support was balanced, however, by a range of countervailing interests. For one thing, the long-term tradition of a military culture predisposed toward offense was now coupled to a nuclear-age legacy of strategic offense dominance spanning two decades. Moreover, the Navy, which had opposed strategic bombing in the early 1950s, had by now acquired a major share of that mission (missile-carrying submarines).

Thus, by the mid-1960s the other armed services were reluctant to join the Army in endorsing ABM deployment, especially in an arms control context that would reduce their own strategic roles. The Army garnered support for ABM from the other service chiefs only by offering as a quid pro quo support for their own favored strategic programs. That arrangement removed any prospect that the Army would seriously press the MDE argument.[45]

In addition to the services' predictable resistance to MDE, a new domestic obstacle to such an approach arose in the 1960s. Unlike the situation in the 1950s, a lack of candor to the American people was no longer a roadblock to the arms control effort. Public confusion caused by a dearth of information in the 1950s now yielded to confusion caused by a barrage of violently contradictory expert commentary. Whereas the pro–strategic defense arms controllers of the 1950s had bemoaned the absence of a national debate over nuclear policy, the antidefense arms controllers of the 1960s now undertook an intense national campaign to drive home the futility, enormous cost, and possible danger of adding ABM to the U.S. nuclear war-fighting arsenal.

Here they were aided by factors unrelated to the merits of particular technical arguments about nuclear policy. By the late 1960s, ABM suffered from a degree of "guilt by association" as the Vietnam stalemate stimulated generalized opposition to what was now widely la-

45. Thus Morton Halperin's study of ABM decision making concluded: "In return for Army support of continuing development of the Navy sea-based ballistic missile system, the Navy was prepared to support an Army land-based system." He added that while the Air Force might have resisted a system designed principally for defending the Minuteman ICBMs (out of concern that funds might have then been diverted from new strategic offenses), it was "prepared to go along" as long as the Army's ABM system was designed for area defense. Morton Halperin, *National Security Policy-Making: Analyses, Cases, and Proposals* (Lexington, Mass.: D. C. Heath, 1975), pp. 116–17.

Similarly, two pairs of researchers on strategic weapons decision making during this period each concluded that Navy and Air Force support for ABM was weak. From John Steinbrunner and Barry Carter: "Rather than a solid front, the unanimity of the Joint Chiefs was merely a fragile coalition, with only certain groups in the Army strongly supporting deployment." "Organizational and Political Dimensions of the Strategic Posture: The Problems of Reform," *Daedalus* 104 (Summer 1975): 136. Graham T. Allison and Frederic A. Morris also concluded that the Navy and Air Force were not "attracted to ABM." "Armaments and Arms Control: Exploring the Determinants of Military Weapons," *Daedalus* 104 (Summer 1975): 116.

beled the "military-industrial complex."[46] Domestic receptivity to McNamara's mutual vulnerability approach was also enhanced by an evolving public response to the nuclear danger itself.

One legacy of the decade preceding the ABM debates was a growing public preoccupation with apocalyptic visions of nuclear war. Although the fear was rooted initially in the images of Hiroshima and Nagasaki, subsequent events and cultural responses created a deep and widespread impression that the possibility of assured destruction was inherent in the nuclear age. A significant contribution to that mind-set was the 1957 book (and subsequent film) *On the Beach*, whose representation of nuclear war as the end of human existence was to became a major theme in popular culture.[47] The persuasiveness of these images was rooted in real developments in the arms race: massive retaliation doctrine and the attendent nuclear buildup, and in particular the atmospheric test programs of the superpowers. Thus fictional depictions of wartime survivors waiting for death from fallout were now coupled to the reality of measurable contamination of the atmosphere and food chain.

The power of apocalyptic imagery showed its force in the first real national debate over population defense, which concerned not ballistic missile defense but civil defense. The most intense phase of the debate was provoked by President Kennedy's call, in the summer of 1961, for a nationwide shelter program. It was the civil defense debate that first inspired what became an important psychological underpinning for the doctrine of assured destruction: the claim that decision makers *must* believe that nuclear war meant total destruction. Thus, in arguing against any effort at civil defense, the noted psychologist Erich Fromm wrote in 1962 that "thermonuclear war has been avoided until now because neither side believed that it was possible to survive such a war. . . . It is precisely for this reason that we consider it so dangerous to underemphasize the fantastic damage that a thermonuclear war would surely bring about."[48]

46. For an interesting effort to explain opposition to ABM in terms of the political culture of the late 1960s, see Herman Kahn, "The Missile Defense Debate in Perspective," in Holst and Schneider (n. 1), pp. 285–94. For an argument identifying U.S. involvement in Vietnam and ABM as linked evils, see David R. Inglis, "Missile Defense, Nuclear Spread and Vietnam," *Bulletin of the Atomic Scientists* 23 (May 1967): 49–52.

47. For an extensive review of public perceptions of the nuclear menace, see Spencer R. Weart, *Nuclear Fear: A History of Images* (Cambridge: Harvard University Press, 1988).

48. Erich Fromm and Michael Maccoby, "The Case against Shelters," in *No Place to*

That analysis was seriously flawed. First, the United States had not launched a nuclear war during the 1950s even when highly confident that it could "survive"; war had been avoided across the whole range of growing U.S., and later Soviet, offensive capabilities. That empirical error became the basis for a misconception of far greater consequence. To be deterred, a rationally acting state obviously does not need to know that it will be utterly destroyed; what is required is a conviction that any possible gains from aggression are outweighed by the prospective costs and risks.[49] Indeed, it is plausible that anyone whose restraint from launching nuclear war depends on nothing less than the certainty of national "death" may not even be deterred by that prospect.

The civil defense debate represented the onset of a tendency to rely on the worst possible war outcome as a hedge against what was believed to be the irrational militarism of leaders (particularly U.S. leaders). Inadvertent support for those invoking these fears was provided by Herman Kahn and Edward Teller, who were speaking and writing with breezy optimism about how civil defense could make nuclear war tolerable.[50]

The controversy over civil defense affected the later ABM debates

---

Hide: Fallout Shelters—Fact and Fiction, ed. Seymour Melman (New York: Grove Press, 1962), pp. 90–91.

49. This point paraphrases Glenn Snyder's precise formulation of the essential meaning of deterrence: "discouraging the enemy from taking military action by posing for him a prospect of cost and risk which outweighs his prospective gain." *Deterrence and Defense: Toward a Theory of National Security* (Princeton: Princeton University Press, 1961), p. 3.

50. Kahn's negative response to the question, Will the survivors envy the dead? was backed up, for example, by the following upbeat speculation: "Now just imagine yourself in the postwar situation. Everybody will have been subjected to extremes of anxiety, unfamiliar environment, strange foods, minimum toilet facilities, inadequate shelters, and the like. Under these conditions some high percentage of the population is going to become nauseated, and nausea is very catching. If one man vomits, everybody vomits. Almost everyone is likely to think he has received too much radiation. Morale may be so affected that many survivors may refuse to participate in constructive activities, but would content themselves with sitting down and waiting to die. . . . However, the situation would be quite different if radiation meters were distributed. Assume now that a man gets sick from a cause other than radiation. Not believing this, his morale begins to drop. You look at his meter and say, "You have received only ten roentgens, why are you vomiting? Pull yourself together and get to work." Herman Kahn, *On Thermonuclear War*, 2d ed. (New York: Free Press, 1969), p. 86.

Teller's writings struck a similar tone of unintentional black humor. In a chapter titled "Off the Beach," Teller endorsed civil defense as the key to U.S. supremacy in a post–nuclear war era: "With adequate civil defense . . . , we can assure ourselves and the world that after an all-out war the United States would be able to re-establish

in another way. In the early 1950s, Oppenheimer and the Panel of Consultants on Disarmament hoped that a national continental defense effort would raise concern over the emergent Soviet threat and thus inspire public support for arms control. Subsequent major campaigns for civil defense, then ABM, proved them right in one sense. Fear of the arms race was heightened by the prospect of seriously preparing for nuclear attack. They failed to anticipate, however, that this fear might largely be directed against the defenses themselves. As one debate participant observed,

> Already the mere beginnings of a civil defense have led to loud threats from Nevada to shoot down "invading" Californians, to unpublicized but uneasy questions about racial segregation or integration in fallout shelters, and to angry remarks about the expendability of city residents as against suburban or country folk. The question of survival . . . will inevitably divide Americans far more sharply than we have ever known. Making concrete decisions about civil defense will rub our old divisions to the raw.[51]

Although the debate over civil defense ground on throughout the 1960s, its outcome was largely decided by the end of 1961. "Let us concentrate more on keeping enemy bombers and missiles away from our shores," suggested President Kennedy, "and concentrate less on keeping neighbors away from our shelters."[52]

The potential of defensive measures to generate fear was spurred by the particular design of the ABM technology that evolved in the 1960s. Nike-X was originally designed as a heavy city-defense system, and the prospect of surrounding cities with interceptor missiles carrying nuclear warheads generated intense grass-roots opposition from inhabitants of the designated cities.[53] In general, defensive measures were now widely associated with the very apocalypse that defense (according to its proponents) was meant to prevent.

Given the bureaucratic and public attitudes described above, McNamara's MAD approach certainly appeared to be the path of least resistance in garnering domestic support for an arms control agreement. This was particularly true in light of his decision to apply the concept selectively: targeting ABM and exempting offensive

economic strength sooner than Russia—and so the United States would remain by far the strongest nation in the world." Edward Teller with Allen Brown, *The Legacy of Hiroshima* (New York: Doubleday, 1962), pp. 259–60.

51. Arthur Waskow, "Both Red and Dead," in Melman (n. 48), p. 46.

52. Cited in Ralph E. Lapp, *The Weapons Culture* (Baltimore: Penguin Books, 1969), p. 56.

53. See Yanarella (n. 6), pp. 146–47.

damage-limitation programs. But that domestic environment did not evolve in a leadership vacuum. McNamara and his supporters inside government had powerful tools for shaping attitudes toward offensive and defensive measures.

Political Leadership and the Nuclear Debate in the 1960s

Governmental Politics

Although the overall preference of the armed services remained with strategic offense, the capacity of the military to pursue any particular version of war-fighting had now been dramatically constrained by major new influences on strategic policy. By the late 1960s, supporters of nuclear war-fighting doctrines were facing an emergent arms control coalition whose constituents in the 1950s had been either nonexistent (the Arms Control and Disarmament Agency), largely unorganized (the "dove" segment of the American populace), or formerly supportive of new strategic programs (congressional liberals, the Office of the Secretary of Defense). Of greatest importance was the progressive defection of the chief executive, as Kennedy's tentative embrace of arms control (the Partial Test-Ban Treaty) gave way to Johnson's willingness, by the end of his administration, to end the arms race based on nuclear parity.

The chief difference between the Eisenhower and Kennedy administrations was the decisive shift of nuclear policy-making influence from military (notably SAC) to civilian control under a greatly strengthened Office of the Secretary of Defense. McNamara later provided a dramatic recounting of SAC's confrontation with that transfer of authority:

> I remember being with President Kennedy in May of 1962, in California. We were visiting Vandenberg Air Force Base, and the Commander of the Strategic Air Command met us when our plane landed. As we got into his car, he turned to the President and said, "When we get the 10,000 Minutemen, Mr. President, I . . ."
>
> At that moment the President said, "What did you say?"
>
> "Well, I started to say when we get the 10,000 Minutemen, we're going to do . . ."
>
> The President said, "I thought that's what you said." And he turned to me and said, "Bob, we're not going to get 10,000 Minutemen, are we?"
>
> I said, "No, Mr. President, we're limiting it to 1000."[54]

54. Charlton (n. 15), pp. 9–10.

Throughout the McNamara era, decisions over the size and shape of the U.S. strategic force posture were largely determined by the centralized control exerted from the OSD.[55] Nevertheless, any agreement that would actually "halt the arms race" (which is what McNamara claimed for a MAD framework in 1967) would have posed a major challenge to those segments of the armed services with a stake in the offensive strategic mission. To assume that a freeze or reduction of strategic offenses (whether accompanied by defensive deployments or not) would have been precluded by the opposition of the military establishment and its congressional allies is tantamount to concluding that the strategic offensive buildup was politically unstoppable.

SALT I, of course, did not provide a decisive test of that possibility. It is at least plausible, however, that confronted with a choice between two frameworks for ending the strategic arms race—"mutual assured vulnerability" or mutual defense emphasis—the defense establishment on balance might have preferred the latter. Note Brennan's assessment of the "bureaucratic politics" explanation for the impossibility of MDE:

> Many opponents of BMD have agreed that an arms-control program of this form seems fundamentally preferable to a posture of abstaining from defenses and leaving the offensive forces unconstrained; they argue that a program of the type suggested here will not prove feasible, because it will not prove acceptable to the U.S. military "establishment." This assertion is subject to investigation, and considerable investigation suggests it is incorrect. Many senior military officers, in the U.S. Air Force as well as in other services, are favorably disposed to a suitable ceiling on offensive forces (at prevailing levels) providing it is possible to deploy defenses.[56]

Even Brennan, who was clearly predisposed toward optimism about MDE's acceptability, appeared to acknowledge that there would be considerable resistance to significantly *lowering* offensive forces in an MDE arms control regime. Had a U.S. administration chosen to wage that battle, public opinion might have proved decisive. Although one legacy of the offensive arms race was a widespread public fear that defensive measures represented a step closer

55. For an extended argument emphasizing the power of the Office of the Secretary of Defense during the McNamara years, see Murdock (n. 6). For a view depicting a range of domestic and bureaucratic political determinants of policy, see Desmond Ball, *Politics and Force Levels* (Berkeley and Los Angeles: University of California Press, 1980).

56. Brennan (n. 1), p. 113.

to nuclear war, it is far from certain that defenses proposed as part of a superpower disarmament regime would have engendered the same response.

Public Attitudes toward Defense

There was indeed an organized and articulate antidefense campaign as early as the 1961 debate over civil defense, yet a sizable majority of the public during this period supported efforts to defend against nuclear attack.[57] Skepticism over the significance of that support is warranted, however, when one considers that as of 1965, two-thirds of Americans believed they were already protected by an ABM system.[58]

Within the relatively narrow spectrum comprising the attentive public, attitudes were (and are) strongly influenced by an elite community of nuclear policymakers and nongovernment experts. The arms control lobby sought both to stimulate and to draw upon public concerns over the arms race and nuclear war. The war-fighting lobby, at various points, emphasized a range of justifications for new strategic programs: the need for U.S. nuclear superiority, claims that the United States was falling dangerously behind (the "bomber gap," the "missile gap," and later the "window of vulnerability"), and the need to "negotiate from strength."

If citizens attentive to nuclear policy issues were left in the dark by a lack of government candor in the 1950s, confusion in the 1960s was caused by wildly contradictory empirical claims by the community of "experts" concerning Soviet nuclear doctrine, the state of the nuclear balance, the nature of nuclear deterrence, and in particular the technological capabilities of defenses against Soviet attack.

The public had to contend with one group of experts expressing certainty that defenses would work extremely well while another proclaimed that ABM technology was almost self- evidently useless. (Aside from Aaron Wildavsky, few commentators directed attention to the strange circumstance that none of the scientists working to "inform" Congress and the public occupied a middle ground regarding either the current or the prospective capabilities of defensive technologies.)[59]

57. A Harris poll in April 1969 (when opposition to Safeguard was nearing its peak) showed 47 percent favoring ABM deployment, 26 percent opposed, and 27 percent undecided. Adams (n. 6), p. 213. Generally, surveys showed a majority in support.

58. "Public Opinion and Ballistic Missile Defense: Report of an Exploratory Study," RM 64TMP-50, General Electric TEMPO, Santa Barbara, Calif., 1964, p. 88. Cited by Adams (n. 6), p. 117.

59. Aaron Wildavsky, "The Politics of ABM," *Commentary*, November 1969.

When eminent physicists like Edward Teller and Hans Bethe were starkly opposed on nearly every relevant technical point, there was no way a layman could sort out the truth. (Many undoubtedly persuaded themselves that they had done so, presumably based on a mysterious process of "evaluating" such issues as the cost, feasibility, and value of dummy warheads, salvage fusing, maneuverable warheads, "boost-glide" reentry vehicles, etc.) The lay public was evidently basing its conclusions not on the technical jargon of defensive measures and offensive countermeasures, but on the overall approach to nuclear policy that the scientific experts represented.

Here they were assisted by the fact that the two clusters of experts generally agreed on two crucial points. First, that with or without arms control, having a huge arsenal of strategic offenses was vital for national security. Second, that the purpose of deploying defenses was to sustain an ability to wage and survive a nuclear war (though ABM supporters, of course, stressed that the aim was to strengthen deterrence). The clear implication of both sides' positions was that ABM should be decided based on how one felt about continuing the nuclear arms race. Indeed, members of the pro-ABM lobby hardly disguised their skepticism toward arms control. Inspiring public distrust of the Soviets was, after all, simply another part of their political agenda.

The significant shift in attitudes in the 1960s was the growing support for arms control within the attentive and politically active segment of the public. Whether that movement would find itself supporting or opposing strategic defense almost certainly depended on perceptions of the impact of defense on arms control. That perception in turn was largely shaped by the particular theory developed by the comprehensive arms control theorists at the dawn of the missile age, and given authoritative validation by a powerful secretary of defense. There is simply no reason for interpreting the enthusiastic public and congressional support for the 1972 SALT agreements as decisive public support for preserving threats of mutual extinction. Similarly, had those agreements been based on an MDE transition toward mutual survival, it is hard to believe that ratification would have foundered on liberals' opposition to strategic defense.

In 1969 Herman Kahn recognized the success of the anti-ABM movement in appropriating the general appeal of arms control, and he advised the ABM lobby, "It would greatly and appropriately help the cause of the proponents of ABM if ABM were generally perceived (and presented) as a shield designed to facilitate both current arms control negotiations and, eventually, comprehensive and lasting arms control measures. It is important for the two objectives to be pursued in parallel and jointly."[60] If McNamara and the mainstream arms control theorists of the 1960s had encouraged serious consideration of defense as an instrument of arms control (while confronting war-fighters on the issue of offensive damage limitation), it is unlikely that national sentiments against the arms race would would have been channeled into opposition to strategic defense.

Instead, the U.S. leaders during the McNamara years managed to undercut prospects for both a domestic and a superpower dialogue. Earlier, I noted that domestic resistance to homeland defense emerged as an important political force during the civil defense debate. Yet the near hysteria attending the 1961 civil defense proposal can be attributed in part to the context of its presentation. As McGeorge Bundy (then national security adviser) recounted, "The civil defense proposal was put forward with inadequate preparation, and Kennedy's most important statement about it was unwisely placed in a speech about decisions on the Berlin crisis, with the result that it was wrongly perceived as a means of response to imminent danger. There were panicky and uninformed reactions."[61]

Besides calling for civil defense in the midst of a superpower crisis, the president simultaneously announced that the United States was seeking the ability to wage a limited nuclear war. That call for a "wider choice than humiliation or all-out nuclear action"[62] received its fullest expression in July 1962, when McNamara publicly endorsed what amounted to a nuclear victory strategy based primarily on counterforce damage limitation (the "no cities" doctrine).[63] Had civil defense been presented as a fully conceived program, at a calmer moment in U.S.–Soviet relations and shorn of its association with an apparent willingness to wage nuclear war, it is likely it would have evoked far less resistance. As Bundy conceded, "The risk of public misunderstanding was grossly neglected by all of us."[64]

McNamara, after changing his mind about the viability of a war-fighting strategy, later used the national antipathy to civil defense as

60. Kahn (n. 46), p. 293.

61. McGeorge Bundy, *Danger and Survival: Choices about the Bomb in the First Fifty Years* (New York: Random House, 1988), p. 355.

62. For a description of the background and context of Kennedy's statements on civil defense and war-fighting, see Lapp (n. 52), pp. 51–57.

63. Jerome Kahan noted that official rationales for the "no cities" doctrine stressed that the United States "would attempt to limit damage by means of *second strike* counterforce attacks." Critics, however, argued "that a second-strike counterforce capability was indistinguishable from a first-strike strategy" (n. 31), pp. 91–92.

64. Bundy (n. 61), p. 358.

a political lever against ABM. Thus he told Congress in 1963 that "I personally will never recommend an anti-ICBM program unless a fallout program does accompany it."[65] Given McNamara's subsequent arguments against the very principle of homeland defense, there is reason to doubt that the absence of a large-scale civil defense program contributed to his opposition to ABM. Nor did it make sense to imply that ABM could be worthwhile only if accompanied by a fallout program. (If the Soviets subscribed to assured destruction, they would expand their offenses to offset any type of population defense. If they instead preferred "live Russians" over "dead Americans," they could allow the prospective lowering of fatalities by active or passive defense.)

Whatever its intellectual merit, McNamara's 1963 precondition for supporting an ABM program was to prove politically useful. Three years later, having done nothing to change the widespread perception that civil defense represented a step closer to nuclear war, McNamara began to draw on the public response as evidence of a general rejection of defense: "If you wished to increase our defensive posture in relation to a Soviet attack, the first and by far the most important action to take, and certainly the cheapest action to take, would be to support a full fallout shelter program for the Nation. The Congress, and in a very real sense I think the people, have turned down such a program on a number of occasions."[66]

In considering why the nation turned down such a program, we can reject the existence of some universal human aversion to defense against catastrophic threats. Aside from the persistent Soviet effort in passive defense measures, Switzerland since 1950 had required that a fully equipped blast shelter be included in every new home and public building—a program that drew consistent public support.[67] Indeed, the case of Switzerland can help explain the very

65. "The Nuclear Test Ban Treaty," Report of the Senate Committee on Foreign Relations, 88th Cong., 1st sess., p. 13.

66. Cited in Murdock (n. 6), p. 122.

67. From Freeman Dyson's account: "Swiss shelters are massive reinforced-concrete structures built into the foundations of buildings. They are intended to protect people against blast and fire as well as fallout. The civil defense authority makes sure that they are kept in working order." He concludes that "two aspects of the Swiss shelter program are extraordinary: its technical thoroughness and its political quietness." *Weapons and Hope* (New York: Harper and Row, 1984), pp. 86, 88.

Surprisingly, McGeorge Bundy has recently made a strong appeal for a nationwide shelter program, arguing that it would be "imperfect but relatively cheap—a way of mitigating a possible disaster, not a way of avoiding it or making it acceptable." Bundy (n. 61), p. 365. Bundy makes no effort to explain why an "imperfect" shelter

different view that prevailed in the United States. Switzerland's defensive tradition preceded the nuclear age, paving the way for its unique response to the nuclear danger. For the United States to have moved in a similar direction would have required a significant shift in military and political culture.

As Oppenheimer realized, the best prospect for such a shift would have been a very early recognition by U.S. leaders that the only long-term hope for limiting the catastrophic consequences of a nuclear attack required a combination of defense and offensive arms control. By the time of Kennedy's call for a nationwide shelter program, the lack of a national defensive tradition was compounded by the association of homeland defense with irrational visions of nuclear victory. However inadvertently, that association was reinforced by the Kennedy administration. Thus, while McNamara may have been correct in his 1966 assertion that the nation had turned down the option of substantial civil defense, that national judgment cannot be separated from the historical lack of leadership in offering a coherent program in which defense could contribute to national security.

It is plausible, moreover, that if the civil defense option had been presented in the context of pursuing MDE-based offensive disarmament, the U.S. legacy of viewing blast and fallout shelters as futile or even dangerous might gradually have lost its impact. One result of the MAD versus war-fighting debate that began in the 1960s has been the United States' incapacity to direct meaningful attention to some of the "minor" permanent risks of the nuclear age—such as the danger of nuclear blackmail or use by terrorist groups (or deranged leaders of small nuclear powers), or the fallout from a major nuclear power plant catastrophe. Americans react with appropriate ridicule to civil defense "plans" that rely solely on the rapid evacuation of major urban areas. Should homeland defense be credibly separated from an association with provocative militarism, Switzerland's gradual, sustained shelter program might well provide a model that the United States would wish to emulate.

---

program would be compatible with MAD-based arms control whereas imperfect active population defenses would fuel the arms race. He might have addressed Dyson's observation that "shelters are perceived to be futile because the assured destruction strategy demands that they be ineffective. Shelters are perceived to be threatening because they suggest an intention to make the operation of assured destruction unilateral. If the United States ever wishes to build shelters in a serious fashion . . . the doctrine of assured destruction must be abandoned." Dyson (n. 67), p. 90.

The same anxieties originally raised by the abortive national shelter program in 1961 resurfaced when the United States began to move toward construction of the Sentinel ABM system. Grass-roots opposition to ABM was spurred when the Army sought to purchase land for Sentinel sites in major American cities. Actually, the Army's provocation was largely unnecessary, since the abandonment of the original Nike-X plan for a terminal defense of cities (in favor of a light nationwide area defense) had reduced the need to place missiles in heavily populated areas.[68] Nevertheless, the public reaction raised the possibility that any significant introduction of ballistic missile defenses using 1960s technology would founder on local opposition.

Of particular concern was that interception of warheads that had penetrated the atmosphere relied on Sprint missiles, whose twenty-five-mile range and nuclear warheads (of several kilotons) meant that nuclear-tipped missiles would have to be based very close to any heavily defended cities. (Sprint and Spartan missiles required a special command from the ground to detonate when they were near their targets, providing a safeguard in the case of accidental launch. Strategic offensive missiles cannot be disarmed after launch.)[69] Regardless of the level of actual risk, it is possible that no rationale for population defense would have allayed public concerns over Sprint.

On the other hand, those public concerns would not necessarily have derailed superpower negotiations on MDE. First, there would have been no reason not to move first toward protecting missile bases. In fact, that is the direction U.S. policy took when public opposition stimulated the Nixon administration's decision to adopt the "Safeguard" deployment plan. Second, the Soviets had not yet developed a short-range interceptor. The Soviet Galosh was roughly comparable to the U.S. Spartan, so that any bilateral move toward a nationwide defense would almost certainly have been built intially around the "light area defense" concept underlying Sentinel. Negotiated bilateral deployments on the scale of Sentinel could have provided protection against accidental or small-scale attacks without challenging anyone's attachment to mutual assured destruction. Moreover, such a limited step toward MDE would have been a con-

68. Yanarella (n. 6), pp. 146–67.

69. In March 1969 Secretary of Defense Melvin Laird had mistakenly testified that U.S. strategic missiles could be disarmed in flight. See "Strategic and Foreign Policy Implications" (n. 32), pp. 382–83.

crete repudiation of the axiom that defenses were "inherently" destabilizing and could have set the stage for later, more far-reaching agreements.[70]

It may be that any favorable public consensus on a nationwide population defense would have been contingent on development of a means for nonnuclear interception of missiles—an entirely remote prospect in the 1960s. But it is important to remember that popular resistance to strategic defense in general was molded during an era when most proponents of population defense were motivated by a desire to sustain a viable nuclear war-fighting capability. In that sense, there was a certain underlying validity to the antidefense sentiments of a segment of the American public. Opponents of defense were given no reason to believe that a national defensive effort would be accompanied by a reversal of the offensive strategic buildup of the superpowers, and there is no way to assess how such a negotiated regime would have altered public reactions.

70. When McNamara was compelled to announce a limited ABM deployment in September 1967, he supplemented the anti-Chinese rationale for deployment by adding, "Such a reliable ABM system will add protection of our population against the improbable but possible accidental launching of an intercontinental missile by any one of the nuclear powers." McNamara (n. 17), p. 165. Since bilateral deployments limited to protection against accidental attack need not interfere with MAD, the main argument against such an approach is reflected in the warning McNamara added to his Sentinel deployment proposal: "There is a kind of mad momentum intrinsic to the development of all new nuclear weaponry. If a weapons system works and works well, there is strong pressure from many directions to procure and deploy the weapon out of all proportion to the prudent level required. The danger of deploying this relatively light and reliable . . . ABM system is going to be that pressures will develop to expand it into a heavy Soviet-oriented ABM system" (p. 166).

Although the Nixon administration often stressed the value of its Safeguard deployment plan for defending against accidental attack, one consequence of the 1972 ABM Treaty was the dropping of all references to that danger. The case for such a limited role for BMD resurfaced from an unexpected source in 1988, when Senator Sam Nunn called for exploring a negotiated implementation of an "Accidental Launch Protection System" (ALPS) "to deal with the frightening possibility of an accidental or unauthorized missile launch." Nunn argued that this approach would require no more than "a modest amendment" to the ABM Treaty. Sam Nunn, "Arms Control in the Last Year of the Reagan Administration," speech before the Arms Control Association, January 19, 1988 (see pp. 10–13).

For consideration of the case for a negotiated deployment of limited defenses, see Jerome Slater and David Goldfischer, "Can SDI Provide a Defense?" *Political Science Quarterly* 101, no. 5 (1986): 839–56, and David Goldfischer, "Strategic Defense, Arms Control and Proliferation after the Cold War," in *Nuclear Deterrence and Global Security in Transition*, ed. David Goldfischer and Thomas W. Graham (Boulder, Colo.: Westview Press, 1992), pp. 171–85. For an opposing view, see Matthew Bunn, "Star Wars Redux: Limited Defenses, Unlimited Dilemmas," *Arms Control Today* 21 (May 1991): 12–18.

The preceding analysis has suggested that the U.S. rejection of MDE in the 1960s can be explained largely by the influence of a flawed approach to arms control, and particularly by the embrace of that approach by a powerful secretary of defense. Ironically, what probably would have been the most difficult hurdle confronting MDE is one that McNamara himself tried unsuccessfully to overcome: the U.S. nuclear guarantee of Europe's security against invasion by the Red Army.

MDE and the Defense of Europe

As I described earlier, Jerome Wiesner's 1967 response to Brennan acknowledged that "from a technical point of view" MDE could make feasible the nuclear disarmament regime he had worked toward since participating in the Gaither Study in 1957. But the "real problem," he concluded, "is to create a military-political situation in which the strategic weapons threats and the danger of major war are not needed to provide a restraining influence on the behavior of the major powers in their dealings on other problems."[71]

In the early Cold War years, the decision to rely on nuclear weapons to contain Communism could be regarded as a rapidly improvised response to a frightening range of threats. Although the growth of Soviet nuclear strength had eroded the credibility—and the policy—of massive retaliation, the West had proved unwilling to seriously reexamine the concept of extended nuclear deterrence. As indicated by Wiesner's statement above (and the passage by Erich Fromm cited earlier), the specifically anti-Soviet rationale of the original nuclear buildup had yielded in part to a more generalized belief that peace between the superpowers depended on making war seem wholly suicidal. That general adaptation to the nuclear world had become most evident in Western Europe, where the novelty of extended nuclear deterrence in the late 1940s had been transformed into the traditional foundation of Atlantic Alliance defense policy. McNamara had struggled since his early years as defense secretary to overcome NATO's reliance on nuclear threats by garnering support for a credible conventional defense of Europe. But even the achievement of the 1967 "flexible response" compromise had no fundamental effect on European policy.

McNamara expressed his basic perspective on extended nuclear

71. Wiesner (n. 30)

deterrence in the same 1967 speech in which he outlined the rationale for MAD-based arms control. Here he called for the United States and its allies to maintain forces that were "fully capable of dealing with a wide spectrum of lesser forms of political and military aggression." Strategic nuclear threats would not provide protection against such aggression, since "one cannot fashion a credible deterrent out of an incredible action."[72]

Long after he left government, McNamara proposed (in 1982) a formal renunciation of NATO's reliance on nuclear deterrence against conventional attack, calling for a policy of "no first use." Among the other rationales for that policy, he noted that it could "open the path toward serious reduction of nuclear armaments."[73] That was because much of the pressure in the United States for "massive new nuclear forces" had stemmed from the effort to make extended deterrence credible. At worst, first-use threats justified pursuit of nuclear "escalation dominance," that is, a doctrine of victory in a nuclear war. At a minimum, it provided the primary rationale for flexible nuclear response options, which McNamara was convinced would lead in practice to uncontrollable escalation.[74]

It had been impossible for McNamara to state these arguments explictly in the 1960s. Neither of the presidents he served showed a willingness to risk a crisis in U.S.–European relations by renouncing strategic nuclear threats as the foundation of containment in Europe. The fear was that Europe would react not with an improved conventional defense, but with a loss of will to resist the Soviets. Indeed, beginning with Charles de Gaulle's overtures to the Soviet Union in 1966 (and followed shortly thereafter by the onset of West Germany's Ostpolitik), U.S. leaders were growing increasingly concerned over a prospective European détente with the Soviet Union that—it was feared—could gravely weaken the Atlantic Alliance.[75]

The European dimension of U.S. nuclear policy limited the arms control options the United States was willing to consider. The primary constraint was that the ultimate threat of massive retaliation would be preserved, its credibility presumably bolstered by a policy

72. McNamara (n. 17), p. 60.

73. McGeorge Bundy, George F. Kennan, Robert S. McNamara, and Gerard Smith, "Nuclear Weapons and the Atlantic Alliance," *Foreign Affairs* 60 (Spring 1982): 767.

74. Thus: "It is time to recognize that no one has ever succeeded in advancing any persuasive reason to believe that any use of nuclear weapons, even on the smallest scale, could reliably be expected to remain limited." Ibid., p. 757.

75. See Raymond L. Garthoff, *Detente and Confrontation: American-Soviet Relations from Nixon to Reagan* (Washington, D.C.: Brookings Institution, 1985), pp. 106–12.

based on flexible response. In that context, even a limited bilateral introduction of population defenses against missiles would have posed a direct challenge to NATO policy. Thus, in his critique of MDE described earlier, Jerome Kahan argued that "to make matters worse, with ABMs deployed on both sides, neither nation could employ selective strategic options. A defense emphasis approach would force both nations into using their strategic capabilities massively, once deterrence failed, in order to penetrate an opponent's ABM system."[76]

Despite McNamara's long-standing opposition to ABM, he could not have shared Kahan's disapproval of that particular consequence of MDE. McNamara feared and opposed the concept of selective strategic options, given "the appalling consequences of even the most limited use of nuclear weapons and the total impossibility for both sides of any guarantee against unlimited escalation."[77] One might add that MDE would have discouraged limited nuclear attacks (e.g., "demonstration strikes" against Soviet territory) more effectively than the declaratory policy of "no first use" McNamara proposed.

Kahan's observation points to another reason some Europeans opposed MDE: that growing Soviet BMD of its population could erode the independent nuclear deterrent forces of England and France. (The French nuclear deterrent in 1969 consisted solely of approximately sixty bombers, which had to confront the substantial Soviet air defense system. Thus, since France was undertaking construction of missile-carrying submarines, a large-scale Soviet BMD would simply have resurrected the same basic situation France already faced.)

In terms of U.S. NATO policy, assured destruction arms control represented the same blurring of objectives that it served domestically. Just as the emergent SALT framework would allow the United States to exploit its (short-lived) MIRV monopoly in the pursuit of counterforce damage limitation, it similarly preserved the limited strategic options that were being adopted by NATO.

Thus any truly comprehensive strategic arms control regime—whether based on MAD-only, minimum deterrence, or MDE—would have pressured the United States to separate its strategic deterrent from anything less than a Soviet nuclear attack. Favoring such a policy departure was the fact that the world had changed in

76. Kahan (n. 31), pp. 258–59.
77. Bundy et al. (n. 73), p. 757.

two fundamental ways. First, the intense fears of an imminent Soviet invasion that had characterized the early Cold War years had substantially receded. Second, usable U.S. nuclear superiority, whose preservation had been the crucial justification for the original decision to rely on a strategic airpower buildup, was gone forever.

In the early 1950s, MDE advocates had argued that the United States should not adopt massive retaliation precisely because it would ensure future vulnerability to complete nuclear devastation. Yet now that the United States was arriving at that point, the world of total offense dominance had become a familiar—if uncomfortable—feature of the political landscape. The Europeans' refusal to seriously explore alternative paths to security was another reason for the United States to avoid reexamining the war-fighters' and arms controllers' rationales for an offense-dominant nuclear policy, especially since all their motivations could now be lumped (however awkwardly) under the banner of assured destruction.

Basing arms control on MAD thus had the undeniable political advantage of forestalling a painful debate in the West over extended nuclear deterrence. Even embarking on MDE negotiations with the Soviets would have thrown into question that most critical United States foreign policy commitment of the postwar era. Although we cannot know whether arms control experts could have devised a transition to MDE in the 1960s, it seems certain that any serious superpower dialogue on resolving the nuclear danger would have jeopardized Western Europe's confidence in the United States.

Was there a way out of that impasse? If so, it would have taken one of two forms. First, the United States might have simply declared (as McNamara might have wished) that the prospective reduction in the role of strategic nuclear weapons did not mean the abandonment of Europe. The United States, in effect, would have adopted as policy the perspective on nuclear-age deterrence outlined by British analyst Laurence Martin: "Caution about getting into war with a nuclear power at any state of the technical balance may well be a more potent deterrent than any particular force posture."[78] A strategic balance of bilateral defense emphasis, Martin noted, would

78. Laurence Martin, "The Determinants of Change: Deterrence and Technology," in *The Future of Strategic Deterrence, Part II*, Adelphi Paper no. 161 (London: International Institute for Strategic Studies, 1980), p. 11. McGeorge Bundy makes the same point, that the principal disincentive for launching a nuclear attack is "not the result of estimates of each other's first or second-strike counter-force capability, or a consequence of the possession or absence of escalation dominance." The superpowers simply fear a nuclear war. Bundy (n. 44), p. 11.

"surely perpetuate more than enough uncertainty and residual horror to inspire the kind of overall caution that has hitherto characterized the behaviour of the nuclear powers."[79]

Unfortunately, however cogent that observation, a U.S. move toward substantial offensive disarmament would have provoked a full-blown crisis in the Atlantic Alliance. In the late 1960s, the United States (at the peak of its involvement in Vietnam) was simply not prepared for steps that could be interpreted as the nuclear abandonment of Europe. A second alternative would have been to link the prospect of MDE in the strategic balance to a Soviet abandonment of an offensive force posture in Europe. The U.S. insistence on MAD-based arms control gave the Soviets little incentive to resolve the imbalance in the European theater. After all, by the end of the 1960s, they had achieved nuclear parity without any U.S. arms control concessions. Indeed, the only real remaining bargaining leverage provided by the U.S. strategic arsenal would have depended on the United States' willingness to greatly reduce the nuclear threat against the Soviet homeland.

Such an approach still might have failed to generate European receptivity to the Soviets' BMD of their population. But the prospect of major reductions in overall Soviet offensive capabilities—from conventional force projection to nuclear—would certainly have dramatically changed the terms of debate. So long as the upper limit on superpower defenses left a potential for British and French retaliation against even a few Soviet cities, MDE would have perpetuated the inherent inequality of European and Soviet nuclear capabilities. Although heavier Soviet defenses would have in effect returned Europe to its position before the development of independent nuclear forces, a corresponding Soviet shift to a defensive conventional posture would have removed the primary original British and French incentive to acquire nuclear weapons.

The United States, of course, never considered offering a meaningful bilateral reduction of strategic capabilities in return for Soviet reductions in offensive conventional strength. Instead, the association of arms control theory with MAD was coupled to a failure to develop a guiding concept in conventional arms control, where an unproductive preoccupation with levels of troops was leading toward a fruitless decade of "mutual and balanced force reductions" negotiations. The link between Western nuclear threats and European defense policy was already deeply established—and as yet

79. Martin (n. 78), p. 16.

scarcely challenged—in the 1960s. As a result, MDE could not have been seriously explored without the daunting prospect of simultaneously engaging the spectrum of sensitive political relationships and entrenched military policies that shaped the Atlantic Alliance.

Thus, even had the United States in 1967 accepted the strategic concept that, as Kosygin put it, "Defense is moral, offense is immoral," negotiations would likely have foundered on the apparent intractability of the military imbalance in Europe. In the early 1950s Truman and Eisenhower had failed to heed the warning of MDE advocates that the atomic bomb works both ways. More than a decade later, even the realization of that warning failed to inspire the will—let alone serious inquiry into the means—to overcome reliance on threats and on the power to unleash a nuclear holocaust.

Clearly, to the extent that either superpower in the 1960s clung to dreams of nuclear superiority, any comprehensive arms control approach would have been stillborn. It is possible that once the Soviets achieved strategic parity in the late 1960s, they were tempted to pursue a politically useful nuclear advantage. The SALT I Interim Agreement and the ABM Treaty hardly proved otherwise.

Technological uncertainty (or a belief that the United States had the edge) might explain Soviet willingness to forgo ABM. That decision could also be explained by concern that U.S. missile-site defenses would jeopardize plans for acquiring a counterforce capability against U.S. ICBMs. Yet there may have been nothing inevitable about the subsequent Soviet decision to shift toward a counterforce strategy. One could point out that the MIRV race was initiated by the United States, just as one could argue that a more comprehensive SALT I framework might have contained both sides' preoccupation with offensive forms of damage limitation.

Unless we assume that expressions of the Soviets' interest in defense emphasis arms control were meaningless rhetoric (and no one who interacted with Soviet officials during this period has made that claim), it seems reasonable to conclude that U.S. policy played a major role in their abandonment of that idea. An intense interest in overcoming Soviet defenses, after all, was the single strategic objective that united both U.S. war-fighters and U.S. arms controllers.

Whatever the Soviets' motives for proposing an ABM ban (as they did in 1970), they certainly realized that doing so weakened the prospects for U.S. war-fighters to derail any form of arms limitation. Indeed, their attacks on U.S. ABM deployment (which began two years after the 1967 Sentinel deployment decision) were never based on any endorsement of MAD. Instead, they rested, as Johan Holst testified, on "the political observation that Safeguard is being supported primarily by what is perceived as a hostile military-industrial complex which has no interest in an arms control agreement with the Soviet Union."[80]

The U.S. agreement on the ABM Treaty, of course, occurred long after McNamara's departure. In principle, Richard Nixon and Henry Kissinger had an opportunity to revise the arms control foundation laid by McNamara. In fact, their effort even to sustain Safeguard (with its emphasis on defending retaliatory forces) was on the verge of defeat in the Senate. Aside from domestic constraints on ABM, the administration's overriding concern with disengaging from Vietnam undercut any possibility of reexamining the near consensus of the U.S. arms control community.

Although Kissinger had a background as a nuclear policy analyst, his own ideas were in flux. Having rejected his earlier commitment to a theory of limited nuclear war-fighting, he did not bring to the new administration any clearly formulated nuclear doctrine. Clearly, his and Nixon's chief arms control priority was to hammer out an agreement that was acceptable domestically and also could advance the overall search for a limited détente with the Soviet Union. To attempt that on any basis other than MAD would have meant an assault on the entire U.S. arms control establishment: ACDA, the State Department, congressional arms control supporters, and the nongovernment community of experts.

Nevertheless, given his background and influence, Kissinger was the single individual who might have undertaken the effort to supplant MAD with MDE as the basis for strategic arms control before the former approach became even more deeply institutionalized. It is of great interest that Kissinger subsequently expressed profound regret that he failed to do so. In 1984 Kissinger wrote:

> Since the ABM Treaty was signed, it has become clear that to rely on a strategy of mutual annihilation based on unopposed offensive weapons raises profound and political issues. Has a president the right to expose our people forever to the vagaries of an increasing number of volatile decision-makers? Such a course involves . . . the risk of a holocaust as a result of miscalculation or the gradual escalation of peripheral crises.[81]

80. "Strategic and Foreign Policy Implications" (n. 32), p. 478.

81. Henry A. Kissinger, "Should We Try to Defend against Russia's Missiles?" *Washington Post*, September 23, 1984, p. C8.

Noting the irony that he was writing "as one of the architects of the existing ABM Treaty," Kissinger now made the case for strategic defense, concluding that "perhaps the most compelling argument is the possible beneficial effect of some missile defense on arms control. Arms control theory is now at a dead end; the stalemate in negotiations reflects an impasse in thought." Oppenheimer had written in 1953 that MDE-based disarmament could make offenses "far too vast too conceal, or far too small to have a decisive strategic effect." Kissinger would now write that with MDE, "much larger numbers would be needed for a strategically decisive evasion, and those numbers could be detected."[82]

Some months later, having described his plan as a "revolutionary approach to reduction of offensive forces by agreement," Kissinger submitted an MDE proposal that could easily have been written by Brennan.[83] By then, however, MDE's status as an alternative approach to arms control had changed in two unprecedented ways. First, as of January 1985, MDE had become the declaratory arms control doctrine of the United States. Second, the relation of the U.S. plan to the traditional advocacy of MDE was almost purely rhetorical, as war-fighters seized on the appeal of the concept to try to destroy the domestic consensus for nuclear arms control.

82. Ibid.

83. Henry A. Kissinger, "We Need Star Wars," *Washington Post*, September 8, 1985.

[7]

Strategic Defense without Star Wars: Defense Emphasis in the 1980s and Beyond

In the 1980s, the promotion of mutual defense emphasis took two distinct forms. One was a further exposition of the same basic outlook that had prompted calls for MDE in the 1950s and 1960s. The second had its roots in nuclear war-fighting doctrine, with support for MDE based on the claim that the United States could use technological breakthroughs in defense to impose a defense-dominant strategic environment on the Soviet Union.

The leading advocate of the traditional approach to MDE was physicist Freeman Dyson. Although Dyson drew directly on the earlier contribution of Donald Brennan (who had died in 1980), he avoided Brennan's stress on technical arguments for MDE. In emphasizing the technical feasibility of "parity plus damage limitation," Dyson suggested, Brennan had failed to reach beyond the narrow (and largely uninterested) community of experts. Dyson's work, by contrast, provided a broad historical, cultural, and moral perspective on contending views of technology and strategy.

Comparing the advantages and risks of the basic approaches to nuclear policy—disarmament, MAD, war-fighting, and defense emphasis—he attempted to show that MDE was the most "robust concept" for ensuring survival in the nuclear age, presenting it in terms of a fundamental injunction to "live and let live."[1] Dyson's work

1. Freeman Dyson, *Weapons and Hope* (New York: Harper and Row, 1984), p. 274. Dyson's interest in mutual defense emphasis dates back to 1969, when he expressed his belief that "the long-term prospects for coming to an informal or even formal stabilization of the arms race are much better if both we and the Soviet Union have a

helped stimulate an unprecedented amount of serious inquiry into MDE in the 1980s. Nevertheless, it was the war-fighters' version of the approach that attracted the most attention.

As I noted earlier, Johan Holst had observed in 1969 that MDE supporters had "good reason to feel uncomfortable about their 'allies' on the subject" who proposed defenses as instruments of war-fighting. In the 1980s, two new factors dramatically increased that cause for concern. First, even before Ronald Reagan's March 1983 "Star Wars" speech, prominent supporters of nuclear war-fighting doctrines had taken heed of Herman Kahn's advice that they had disregarded in 1969: that "it would greatly . . . help the cause of the proponents of ABM if ABM were generally perceived (and presented) as a shield designed to facilitate . . . comprehensive and lasting arms control measures."[2] Second, the Reagan administration, having endorsed a doctrine of "prevailing" in a nuclear war, sought to defuse widespread domestic hostility to its apparent rejection of arms control. A chief means for doing so was to emphasize that the real purpose of the president's Strategic Defense Initiative was a mutual defense emphasis arms control regime.

A change had also occurred in the rationale that war-fighters now offered for strategic defense. With the exception of Paul Nitze and the Policy Planning Staff in the early 1950s, no qualified expert had raised the possibility of decisive defensive supremacy in an offense-defense arms race. Now, beginning with a small group of scientists (led by Edward Teller) and political activists on the extreme right (including columnist Phyllis Schlafly and retired Lieutenant General Daniel O. Graham), a campaign was launched to popularize the notion that defensive technologies were on the verge of wholly negating the nuclear revolution.

Not only did that claim become the explicit rationale for the 1983 Strategic Defense Initiative, it was later built into the 1985 U.S. proposal (labeled the U.S. "Strategic Concept") for mutual defense emphasis arms control. Thus, in a radical departure from anyone's prior advocacy of MDE, Paul Nitze maintained that such a regime depended on the "practical" objective of achieving defenses that

---

preponderantly defensive orientation. I think it may be true that their sensitivity to the moral aspects of this is to some extent genuine—that is, I don't think it is only propaganda." "A Case for Missile Defense," *Bulletin of the Atomic Scientists* 25 (April 1969): 33.

2. Herman Kahn, "The Missile Defense Debate in Perspective," in *Why ABM? Policy Issues in the Missile Defense Controversy*, ed. Johan J. Holst and William Schneider, Jr. (New York: Pergamon Press, 1969), p. 293.

were both highly effective and "cost-effective at the margin."[3] Given the lack of a serious commitment to MDE by the Reagan administration, the "Star Wars" debate predictably became nearly an exact replica of the 1960s ABM debates, with MAD advocates sharply challenging war-fighting rationales for strategic defense.

By 1986, however, President Reagan began to demonstrate that his support for a war-fighting strategy was not unconditional. Two years later he was denouncing opponents of arms control as irrationally preoccupied with the inevitability of war with the Soviet Union.[4] Indeed, there was reason to believe that his earlier rhetorical commitment to MDE-based nuclear disarmament had attained the status of real conviction. In a remarkable encounter with Mikhail Gorbachev in Reykjavik, the two leaders found themselves grappling with how to achieve complete nuclear disarmament, with their only substantive difference based on the president's claim that defense was an essential precondition for such a regime.

That first direct superpower dialogue on nuclear disarmament was rendered incoherent by two competing misconceptions about strategic defense. The first was the president's inability to acknowledge the dangers of unilateral efforts at defense. The second was the Soviet leader's failure to recognize that, notwithstanding legitimate concerns over Star Wars, the feasibility of his own disarmament plan might depend on a negotiated deployment of defenses. Serious offensive disarmament talks were not precluded solely by the lack of a usable technical framework, however. Those who remained convinced that Europe's defense rested on U.S. assured destruction threats were dismayed not by the "failure" of Reykjavik but by its success in raising a profound issue as a U.S. administration briefly confronted the West with a call for overcoming Europe's reliance on extended nuclear deterrence.

By the end of the decade, the argument that Europe's security

3. Paul Nitze, "On the Road to a More Stable Peace," *Department of State Bulletin*, April 1985, p. 28.

4. Referring to opponents of the Intermediate Nuclear Forces (INF) Treaty, Reagan stated: "I think that some of the people who are objecting the most and just refusing even to accede to the idea of ever getting any understanding, whether they realize it or not, those people—basically down in their deepest thoughts—have accepted that war is inevitable and that there must come to be a war between the superpowers." That comment produced the following reply from Howard Phillips (chairman of the Conservative Caucus): "Ronald Reagan is a very weak man with a strong wife and a strong staff. He becomes a useful idiot for Kremlin propaganda." Quoted in David K. Shipler, "The Mood Is Genuinely Hopeful for This Summit," *New York Times*, December 6, 1987, p. E1.

depended on U.S. nuclear threats had been overtaken by events. With the end of the Cold War, the only apparently compelling argument for preserving threats of mutual annihilation was the absence of a viable path to a less destructive nuclear balance. Critics of MDE since the 1960s had often maintained that the decisive weakness of the approach was its inability to recognize the limits of superpower cooperation in a cold war. Charles Glaser, for example, raised that issue in 1988 (in a revised version of a 1984 article called "Why Even Good Defenses May Be Bad"): "Defenses might help the superpowers to reduce their vulnerability if combined with limits on their offenses. . . . [O]nce the superpowers are already committed to . . . cooperation, defenses might help reduce the risks of cooperating. But these necessary conditions for ambitious arms control agreements do not exist in today's world."[5]

At the end of the decade, few would so readily dismiss the prospects for far-reaching nuclear cooperation. Yet though the end of the Cold War created the political preconditions for dispassionate inquiry into MDE, the association of defense with the search for nuclear superiority continued to influence the mind-set of the mainstream arms control community. That legacy, dating back to the massive retaliation doctrine of the 1950s, had only been strengthened by the effort in the 1980s to promote the notion of achieving MDE through technological defense dominance.

With more thoughtful arguments for MDE largely ignored in the sound and fury of the Star Wars debate, the Reagan administration's version of the approach seemed to confirm that defense was incompatible with basic arms control standards of parity and deterrence stability. As the nuclear superpowers move beyond the conflict that produced the capacity for societal extinction, we should consider both the weaknesses of SDI from an MDE perspective and the serious arms control rationales for defense that appeared in the technological environment of the 1980s. With the fading of the final debate between MAD and war-fighting, it is possible that these most recent approaches to MDE may provide long-term direction for nuclear policy.

The Revival of the MDE Tradition in the 1980s

Freeman Dyson's effort to revive consideration of mutual defense emphasis began with the 1978 publication of an essay entitled "The

5. Charles L. Glaser, "Defense Dominance," in *Fateful Visions: Avoiding Nuclear Catastrophe*, ed. Joseph S. Nye, Jr., Graham T. Allison, and Albert Carnesale (Cambridge, Mass.: Ballinger, 1988), pp. 60–61. For the original version, see "Why Even Good Defenses May Be Bad," *International Security* 9 (Fall 1984): 93–123.

Ethics of Defense."[6] Defense emphasis, he maintained, should be adopted as a general principle of international relations:

> In the long run, the survival of human society on this planet requires that one of two things happens. Either we establish some kind of world government with a monopoly of military power. Or we achieve a stable division of the world into independent sovereign states, with the armed force of each state strictly confined to the mission of defending its own territory. . . . If we consider world government either undesirable or unattainable, then the aim of our military and diplomatic efforts should be . . . to guide the forces of nationalism into truly defensive channels.[7]

Although he adocated defense emphasis as a general approach, Dyson's chief concern was with the nuclear doctrine of MAD:

> The scientists . . . argue that because the supremacy of the offensive is unalterable, the strategy of Mutual Assured Destruction is the best among the dismal alternatives that are open to us. But their basic dogma is in fact a falsehood. . . . If we were to make the political decision to switch from an offense-dominated to a defense-dominated strategy, to redirect our weapons procurement and research and development, together with our diplomacy, toward the ultimate nullification of offensive weapons, there is nothing in the laws of physics and chemistry that would prevent us from doing so.[8]

Dyson developed his approach more fully in his 1984 book *Weapons and Hope*. Writing before President Reagan's March 1983 Star Wars speech, Dyson had already noted the appearance of a new technological "dogma." That dogma was the antithesis of the MAD conception of a technological plateau. The new claim was that by overcoming the MAD-inspired effort to stifle defense-oriented research and development, defense would emerge as technologically dominant. The arms competition would then be driven "naturally" in the direction of "assured survival."

It was clear, Dyson pointed out, that adherents of defense dominance were interested primarily in the ability to win a war. For example, the 1982 "High Frontier" report by strategic defense lobbyists maintained that "a bold and rapid entry into space . . . would end-run the Soviets. . . . When we look to space for the technological end-run on the Soviets, we find all factors call for an emphasis on strategic

6. Serialized in the *New Yorker* in 1978 and reprinted in Freeman Dyson, *Disturbing the Universe* (New York: Harper and Row, 1979), pp. 142–54.

7. Ibid., p. 151.

8. Ibid., p. 144.

defense."[9] Taking note of the report's claim that "we would, of course, not object" should the "Soviet Union wish to . . . make Assured Survival a mutual endeavor,"[10] Dyson argued that the High Frontier agenda rendered that sentiment meaningless. Trying for an "end run" obviously entailed an arms race—a context in which Dyson shared the MAD view that defense could never prevent total catastrophe in a nuclear war. After describing the technical obstacles confronting space-based defenses in a war-fighting environment, Dyson concluded that the High Frontier concept pointed toward a "technical follies future": "It is a future of double folly, the small-scale folly of militarily useless weapons, and the large-scale folly of unattainable strategic objectives."[11]

Coupled to his attack on that new version of war-fighting, which Dyson labeled "defense unlimited," was a critique of MAD-based arms control:

> The concept rests on the belief that . . . our weapons will never be used. . . . But who, looking at the historical record of human folly and accident which led us into the international catastrophes of the past, can believe that careful calculation and rational decision will prevail in all the crises of the future? Inevitably, if we maintain assured destruction as a permanent policy, there will come a time when folly and accident will surprise us again as they surprised us in 1914. And this time the guns of August will be shooting with thermonuclear warheads.[12]

By the time *Weapons and Hope* was published, President Reagan's Star Wars speech had launched a new national debate over strategic defense. The original SDI proposal and its subsequent promotion reflected the same basic perspective as the High Frontier plan. (Daniel Graham, who led the High Frontier project, had been a defense policy adviser to Reagan in the 1976 and 1980 presidential campaigns.) First, the president's call to render offenses "impotent and obsolete" raised the prospect of complete protection against all means of delivering nuclear weapons. Second, Reagan made it clear that he had no intention of allowing United States offenses to be rendered "impotent and obsolete." "As we pursue our goal of defensive technologies, we recognize

9. Dyson (n. 1), p. 253. For the High Frontier argument see Daniel O. Graham, "The High Frontier Study: A Summary," in *Understanding U.S. Strategy: A Reader*, ed. Terry L. Heyns (Washington, D.C.: National Defense University Press, 1983), pp. 93–133 (quotation cited by Dyson is on p. 97).

10. Dyson (n. 1), p. 254.

11. Ibid., p. 70.

12. Ibid., pp. 245–46.

that our allies rely upon our strategic offensive power to deter attacks against them. . . . We must and shall continue to honor our commitments." Finally, in a fashion similar to the High Frontier study, the president contradicted his apparent endorsement of a U.S. war-fighting advantage with an unexplained suggestion that SDI "would pave the way for arms control measures to eliminate the [nuclear] weapons themselves."[13]

After the speech, Soviet general secretary Yuriy Andropov reacted predictably to the threat of being unilaterally disarmed: "Should this conception be converted into reality, this would actually open the floodgates of a runaway race in all kinds of weapons, both offensive and defensive."[14] The Soviet leader's response was matched by widespread skepticism in the United States over a major new arms program. Almost immediately, members of the Reagan administration began to mention the desirability of bilateral defenses. Defense Secretary Caspar Weinberger went so far as to state that "we would hope and assume that the Soviets . . . would develop about the same time we did the same kind of effective defense."[15]

Such benign sentiments, however, had to be considered in the context of other nuclear policy pronouncements by the Reagan administration during this period. Most notable was Weinberger's Defense Guidance Plan for fiscal years 1984–88, which called for the ability to "prevail" in a protracted nuclear war. It proposed an intensified arms race as a deliberate policy, as the United States would develop weapons that "are difficult for the Soviets to counter, impose disproportionate costs, open up new areas of major military competition, and obsolesce previous Soviet investment." Finally, lest anyone imagine that the strategy would emphasize defense, Weinberger called for the United States to maintain "through a protracted conflict period and afterward, the capability to inflict very high levels of damage" on the Soviet Union.[16]

Although the president promoted SDI as a "peace shield," Soviet decision makers could also contemplate the 1982 manual titled "Military Space Doctrine," written by Air Force chief of staff Charles Gabriel, whose foreword noted: "The nation's highest defense priority—deterrence—requires a credible warfighting capability across the spec-

13. The relevant portion of the Reagan speech is reprinted in *Survival* 24 (May–June 1983): 129–30.

14. Ibid., p. 131.

15. Cited by Richard Garwin, "Reagan's Riskiness," *New York Times*, March 30, 1983, p. A31.

16. *New York Times*, May 30, 1982, p. 12.

trum of conflict. . . . Space provides an unlimited potential and opportunity for military operations and a place where the Air Force can perform or support all of its missions and tasks."[17] In case the Soviets remained confused about where SDI fit into that U.S. strategy, Weinberger explained it explicitly. Once the peace shield was deployed, he noted, "we could be back in a situation we were in . . . when we were the only nation with a nuclear weapon."[18]

By 1984 it had become clear that it was politically unwise to characterize strategic defense as the missing element in a complete U.S. war-fighting strategy. The chief domestic effect of the war-fighting rhetoric associated with the Reagan defense buildup was the resurgence of widespread antinuclear activism under the banner of a "nuclear freeze." The president and his associates appeared to conclude that a viable presidency required at least the appearance of a serious commitment to arms control.

Calls to "prevail" in a nuclear war ceased, and the administration moved to recast its nebulous rhetoric linking strategic defense to disarmament into a concrete arms control plan. That task fell to Paul Nitze, who drafted a mutual defense emphasis arms control proposal in mid-December 1984. A slightly revised draft was unanimously endorsed by the Senior Arms Control Policy Group, comprising representatives from the Defense Department, the Joint Chiefs of Staff, the State Department, ACDA, and the Central Intelligence Agency.[19] Approved by President Reagan on January 1, 1985, it was presented three weeks later to the Soviet arms control delegation at Geneva under the label "U.S. Strategic Concept." It consisted of the following four sentences:

> During the next ten years, we should seek a radical reduction in the number and power of existing and planned offensive and defensive nuclear arms, whether land-based, space-based or otherwise. We should even now be looking forward to a period of transition, beginning possibly ten years from now, to effective non-nuclear defensive forces, including defenses against offensive nuclear arms. This period of transition should lead to the eventual elimination of nuclear arms, both offensive and defensive. A nuclear free world is an ultimate objective to which we, the Soviet Union and all other nations can agree.[20]

17. *Washington Post*, January 15, 1985, p. A13.
18. George W. Ball, "The War for Star Wars," *New York Review of Books* 32 (April 11, 1985): 40.
19. Paul H. Nitze, *From Hiroshima to Glasnost: At the Center of Decision* (New York: Grove Weidenfeld, 1989), pp. 403–5.
20. For a description of the preparation and presentation of the "U.S. Strategic Concept," see *Washington Post*, January 26, 1985, p. A1.

As Nitze described the approach in a speech in February 1985, the administration's proposal shared the same perspective that had originated with Oppenheimer and the Panel of Consultants on Disarmament in the 1950s and was later refined by Brennan and the Hudson Institute's "arms control through defense" project in the 1960s.

First, it shared the key premise that the world of nuclear offense dominance was intolerably dangerous. Although there would be risks of cheating in an MDE arms control regime, Nitze noted, they "would be orders of magnitude less than the risks and potential costs posed by a possible breakdown in the present deterrence regime based upon the ultimate threat of massive nuclear retaliation."

Second, it implicitly adopted Brennan's deterrence standard of relative damage as the guiding principle of the transition toward MDE: "We recognize that the transition period . . . could be tricky. We would have to avoid a mix of offensive and defensive forces that . . . would give one side or the other an incentive to strike first."

Third, it clearly indicated that the deployment of defenses would take place in the context of U.S.–Soviet arms control negotiations: "We would see the transition period as a cooperative endeavor with the Soviets. Arms control would play a critical role."

Finally, it revived complete nuclear disarmament as the "practical goal" of U.S. policy. As Oppenheimer had first maintained in 1953, Nitze now noted that "defenses would provide assurance that were one country to cheat . . . it would not be able to achieve any exploitable military advantage. To overcome the deployed defenses, cheating would have to be on such a large scale that there would be sufficient notice so that countermeasures could be taken." The ultimate goal, Nitze maintained, was a strategic relationship based on "mutual assured security."

Nitze, whose involvement with nuclear policy had begun with an inspection of the damage done to Hiroshima in 1945, ended his speech with an appeal to emotion: "We owe it to our children, our grandchildren, and—in my case—to my great-grandchild to hold out for and to work toward some brighter vision for the future."[21]

Given that the U.S. Strategic Concept followed nearly two years of sustained promotion of war-fighting rationales for strategic defense, it would have been truly remarkable for the Soviets to have welcomed it as a substantive arms control initiative. Nevertheless, the formal presentation of MDE as U.S. arms control doctrine represented a radical break with the entire history of U.S. nuclear policy. Indeed, since the Strategic Concept called for a prolonged period of

21. Nitze (n. 3), p. 29.

superpower negotiations, one might expect that the initial skepticism it deservedly received would eventually yield to a serious examination of the substantive arguments for the new approach.

That would have meant, however, that the Reagan administration was prepared to back up its Strategic Concept with a coherent exposition of how a Strategic Defense Initiative (presumably to be pursued by both superpowers) would provide a path toward MDE arms control. Considering its unprecedented promise of making nuclear disarmament a "practical goal" for the first time, we should examine how far the Strategic Concept—independent of the prior nuclear policy preferences of its chief advocates—in fact represented a plausible approach to strategic arms control.

Evaluating the Strategic Concept as an Arms Control Approach

Despite the high level of abstraction of this revolutionary plan, the Reagan administration managed repeatedly to contradict both its specific content and its general guidelines. A relatively minor example was the Strategic Defense Initiative's pursuit of nuclear-pumped X-ray lasers despite the explicit renunciation of nuclear defensive forces called for in the Strategic Concept.[22]

Of greater significance was that subsequent statements by the president and administration officials in effect rewrote the "concept" so as to render it almost absurd. Thus, in lieu of explanations of how a transition from offense to defense might be negotiated, they asserted that after developing a highly effective (and cost-effective) defensive system, the United States would then give (or sell at cost!) that system to the Soviets.[23] That idea in itself reduced any prospective superpower dialogue to farce, as was reflected in Soviet leader Gorbachev's appropriate response: "You don't want to share with us even equipment for dairy plants at this point, and now you're promising us that you're going to share results on SDI development?"[24]

Besides the fact that a promise to eventually share missile defense

22. One example of the administration's early confusion about the strategic defense research program was Weinberger's apparent ignorance that the X-ray laser required nuclear weapons. See Janne E. Nolan, *Guardians of the Arsenal: The Politics of Nuclear Strategy* (New York: Basic Books, 1989), p. 166.

23. In a November 12, 1985, interview with foreign journalists, Reagan qualified his promise to share strategic defense technology by offering to sell it at cost. *Star Wars Quotes* (Washington, D.C.: Arms Control Association, 1986).

24. *New York Times*, October 15, 1986, p. A12.

technology provided a dubious incentive for the Soviets to welcome a U.S. bid for defensive supremacy, the administration made no effort to explain how the types of defensive systems being pursued could be reconciled with the essential arms control requirements of parity and stability. Indeed, SDI's emphasis on what the Soviets call "space-strike arms" seemed calculated to render the arms control process unmanageable. For one thing, it was unrealistic to assume that a race to develop and apply a range of exotic technology would result in technological parity between the superpowers' defensive systems. Moreover, there were several reasons for suspecting that the particular kinds of technology emphasized by SDI were inherently incompatible with the requirements of arms control.

First, space-based weapons that can penetrate the atmosphere could also attack ground targets without warning. Some experts maintained that the system originally proposed as the first phase of space-based BMD deployment (based on homing rockets placed in orbit) would have such an offensive potential.[25] Obviously, no arms control regime could allow for such an ability.

Second, aside from the likely difficulties in comparing the capabilities of independently developed directed energy weapons, the prospective deployment of such weapons in a multilayered defensive screen seemed bound to inspire radical uncertainty about the relative overall capacity of the two sides' defensive systems. That uncertainty might not in itself undermine deterrence stability, yet it would clearly stimulate the arms competition, since arms control requires establishing and implementing standards of parity in which both parties have reasonable confidence.

Finally, it was widely agreed that weapons capable of destroying ballistic missiles in early flight would be most effective against objects already based in space—that is, the space-based component of the adversary's defense,[26] as well as satellites used for military com-

25. For a brief consideration of this problem, see Office of Technology Assessment, "Ballistic Missile Defense Technologies," in *Strategic Defenses* (Princeton: Princeton University Press, 1986), pp. 192–93. The OTA study concluded that "although the optimal weapons for space-to-earth attack may not be the best for ballistic missile defense, they would probably be difficult to ban under an arms control regime which allowed space-based BMD weapons." For a discussion of the space-to-earth capabilities of the Reagan administration's proposed "homing rockets," see *New York Times*, February 22, 1987, p. 1.

26. SDI was thus both a strategic defense initiative and an anti–strategic defense initiative. The nuclear-pumped X-ray laser, for example, was pursued both for its potential as a BMD system and for its ability to destroy the adversary's space-based defenses. See Gerold Yonas, "The Strategic Defense Initiative," in *Weapons in Space*,

munication, reconnaissance, navigation, and early warning of a nuclear strike.[27] Thus, unlike the "traditional" ground-based ABMs developed in the 1960s, space-based defenses introduced the possibility of a defense-initiated attack—an attack that could alone decisively affect the strategic balance and that could pave the way for a follow-on strike by offensive forces. The simultaneous deployment of such "defenses" by the superpowers would progressively undermine each side's security, even creating pressures for a preemptive attack on the other's space-based defenses and satellites.[28]

The potential vulnerability of space-based defenses would be especially dangerous if heavy defensive deployments were combined with low levels of offensive forces, presumably the direction of the transition called for in the U.S. Strategic Concept. In that situation the rewards of a successful first strike against the other side's defenses could be enormous, possibly leaving the victim incapable of penetrating the intact defensive shield of the attacker and largely if not totally defenseless against an attack on its own homeland. There would be no incentive to "manage" such a transition; the only shared interest between the superpowers regarding such weapons would be a mutual ban.

It did not seem likely that those problems could be overcome.[29] Not only might it be impossible to combine high effectiveness against missiles with no effectiveness against other space-based systems, but space-based defenses may be highly vulnerable to a range of antidefense weapons whose future efficacy is impossible to determine. Indeed, the pursuit of space-based defenses began spawning simultaneous research into yet another category of weaponry—antidefense systems—whose development is antithetical to the concept of a bilateral transition to defense dominance.

---

ed. Franklin Long, Donald Hafner, and Jeffrey Boutwell (New York: W. W. Norton, 1986), p. 83.

27. Ashton Carter has noted that space-based laser or particle-beam BMD systems would probably be "capable of attack on satellites at all altitudes." Ashton Carter, "The Relationship of ASAT and BMD Systems," in Long, Hafner, and Boutwell (n. 26), p. 176. Moreover, the OTA study notes that since a space-based defense will be vulnerable to attack by orbiting antidefense systems, it "will almost certainly require ASAT capability to defend itself." Office of Technology Assessment (n. 25), p. 191.

28. These dangers are discussed in Office of Technology Assessment (n. 25), pp. 186–87.

29. Remarkably, as late as 1987, the Office of Technology Assessment reported: "SDIO and its contractors have conducted no serious study of the situation in which the United States and the Soviet Union both occupy space with comparable BMD systems." Office of Technology Assessment, *SDI: Technology, Survivability, and Software* (Princeton: Princeton University Press, 1988), p. 4.

For arms control purposes, that amounted to a Catch-22 situation. Meaningful arms control negotiations over defensive deployment could not proceed until both sides had fully developed space-based defensive systems. Yet in the absence of an arms control agreement, hedging aginst a defensive advantage by the other side dictated pursuit of an ability to destroy the adversary's defense. Presumably, an arms control agreement could occur upon arrival at a technological plateau in which all these technologies simultaneously matured. At this point, negotiating parity in defensive capabilities could be combined with negotiating parity in survivability.

Not only did that seem an absurdly indirect path toward an arms control regime, it was almost certain that such a technological plateau would never be reached. Instead, by focusing on nonexistent defensive systems whose future effectiveness and vulnerability were entirely unknown, SDI pointed toward a fear-driven race to develop the defenses themselves, the offenses to overwhelm them, and the "antidefenses" to destroy them.

All the possibilities mentioned above resulted from the fact that SDI was clearly designed to explore the idea of coping with an unconstrained offense-defense arms race. "The challenge," as the SDI chief scientist Gerold Yonas put it in 1986, "is to develop technology that would evolve at least one step ahead and hopefully far ahead of any possible response."[30] Yonas also recognized that defining the challenge in that manner dictated a particular technological solution, since "the ability of any defense to respond effectively to an unconstrained Soviet threat is strongly dependent on the feasibility of boost-phase and post-boost interception."[31] Although some attention was given to ground- or sea-based systems that would "pop up" on detecting a Soviet missile launching, there was widespread agreement that interception in early flight would require a heavy reliance on space-based components.

It is significant that SDI's research agenda simply ignored the prospect of a bilateral agreement to reduce offenses while augmenting defenses. (In the context of such an agreement, there would be no need to cope with an "unconstrained Soviet threat.") Of greater import was the absence of any attention to the possibility that the particular technologies vital to winning an offense-defense arms race might *preclude* serious negotiations based on the U.S. Strategic Concept.

30. *New York Times*, December 23, 1984, p. 14.
31. Yonas (n. 26), p. 82.

The incompatibility between the Reagan administration's arms control doctrine and its actual research and development program was similarly reflected in SDI's avowed goal of a defense that is "cost-effective at the margin." Indeed, the inclusion of the standard of cost-effectiveness in Nitze's explanation of the U.S. Strategic Concept went to the heart of the difference between the Reagan administration proposal and the traditional advocacy of MDE. As Nitze explained it,

> New defensive systems must . . . be cost-effective at the margin—that is, they must be cheap enough to add additional defensive capability so that the other side has no incentive to add additional offensive capability to overcome the defense. If this criterion is not met, the defensive systems could encourage a proliferation of countermeasures and additional offensive weapons to overcome deployed defenses instead of a redirection of effort from offense to defense.[32]

Nitze's criterion marked a radical departure from prior arguments for MDE. For the 1953 disarmament panel, the inherent advantage of a nuclear offense was the very basis for insisting that defense and arms control were "necessary complements." Similarly, we may recall Brennan's argument that decisions between offense and defense should not be "driven by the technology" and that prospects for an effective defense would depend on the "preference and conscious decision" of both superpowers.

As I described in chapter 4, Nitze was nearly alone in the early 1950s in arguing that active defensive technology could potentially outpace the adversary's nuclear offense. In the 1980s, however, Nitze was joined by a group of scientists—among them Edward Teller—who now argued that the nuclear revolution could be wholly reversed by a variety of exotic new defensive technologies. It was Teller who first made the point, one week after the Star Wars speech, that achieving a technological advantage for the defense was the only route to a world of MDE:

> To understand what is at stake, one must realize that defense itself is not enough. Defense must also be less expensive than offense. If and when this is clearly demonstrated, our opponents cannot respond effectively by building more destructive weapons. They too will have to emphasize defense. In this way, . . . McNamara's policy of mutually assured destruction may be rendered obsolete.[33]

32. Nitze (n. 3), p. 28.
33. Edward Teller, "Reagan's Courage," *New York Times*, March 30, 1983, p. A31.

That mutual defense emphasis does not require cost-effective defenses was explained by the 1986 Office of Technology Assessment study of strategic defense:

> If both sides could agree . . . on the desirability of reducing offenses and increasing defenses, then the incentive of a favorable "cost-exchange ratio" of defenses over offenses would not be necessary. Or, to put it another way, a favorable ratio could be negotiated: decreasing offenses would make defenses more effective. A "race" between offenses and defenses would be circumvented.[34]

Moreover, the attainment of a cost-effective defense would dramatically undercut incentives to negotiate, since the United States could protect its population despite the Soviets' efforts to restore their retaliatory capability. In principle, of course, the Soviets would also have a chance to win an all-out race for defensive supremacy. One might have thought that strategic defense advocates, after two decades of outrage at the powerful domestic support for MAD, would have been particularly fearful that the United States would lose a race toward an effective defense. But despite their anticipation that most of the envisioned multilayered defense would be space-based, they also ignored the severe difficulties the United States was then having in maintaining even a minimally functional space program.[35]

In this context, recall the 1961 observation by Halperin and Schelling that "either we *or* the Russians may be the victim or beneficiary of technological breakthrough. . . . Each of us may well be willing to relinquish capabilities in future contingencies on condition that the other side do likewise."[36] That incentive for banning ABM deployment was far less powerful in the 1960s, when neither Teller nor other pro-ABM scientists had argued that defenses could render nuclear weapons impotent and obsolete. The stakes of the technological gamble they were now proposing were far higher. Thus a presidential science adviser, George Keyworth, argued:

> Most certainly, when I talk about "cheaper," I'm not talking about ten per cent—not even a factor of two. I am talking about such an over-

34. Office of Technology Assessment (n. 25), p. 22.

35. For an analysis suggesting that Soviet political culture would provide a more supportive environment for "sustain[ing] an effort like SDI over the long-haul," see Sayre Stevens, "The Soviet Factor in SDI," *Orbis* 30 (Winter 1986): 689–700.

36. Thomas C. Schelling and Morton H. Halperin, *Strategy and Arms Control* (New York: Twentieth Century Fund, 1961), p. 13.

> whelming difference in the cost of defense and offense that there would be no question on that issue.
>
> Let me offer an example. . . . [O]ne laser (which we believe could be built within quite reasonable cost) could, in principle defend the West against the entire Soviet ballistic missile fleet today. We are not talking about marginal balances.[37]

Keyworth's enthusiam was equaled by Teller, who wrote to Paul Nitze that "a single X-ray laser module the size of an executive desk" could "potentially shoot down the entire Soviet land-based missile force, if it were to be launched into the module's field of view."[38]

These were the technical assessments that underlay Nitze's incorporation of "cost-effectiveness" as a necessary criterion for mutual defense emphasis arms control. With the Strategic Defense Initiative explicitly seeking decisive victory in the arms race, it was entirely unclear why Nitze would assert that arms control would play a critical role. After all, nations enjoying a decisive and durable military advantage over their adversaries do not typically choose to give it up, and no rational Soviet official could have been expected to presume otherwise. Thus, given the premise that "the Americans manage to put into effect their program," Soviet foreign minister Andrei Gromyko stated: "We told them that in such a situation we have got to rely on your conscience, the conscience of Washington. . . . [W]e said, 'What if we were to change places? Would you think the same way, would our conscience be enough for you?' "[39]

Although the criterion of cost-effectiveness was provocative, its attainment seemed so remote that one could almost suspect that Nitze included it to undercut his own administration's SDI program.[40] Certainly the standard proved an attractive target for critics. By 1986 several Reagan administration officials and SDI scientists had joined in the near consensus of nongovernment experts that a cost-effective population defense against an unconstrained nuclear threat was almost certainly a pipe dream.[41] Once the director of SDI admitted that

37. Michael Charlton, *The Star Wars History, from Deterrence to Defence: The American Strategic Debate* (London: BBC Publications, 1986), p. 102.

38. *New York Times*, July 15, 1988, p. A10.

39. *Washington Post*, January 14, 1985, p. A14.

40. In his memoir, Nitze strongly defends his official position on cost-effectiveness. See Nitze (n. 19), pp. 406–8.

41. The most prominent SDI scientist to cast doubt on Reagan administration assessments of SDI research was Roy D. Woodruff, who served as head of arms devel-

his organization's stated goal of cost-effectiveness "may simply be unobtainable,"[42] determined technological optimism by less-informed strategic defense enthusiasts began to have a hollow ring.

Despite the Reagan administration's manifest unconcern with the issues raised by a prospective negotiated transition, its declaratory support for bilateral defense emphasis was nevertheless a remarkable development. After all, the strategic defense lobby had traditionally argued openly for U.S. nuclear superiority, and Ronald Reagan, despite promoting missile defense as far back as 1966, had never (before the Star Wars speech) publicly proclaimed that strategic defense should in fact be viewed as an arms control concept.[43]

Indeed, as the president displayed a deepening interest in arms control during his second term (fostered by a belief that the Soviets under Gorbachev were now seriously prepared to negotiate), the administration's MDE discourse began to take on a life of its own. In the absence of strident anti-Soviet rhetoric, Reagan's frequent references to a defense-protected nuclear disarmament regime no longer sounded obviously hypocritical. Moreover, some important officials went beyond ritual references to the Strategic Concept to argue energetically and with apparent conviction on its behalf.[44]

What happened at the October 1986 Reykjavik summit and its aftermath cannot be explained without recognizing an element of real presidential interest in the Strategic Concept. When Gorbachev surprisingly pressed his own plan for nuclear disarmament, he evidently encountered genuine responsiveness. Thus, with no real U.S. preparation and no hope of success, the stage was nevertheless set for wandering into substantive negotiations over the attainment of a nonnuclear world.

On one hand, the outcome of Reykjavik made clear the President's desire to preclude meaningful negotiated constraints on strategic defense development. Thus, for most in the arms control community, the impasse at Reykjavik only confirmed a long-held

---

opment at Laurence Livermore Laboratories during the first two years of SDI research. His claim that Teller had given "overly optimistic" and "technically incorrect" information regarding the promise of X-ray lasers became the subject of an inconclusive investigation by the General Accounting Office. See *New York Times*, July 15, 1988, p. A10, and August 1, 1988, p. A14.

42. *New York Times*, May 1, 1986, p. A20.

43. In 1967, Governor Reagan advised Republican candidates to hold the Democrats accountable for an "ABM gap." *New York Times*, September 15, 1967, p. 9.

44. Aside from promotion of the Strategic Concept by Nitze and George Shultz, an apparent true believer in the morality of a shift from offense to defense was the chief of naval operations, Admiral James Watkins. See Nolan (n. 22), p. 168.

conviction that a choice must be made between strategic defense and arms control. Yet there was another dimension to Reykjavik. During the summit and its aftermath, and despite the absence of a usable negotiating framework to guide the first high-level superpower dialogue on nuclear disarmament, the entire history of rationales for strategic offense dominance suddenly seemed open to serious reconsideration.

The Meaning of the 1986 Reykjavik Summit

The willingness of the United States to be lured into disarmament talks can be explained in part by the president's decision to justify SDI as the key to nuclear disarmament. However divided the administration remained on a variety of nuclear policy issues, that the elimination of nuclear weapons had been formally proposed to the Soviets two years earlier at Geneva paved the way for the United States to take up the issue. Moreover, the domestic political value of the Strategic Concept would have been severely eroded had Reagan simply turned his back on disarmament negotiations. One commentator described the political benefits of the U.S. Strategic Concept this way:

> For what were the freezers saying but that deterrence was unstable and dangerous and that something bold had to be done to reduce the threat of nuclear devastation? They built a public for that argument. Reagan bought it. But he put on a different bottom line, calling not for a freeze but for strategic defense, a *non-nuclear* defense, no less, his stated purpose being not simply to reduce offensive arsenals but *to eliminate nuclear weapons altogether*.
>
> No wonder the freezers and traditional arms controllers are pinching themselves, trying to figure out how to reclaim the issues Reagan stole from them: *their* issues.[45]

Finally, aside from Gorbachev's personal skill in setting the summit agenda, the specifics of the Soviet proposal distinguished it from the empty rhetoric normally associated with calls to eliminate nuclear arsenals. Particularly striking was Gorbachev's acknowledgment that a disarmament agreement would require the Soviets

45. Stephen S. Rosenfeld, "A Dizzying Strategy," *Washington Post*, February 1, 1985, p. A19.

to abandon past opposition to comprehensive on-site inspection.[46]

Although how serious the Soviets really were about their disarmament proposal was an open question, it is hard to imagine that any Soviet leader could have fashioned a more concrete or convincing plea to begin a dialogue. From the Soviets' perspective, interest in nuclear disarmament in the mid-1980s could reasonably be explained by several factors: their still formidable conventional advantage in Europe, concern over their long-term competitiveness in strategic arms, or a rational assessment that nuclear weapons are both militarily useless and extremely dangerous.

For decades before Reykjavik, one could explain the impossibility of disarmament simply by pointing out that either one or both sides did not really want it. At Reykjavik, and for a brief period afterward, the whole issue seemed transformed. Two "new" questions now demanded answers: First, if both superpowers wanted to disarm, could they find a means to do so? Second, if they could find the means, was it in the interest of the West to end its reliance on the nuclear threat?

Concerning the first question, the two leaders found themselves at odds on a single technical issue: the role of strategic defense. Gorbachev argued, "The system would be effective only if all missiles were eliminated. But then, one might ask, why the antimissile defense altogether? Why build it?"[47] To that question Reagan had a reasonable reply: defenses (which would not require the elimination of "all missiles" to be effective) would be needed as an "insurance policy" to guard against cheating on a disarmament agreement.

Unfortunately, that last point, repeated across three decades of MDE advocacy, appeared to be the only aspect of the U.S. Strategic Concept that either the president or his advisers had integrated into their thinking on the subject. Thus the Reagan disarmament proposal at Reykjavik utterly bypassed the "period of transition" and

46. Gorbachev's public statement of his position on verification was contained in his October 14 (post-Reykjavik) address on Soviet television. For excerpts from that speech, see *New York Times*, October 15, 1986, p. A12. The Soviet leader's original call for on-site inspection was contained in his January 1986 three-stage proposal for complete nuclear disarmament by the year 2000. For excerpts from that proposal, see *Survival* 28 (March–April 1986): 246–49. Putting aside the issue of Soviet interest in complete nuclear disarmament, the unprecedented verification requirements agreed to in the INF Treaty made it clear that the Soviet change on the issue of on-site inspection was genuine.

47. *New York Times*, October 22, 1986, p. A12.

even inexplicably deferred the deployment of defenses until after all offenses had been scrapped.

With no prior effort to provide the Strategic Concept with substantive content, there were now no guidelines for conducting the talks. That the exchange on disarmament persisted for two days (with staffs working late into the night) can probably best be explained by the remarkable energy unleashed by directly confronting the question of revolutionary disarmament measures and by a momentary sense that statesmen could actually fashion far-reaching solutions to the nuclear danger.

The discovery that the two leaders had agreed in principle to nuclear disarmament had a remarkable impact on the individuals who had fashioned the MAD arms control framework. Thus McNamara, McGeorge Bundy, and Gerard Smith (who had been the chief SALT I negotiator) now joined in describing Reykjavik as the most promising arms control event "since the imperfect effort for international control of atomic energy broke down under Stalin's rejection 40 years ago."

Having advocated MAD for two decades, McNamara might have been expected to remind the Reagan administration never to surrender the ability to ensure "the certainty of suicide to the aggressor." Instead, his only criticism of complete nuclear disarmament was that "both sides in the end may need small offensive forces as general assurances against secret deployments by anyone." Driven instantly back to the "minimum deterrence" arms control theory that predated MAD, McNamara might have raised again Wiesner's 1960 argument that defenses were incompatible with such a regime. Instead, his criticism of the president's claim that strategic defenses should be deployed as insurance against cheating was reduced to the observation that "it can surely wait a little while."[48]

McNamara's statement confirmed that assured destruction had never been a theory regarding the essential requirements of deterrence. It had instead been a political lever against American war-fighters, designed to deny their aspirations for a complete first-strike capability. If the nation's most powerful war-fighter had now embraced nuclear disarmament—as the president seemed to have done—that compromise was no longer necessary. MAD could simply be abandoned.

But there was another element to the original assured destruction compromise: the protection of Europe with options ranging from

48. McGeorge Bundy, George Kennan, Robert McNamara, and Gerard Smith, "Reykjavik's Grounds for Hope," *New York Times*, October 19, 1986, p. E23.

flexible nuclear response to massive retaliation. Thus, even if the superpowers could overcome the technical obstacles to disarmament, the United States would still have to confront the issue of European dependence on U.S. assured destruction capabilities.

Immediately following Reykjavik, the administration encountered a storm of protest from European leaders and important members of the U.S. defense establishment. The most stinging denunciation came in a speech by Senator Sam Nunn, who charged the president and secretary of state with endangering the security of Western Europe. At least briefly, the White House sought to rebut Nunn's accusation, as spokesman Larry Speakes commented, "I don't think Senator Nunn would favor a world with nuclear weapons over a world without. Given a choice . . . I think the American people would favor a world without. I think they would be willing to pay what it takes for conventional forces."[49]

The most impassioned defense of disarmament came from Secretary of State George Shultz. Shultz spent several days appearing before the media, asserting his conviction that both the Reagan administration and the Soviets saw nuclear disarmament as a "good deal." "From our standpoint," the secretary noted, "there's no question about the fact that deterrence based on conventional forces is sharply more expensive than deterrence based on nuclear forces. But it's a safer form of deterrence."[50] Moreover, armed with charts comparing the populations and economic strength of Western Europe, the United States, and the Warsaw Pact, Shultz charged that the only thing standing in the way of dismantling the balance of terror was a lack of "political will" on the part of Western Europe to provide an adequate conventional defense.[51]

In the end, the Reagan administration squelched the incipient disarmament debate by "clarifying" (in fact, altering) the position the president had taken at Reykjavik. The revised U.S. offer was for the elimination of ballistic missiles only (instead of all offensive strategic nuclear forces), with the added reassurance to the allies that even this step would require deep Soviet cuts in conventional forces.

Aside from calming the Europeans, resorting to an offer that the Soviets had little reason to endorse (especially since there was no

49. *New York Times*, October 18, 1986, p. A5.

50. Ibid.

51. Following Senator Nunn's October 17 speech condemning complete nuclear disarmament, Shultz's argument for nuclear disarmament and NATO's capacity to provide an effective conventional deterrent was voiced in his appearances at the National Press Club and on the MacNeil-Lehrer News Hour.

accompanying promise to relinquish the substantial U.S. advantage in bombers and cruise missiles) may have reflected real concern that the Soviets were serious about disarmament.[52] Clearly, the Reagan administration was utterly unprepared to defend the two revolutionary claims the president had asserted at Reykjavik: that nuclear disarmament was in the national interest and that strategic defenses represented a technical instrument for approximating a nonnuclear world. Those propositions are in fact linked: the level of interest in nuclear disarmament depends in part on the plausibility of claims that it could be reliably implemented and verified.

Since the 1960s, two assumptions had been mutually reinforcing. First, that alternatives to MAD were unavailable. Second, that Western Europe's security required AD threats. Even the almost farcical Reykjavik exchange on disarmament proved sufficient to weaken faith in the first belief. As a result, attention swung heavily to the second assumption. Although initial criticism was directed against President Reagan for discussing nuclear MDE, highlighting the linkage between U.S. strategic forces and the Soviet offensive conventional (and theater nuclear) threat also placed pressure on Gorbachev.

At first Gorbachev angrily challenged Reykjavik's critics: "What was being thoroughly disguised previously is now becoming more clear: among U.S. and West European ruling circles, there are powerful forces that seek to frustrate the process of nuclear disarmament. Some people began to assert again that nuclear weapons are almost a boon."[53] Attacking that position, however, did not make it disappear. To sustain his peace initiative, Gorbachev soon began making a series of statements that implicitly acknowledged the Soviet military advantage in Europe.[54] In the nuclear area, he accepted the principle of asymmetrical reductions that led to the 1988 Intermediate Nuclear Forces (INF) Treaty.

Finally, the Soviets announced both that they were going to restructure their conventional forces from an offensive to a defensive

52. Generally, the Reagan administration spent the first two weeks after Reykjavik alternating between acknowledging and denying that the president had endorsed complete nuclear disarmament. A reading of the statements by Soviet officials, Secretary Shultz, and Senator Nunn, and of the more forthright acknowledgments by the White House, leaves no doubt that the United States had agreed in principle to a ban on "all nuclear arms." For a review of these exchanges, see *New York Times*, October 28, 1986, p. A1.

53. *New York Times*, October 23, 1986, p. A12.

54. See Mikhail Gorbachev, *Perestroika: New Thinking for Our Country and the World* (New York: Harper and Row, 1987), p. 203.

posture and that achieving a bilateral "nonoffensive defense" should be the guiding objective of NATO-Warsaw Pact negotiations.[55] In December 1988 Gorbachev's promotion of an MDE conventional balance in Europe was backed up by his announcement of a unilateral withdrawal of half a million troops and the disbanding of ten thousand tanks.[56]

The INF Treaty, combined with the 1990 Treaty on Conventional Armed Forces in Europe (CFE), established force levels that would provide lengthy warning of a renewed Soviet threat to invade Europe.[57] Recognition that the Soviet threat was evaporating did not have to await the culmination of the CFE talks, having been made apparent by the liberation of Eastern Europe and by political change within the Soviet Union.

Western protests over the disarmament negotiations at Reykjavik had helped stimulate crucial attentiveness to the link between strategic arms control and the military balance in Europe. In effect, the subsequent dismantling of the Soviet capacity for an invasion removed the cause of those protests. In principle, reducing and restructuring European conventional forces might have been accompanied by an equally revolutionary effort to address the balance of terror. The incoherence of the two leaders' disarmament exchange at Reykjavik, however, had demonstrated the absence of a framework within which to proceed. Moreover, despite the euphoric initial reaction of McNamara and other key architects of MAD, the concept of minimum deterrence (let alone complete offensive disarmament) was by now utterly foreign to the mainstream arms control community. That strategic defense might even play a role in a cooperative regime flew in the face of beliefs shaped by decades of battle with the (now silenced) nuclear war-fighting lobby. Thus it was decided without reflection to proceed within the MAD framework (now under the heading of START, the Strategic Arms Reduction Treaty) as if massive offensive capabilities were self-evidently worth preserving in the emerging post–Cold War world.

That result was not inevitable, however. After two years of calling for an MDE disarmament regime, the United States had had ample time to flesh out its Strategic Concept with a substantive arms control initiative. A credible proposal would in turn have inspired expert reassessment concerning the technical necessity of assured vul-

55. *New York Times*, March 7, 1988, p. A1.
56. *New York Times*, December 8, 1988, p. A1.
57. *New York Times*, November 18, 1990

nerability arms control, along with a broader national debate over its desirability. The Reagan administration's failure to substantiate its arms control concept contributed to declining support for its bid for a strategic defense and ensured that the first round of post–Cold War strategic arms control talks would proceed (as if nothing fundamental had changed) within the MAD framework.

Nevertheless, we should consider what a U.S. Strategic Concept might have looked like had it been originally conceived as an arms control framework rather than as a public relations ploy for a nuclear war-fighting strategy. After all, views that prevailed in the doctrinal and political struggles over Cold War nuclear policy have become far less compelling in the new international context.

At the same time, events during the aftermath of the Cold War produced far greater attentiveness to the common dangers that have long animated arguments for MDE. One such danger—the emergence of new nuclear powers—was dramatized by visions of some future leader as recklessly aggressive as Saddam Hussein. Another was the risk of inadvertent nuclear use, as Soviet internal crises showed that the very premise of centralized control depends as much on unforseeable political factors as on efforts to design effective technical safeguards.

In response to these events, many U.S. policymakers long hostile to war-fighting rationales for strategic defense began to consider the value of cooperative defensive measures. Moreover, Soviet president Gorbachev, in his response to President George Bush's September 1991 announcement of sweeping unilateral arms control measures, stated that the Soviets were now willing "to consider proposals . . . on non-nuclear anti-ballistic missile defenses."[58] Clearly, that move reflected recognition of the changed context of the U.S. debate and the substantive concerns underlying growing congressional interest in BMD.

Yet even as the Soviet situation stimulated that shift in views, it became questionable whether any entity within the disintegrating Soviet Union would prove capable of negotiating a new strategic relationship. Indeed, from the perspective of those sympathetic to a role for defenses in an arms control context, it was ironic that Gorbachev's reversal of Soviet policy came only weeks before the formal demise of the Soviet state.

The U.S. reaction to that revolutionary development will have profound consequences for the future role of both strategic defense

58. *New York Times*, October 6, 1991, p. 11.

and arms control in general. On one hand, SDI supporters can argue that preferences by the other side have become largely irrelevant, since economic weakness and political disarray would likely prevent an effective response to unilateral defense deployments, including those based in space.[59] It is certainly true that if the former Soviet Union descends into intractable chaos, the issue of defenses will have to be considered in a radically different context than during the era of an essentially bipolar nuclear balance between stable societies. In a long-term situation of fragmenting political and military authority, in which nuclear weapons are prone to change hands at any moment, the case for augmenting defenses unilaterally may become irresistible. (At the same time, internal anarchy in the former Soviet Union would mean that basing deterrence on threats of massive nuclear retaliation would become completely senseless.)

But just as it was dangerous to embrace a nuclear arms control approach that assumed permanent political stability, it would be equally mistaken to pursue a combination of offensive and defensive strategic capabilities that, whatever the motivation, implied a new external threat from the West. The Russian historical experience reflects great resilience in the face of daunting challenges, both internal and external, and it is prudent to anticipate future capabilities consistent with the region's vast human and natural resources—perhaps harnessed far more efficiently than during Communist administration. That same experience suggests that perceptions of threat will strengthen the hand of those contenders for political power likely to be most hostile to the West and least capable of constructing a durably stable political system.

What form would a reconstituted nuclear superpower take? In terms of nuclear and defense policy, will Russia emerge as the sole or predominant authority? Or will power be genuinely shared within the Commonwealth of Independent States? All that is ultimately necessary for continued pursuit of a cooperative approach to the nuclear danger is an emergent political system that is neither chronically unstable nor implacably hostile to the West. At that point, decision makers on both sides, remembering the dangers of the Cold War and its tumultuous aftermath, may reject MAD as an acceptable permanent solution to the nuclear danger.

59. Congressman Les Aspin, chairman of the House Armed Services Committee, responded to this argument by citing ways the Soviets could counter a "Brilliant Pebbles" deployment (see below) even in the near term, despite the "sorry state" of their economy. "Patriots, Scuds and the Future of Ballistic Missile Defense," speech before the National Security Industrial Association, April 24, 1991.

In that context, strategic defense may come to be regarded as an important instrument of arms control and disarmament. Protecting that long-term option will require that the United States think clearly about the near-term direction of its SDI program.

Designing SDI for Arms Control

If we draw on the historical assumptions and arguments of MDE advocates, the goal of preserving the future option of a shift toward MDE would involve the following elements:

1. *A pledge not to deploy defenses unilaterally beyond the confines of the 1972 ABM Treaty.* In 1985 National Security Adviser Robert McFarlane stated: "We don't have any illusions that one side or the other could unilaterally deploy these systems and we have no such intentions."[60] Some MDE advocates in the 1950s and 1960s expressed a belief that MDE could be approached by a tacit agreement between the superpowers, that is, through nonprovocative unilateral deployments. That theoretical possibility, however, is more than outweighed by the fact that withdrawing from a long-standing arms control agreement would cast doubt on the defector's commitment to any form of arms control. In the post–Cold War environment such a move has become highly unlikely. A formal agreement would help clear away unnecessary concerns—for example, among military hard-liners—that might disrupt the disarmament process.

2. *A proposed ban on space-based weapons of all types, including restrictions on development enforced by means of a ban on testing in space.* The specific reasons for this are explained below.

3. *A proposed limitation of future ABM development and deployment to ground-based systems designed for terminal and late midcourse defense.* Ground basing has a number of obvious advantages, which cumulatively make the case for such systems overwhelming:

—In contrast to space-based defenses, ground basing preserves a means of distinguishing between defense of forces and defense of populations, a critical distinction if defensive deployments are to be sucessfully negotiated.

—Unlike space-based defenses, ground-based systems cannot themselves be used to initiate an attack.

—The task of protecting ground-based defenses is incomparably easier and better understood than the protection of space-based de-

60. *New York Times*, January 10, 1985, p. A16

fenses. Ground-based defenses can be destroyed only by using strategic offenses to attack the adversary's homeland, as opposed to the wide range of antidefense systems that might be used specifically to destroy space-based defenses. Thus, bilateral reductions in offensive capabilities would simultaneously enhance the survivability of each side's defensive systems. Since a negotiated transition would also entail the proliferation of defensive weapons by both sides, all aspects of the transition would progressively augment defensive survivability.[61]

—Ground-based systems technology is already in hand. The most important improvement in "traditional" BMD systems, a shift to reliance on nonnuclear interception, is approaching realization.[62]

—Although the altitude of interception necessary for a population defense would provide some antisatellite (ASAT) capability, the restriction of ground-based interceptors to low-orbital range would make it possible to pursue agreements to limit threats to satellites. Space basing of defenses could make it impossible to limit that threat.

—A redirection of research and development priorities to ground-based systems will help slow the momentum of research into novel weapons technologies. It is true that such research will inevitably proceed. Yet making the pursuit of exotic technologies a high priority is a formula for maximizing uncertainty over the future of the military balance. Limitations on testing, combined with the inevitable diversion of expenditures toward systems that both sides have agreed to deploy, can help provide the predictability necessary for submission to far-reaching arms control agreements.

61. The value of MDE negotiations for resolving problems of defensive effectiveness and cost-effectiveness is a recurrent theme in the 1987 OTA study on SDI. For a reference to such negotiations for addressing the survivability problem, see Office of Technology Assessment (n. 29), p. 15.

62. From the 1987 OTA study: "Earlier BMD systems, such as SAFEGUARD, can be characterized as terminal or late mid-course defense systems. The terminal and late mid-course defense part of an SDI BMD system could benefit from experience with these predecessors. There has been no experience, however, with boost phase and post-boost phase, and little experience with early mid-course defenses." The study then goes on to note the potentially decisive value of such experience. Office of Technology Assessment (n. 29), p. 244. Herbert York, who had been skeptical of 1960s ABM technology, wrote in 1987: "All of the new ideas, especially those involving the intercepting of enemy missiles in space, were either well beyond the foreseeable state of the art or easily defeated by countermeasures, or both. The only exception was terminal defense, that is, defense based on the ground in the vicinity of the targets to be defended. It was possible . . . we were approaching the time when that could be made to work." Herbert F. York, *Making Weapons, Talking Peace: A Physicist's Odyssey from Hiroshima to Geneva* (New York: Basic Books, 1987), p. 244.

—If only "traditional" ground-based technologies are developed and deployed, neither side need fear the prospect of being unilaterally deprived of its ability to retaliate. Paradoxically, confidence on both sides that an unconstrained offensive buildup could overwhelm the other's defense is a critical requirement for acceptance of a defense emphasis arms control regime. As long as it is obvious that *both* sides retain a capacity to restore capabilities for assured destruction, neither side will have any rational incentive to do so.

By contrast, as long as either side develops weapons that theoretically could cope with even an "unconstrained" offensive threat, the other must fear the prospect of being unilaterally disarmed. Had Teller's envisioned X-ray laser proved feasible, serious pursuit of a deployable weapon would have derailed the offensive reductions envisioned by START, given Soviet hard-liners a viable rationale for reversing the process of internal reform, and compelled the Soviets to prepare for rapid expansion of their offenses.

The incentive, then, for combining large-scale defenses with deep offensive reductions is not the illusory goal of rendering nuclear offenses technologically "impotent." Indeed, precluding boost-phase and postboost interception by agreement would demonstrate mutual renunciation of that quixotic technological goal. To repeat Oppenheimer's argument, a defense emphasis agreement would be designed to ensure *time* to react to defection, since new offensive deployments could be discovered long before they provided anything approaching a first-strike advantage. Thus the defecting state would be exchanging a measure of real safety for an almost certain return to mutual assured destruction. In contrast to MAD, a survival-oriented arms control regime would provide a powerful incentive for rigorous compliance.

—To the extent that positions long held by the Soviet defense establishment persist in a new political arrangement, receptivity to negotiating expanded defenses will depend on forgoing space-based defenses. During the Defense and Space Talks that coincided with the negotiations leading to a START agreement (1985–91), the Soviets specifically excluded ground-based BMD systems from their definition of space-strike arms.[63] Moreover, that the Soviets modernized their Moscow ABM system during the 1980s (including the addition

63. Paul Nitze, "Arms Control: The First Round in Geneva," *Current Policy* (United States Department of State, Bureau of Public Affairs), no. 698 (May 1985): 3. (Reprint of an address before the National Press Club, May 1, 1985.)

of a short-range interceptor) indicated their defense establishment's strong interest in "traditional" ballistic missile defense technologies.

—Finally, the 1983 Soviet proposal to keep space free of weapons that can destroy "objects on the Earth, in the atmosphere or in outer space"[64] has validity beyond the specific dangers of such deployments. If humankind has a long-term future, the utilization of space will progressively increase. It seems to be an act of minimal sanity to keep space free of capabilities for military attack. The exception would be a distant future in which space-based defenses became an internationalized component of a far-reaching collective security regime. Short of that still-utopian prospect, space-based defenses will be justifiably associated with visions of space as a "high frontier" from which to achieve military domination of the earth. Our capacity to decisively preclude that temptation may be the best test of whether we have collectively learned anything from the consequences of indulging in a nuclear arms race on earth.

By the end of the 1980s, sweeping condemnations of ballistic missile defense by arms controllers were yielding to growing awareness of the distinctions described above. That awareness was reflected in the congressional response to the Bush administration's proposal for a Global Protection against Limited Strikes (GPALS) system.[65] The GPALS plan called for up to 1,000 space-based "Brilliant Pebble" interceptor rockets, combined with 750 to 1,000 ground-based interceptors. Although far more modest than the Strategic Defense Initiative Organization's initial "Phase I" deployment plan, it retained the same fundamental defects. No effort was made to show how the proposed Brilliant Pebbles deployments could be reconciled with the administration's commitment to offensive arms control or its declared endorsement of a cooperative augmentation of defenses.

That omission may be contrasted with the emergent position of Congress. In January 1988 Senator Nunn proposed a "modest amendment" to the ABM Treaty to allow bilateral deployment of an

64. From article 2 of the "Soviet Draft Treaty on the Prohibition of the Use of Force in Outer Space and from Space against the Earth," UN General Assembly document A/38/194, August 22, 1983. Reprinted as appendix A in Office of Technology Assessment, *Strategic Defenses* (n. 25), pp. 145–46.

65. For a description of the GPALS proposal, see "SDI: Test Boosts Limited System," *Defense News*, February 4, 1991, p. 4.

"Accidental Launch Protection System."[66] Denounced initially by both sides in the polarized Star Wars debate, it drew growing support in the aftermath of the Cold War.[67]

In October 1991 the House-Senate Conference on the 1992 Defense Authorization Act endorsed deployment of a treaty-compliant ground-based BMD system by 1996, to be coupled with discussions with the Soviets on "the feasibility and mutual interests of amending the ABM Treaty." At the same time, it rejected language in the Senate bill that raised an implicit threat of treaty withdrawal if those negotiations failed, and it agreed that "deployment of Brilliant Pebbles is not a part of either this initial treaty-compliant deployment or any deployment of ABM defenses supported by the conferees."[68]

Thus the Bush administration's lingering attachment to the dream of a purely technological answer to nuclear threats remained a key obstacle to dispassionate consideration of "mutual interests" in augmenting strategic defenses. In the words of one leading defender of offense-only arms control, referring to the administration's refusal to accept a ground-based-only, treaty-restrained BMD deployment: "The only thing that's saving us is that they won't propose it."[69]

Support for limited nationwide population defenses, of course, does not imply endorsement of a future transition from capabilities for mutual assured destruction. Technical studies have suggested that there is a "window" in which START-constrained offensive forces (e.g., over eight thousand warheads on each side) could coexist with population defenses potentially capable of intercepting up to one thousand warheads without enhancing first-strike incentives and consequent arms race pressures.[70] In other words, MAD-based arms control could coexist with significant protection against acci-

66. Sam Nunn, "Arms Control in the Last Year of the Reagan Administration," speech before the Arms Control Association, January 19, 1988. See also *New York Times*, January 25, 1988, p. 23.

67. For a description of evolving U.S. congressional views on ballistic missile defenses, see Pat Towell, "Bush Carries on Fight for SDI, but Space Weapons in Doubt," *Congressional Quarterly*, July 6, 1991, pp. 1836–44; and idem, "Senate Redirects 'Star Wars' Away from 'Brilliant Pebbles,'" *Congressional Quarterly*, August 11, 1990, pp. 2600–2604.

68. "FY92 Defense Authorization Act: House-Senate Conference Summary of Major Actions," House Armed Services Committee, November 1, 1991.

69. Towell, "Bush Carries on Fight" (n. 67), p. 1844. The statement is by John Pike of the Federation of American Scientists.

70. Glenn A. Kent and David E. Thaler, "First Strike Stability and Strategic Defenses: Part II of a Methodology for Evaluating Strategic Forces," RAND/R-3918–AF, October 1990. See also Dean Wilkening et al., "Strategic Defense and Crisis Stability," RAND/N-2511-AF, April 1989.

dental launches, unauthorized limited strikes, and ballistic missile attacks by small nuclear powers.

Growing political receptivity to such a regime nevertheless suggests a willingness to reappraise the notion of assured vulnerability as a permanent fixture of the nuclear age. When a mainstream arms control analyst invokes "Murphy's law" to explain his recent conversion to limited defense advocacy (adding that "the Earth's inhabitants have been extraordinarily fortunate" in avoiding a nuclear catastrophe "during the first 46 years of the nuclear age"), a step has been taken toward facing the basic danger of a permanent environment of MAD.[71]

Just as with proposals for a limited-defense regime, every effort made by analysts in the 1980s to specifically describe a more substantial negotiated transition has relied solely on capabilities that could be provided by ground-based defenses. Several of these recent proposals can provide a more concrete sense of what a future MDE arms control approach might look like.

MDE Proposals in the 1980s

Given Henry Kissinger's role in devising the treaty that effectively ended consideration of MDE for nearly a decade, it is appropriate to begin with his particular version. In September 1985 Kissinger argued that the Reagan administration "has an opportunity to bring about a historic change in strategic relationships and vastly reduce the threat of a nuclear apocalypse." He then presented the following plan:

a) Both sides would agree to eliminate multiple warhead missiles over an agreed period, say ten years.
b) The number of launchers on both sides would be reduced to less than a thousand, including long-range bombers. These two provisions would bring about a reduction in nuclear warheads of close to 90 per cent.
c) Both sides would agree that strategic defense could be phased in over the same ten year period but confined to the following objectives: (1) protection of the retaliatory force (i.e., ICBM and bomber bases); (2) a

71. Michael Krepon, "Limited ABM Defense: A Prudent Step," *Arms Control Today* 21 (October 1991): 20.

defense of populations against limited attacks and accidental launches by a superpower as well as attacks by third nuclear countries.[72]

Thus Kissinger had belatedly accepted the central argument that Donald Brennan had tried to impress on the Nixon administration beginning in 1969: that allowing MIRV to move forward while largely precluding ABM amounted to a reversal of the proper objectives of strategic arms control. Moreover, he now agreed with Brennan's observation that active defense of retaliatory forces could permit very deep cuts in offenses.

Finally, although Kissinger did not envisage going as far as the "ultimate objective" of the U.S. Strategic Concept, his explanation of the proposal above made it clear that he sought a meaningful reduction of offensive capabilities. Thus he attacked START, whose slated 50 percent cuts, he believed, would only "tend to enshrine" MAD doctrine. Further, he argued that it was no longer in the West's interest to rely on nuclear threats. He wrote that "the policy on which Western defense has been built throughout the postwar period—the equating of security with the threat of massive nuclear devastation—is clearly losing relevance."

Kissinger, however, was vague on two related points. First, how many fewer than one thousand launchers should each side keep? Second, was there any desirable ceiling on the level of population defenses that both sides should deploy? The first question draws attention to the role of active defense of forces. Here it is of interest to examine an MDE proposal that focused exclusively on defense of strategic forces as a means to go below MAD capabilities. In 1984 physicist Alvin Weinberg (who had first called for MDE in 1967) outlined a plan that he labeled "defense-protected build-down" (DPB).[73] DPB's value as an MDE proposal lies in its effort to elaborate in

72. Henry A. Kissinger, "We Need Star Wars," *Washington Post*, September 8, 1985, p. C8. Aside from the proposals discussed in this chapter, see Glenn A. Kent, "A Suggested Policy Framework for Strategic Defenses," RAND Publication Series N-2432-FF/RC, Santa Monica, Calif., RAND Corporation, December 1986. For a proposal incorporating missile-site defenses as a means of enhancing MAD stability, see G. E. Barasch, D. M. Kerr et al., *Ballistic Missile Defense: A Potential Arms Control Initiative* (Los Alamos, N.M.: Los Alamos National Laboratory, 1981).

73. Alvin M. Weinberg and Jack N. Barkenbus, "Stabilizing Star Wars," *Foreign Policy* 54 (Spring 1984): 164–70. For a collection of articles built around consideration of the "defense-protected build-down" concept, see Alvin M. Weinberg and Jack N. Barkenbus, eds., *Strategic Defenses and Arms Control* (New York: Paragon, 1988). In chapter 3 (pp. 89–110) Weinberg provides a sympathetic analysis of the overall implications of a superpower shift to a defense-dominated world.

detail the link between hard-point defense and offensive reductions that Brennan had suggested in the mid-1960s.

Weinberg and his coauthor Jack Barkenbus pointed out that it would be a mistake to pursue a "costly technological gamble" on developing exotic Star Wars BMD systems. Ground-based defenses based on interceptor missiles, they noted, had three major advantages. First, their design and deployment could unambiguously limit their capabilities to hard-point defense. Second, their deployment was a realistic near-term goal. Finally, their relative *ineffectiveness* was the key to making them feasible as instruments of arms control: "Although many strategic defense enthusiasts bemoan the fact that current BMD systems could only provide marginal improvements in U.S. defenses, this characteristic is actually a major advantage of DPB. Its incomplete effectiveness requires policy makers to move incrementally, thereby preventing a sudden destabilization of the strategic balance."[74] Hard-point defenses would allow for progressive reduction in bilateral offenses (explained below), while each side would preserve an unchallenged ability to expand its retaliatory force should the other side cheat: "The reduction in American offensive weapons would give the Soviet Union a powerful incentive not to increase its offensive forces. . . . If Moscow tried to take advantage of the situation, the United States would be forced to restore some or all of its destroyed offensive weapons."[75]

The DBP proposal assumes, in effect, the implementation of the first stage of Kissinger's MDE proposal: the "de-MIRVing" of each side's strategic offenses. Beyond that, the defense-protected build-down would be guided by a standard of "deliverable weapons." Weinberg and Barkenbus give the following example, based on the United States and Soviet Union starting with a force of one thousand weapons each: "A U.S. BMD system capable of destroying 10 per cent of these warheads in an all-out Soviet attack would leave Moscow with only 900 deliverable weapons. This situation would permit Washington to dismantle 100 of its warheads and still maintain the offensive balance."[76]

An interesting feature of DPB is that it makes an entirely tacit arms control regime at least theoretically possible. Thus the United States could demonstrate its defensive intentions with a small (and therefore riskless) reduction of offenses, coupled to a corresponding

74. "Stabilizing Star Wars" (n. 73), p. 166.
75. Ibid., p. 168.
76. Ibid., p. 167.

increase in hard-point defense. The process would continue only if Moscow undertook the same steps. They would have a strong incentive to do so: each time they added BMD and reduced their offenses, they would be rewarded by a further U.S. offensive reduction. In effect, both sides would be cutting their counterforce capabilities without simultaneously endangering their ability to retaliate.

Weinberg and Barkenbus, however, refer to two concerns suggesting why the transition should be negotiated. First, they note that each side is likely to underestimate the performance of its own BMD and overestimate that of its adversary's. That would not affect deterrence stability. Assuming that two warheads would be required to ensure destruction of a single undefended target, preserving even approximate equality in remaining numbers of offensive weapons would preclude a first-strike advantage regardless of the effectiveness of each side's defense. Nevertheless, negotiations would bring needed predictability to the build-down, helping to identify agreed standards of defensive parity and transforming an uncertain, incremental process into a firm expectation that the adversary's offense would be progressively reduced.

The specific rationale the authors cite for relying on arms control is the danger of simply abandoning the ABM Treaty: "Abrogating this treaty would heighten superpower tensions if it were done precipitously and without regard for creating a better substitute. But if the ABM treaty were amended to allow for gradual, explicitly defined phasing in of BMD systems together with DPB, the agreement would stabilize the build-down process."[77]

How far could a defense-protected build-down proceed? Weinberg and Barkenbus suggest that "even one 100–kiloton bomb aimed at each of the 10 largest cities in the United States and the Soviet Union would be a formidable deterrent."[78] Reducing retaliatory forces to so low a level is probably not feasible, however. In this regard, it is useful to examine the most extreme version of DPB that has been suggested: the MDE proposal by Jonathan Schell for achieving the total elimination of nuclear offensive capabilities without any population defense at all.

Although it gained far less attention than *The Fate of the Earth*, Schell's sequel to that work, *The Abolition*, rejected his earlier call for world government. Acknowledging that "most people treasure the

77. Ibid., p. 169.
78. Ibid.

independence of their own countries,"[79] Schell now called on the nuclear powers to "drop their swords . . . and lift their shields."[80] Schell's conversion to MDE is notable in two respects. First, he eloquently restates the rationales for MDE-based disarmament that have been generated since the early 1950s. Second, his treatment of the cheating problem leads him to identify the abolute minimum offensive power to which a nuclear disarmament regime could conceivably aspire.

Schell's initial depiction of cheating seems to imply that he is thinking primarily about population defense: "If defenses were arrayed against the kind of force that could be put together in violation of an abolition agreement they could be crucial. On the one side would be a sharply restricted, untested, and clandestinely produced and maintained offensive force, while on the other side would be a large, fully tested, openly deployed, and technically advanced defensive force."[81] His consideration of a complete breakout from MDE disarmament, however, suggests to him a unique form of "point" defense:

> The worst case . . . is not mere cheating but blatant, open violation of the agreement by a powerful and ruthless nation. . . . The only significant military response to this threat would be . . . a similar nuclear buildup . . . , returning the world to . . . the balance of terror. . . . But in order to achieve that buildup the threatened nations would probably have to have already in existence considerable preparations for the manufacture of nuclear arms. Therefore, a . . . provision of the abolition agreement would permit nations to hold themselves in a particular, defined state of readiness for nuclear rearmament. . . . Under what we might call weaponless deterrence, factory would deter factory. . . .[82]
>
> . . . None of this is to say that defense of the population should be ruled out . . . as a further hedge against cheating.[83]

Schell's argument deserves attention because other MDE advocates had failed to spell out how meaningful cheating could be precluded, even with defenses, in a complete nuclear disarmament regime. In taking "minimal deterrence" to its logical extreme, however, Schell's scenario for complete "abolition" does not appear significantly more feasible than the world government solution he proposed in *The Fate of the Earth*.

79. Jonathan Schell, *The Abolition* (New York: Alfred A. Knopf, 1984), p. 108.
80. Ibid., p. 115.
81. Ibid., p. 116.
82. Ibid., pp. 117–19.
83. Ibid., p. 137.

Schell is certainly right in noting that a party to any arms control regime must be extremely confident that it could react in time to the worst plausible scenario for defection. Unfortunately, the "delayed retaliation" threat Schell envisioned would be unlikely to provide that confidence. Instead, it conjures up visions of factories frantically assembling nuclear weapons as "a powerful ruthless nation" attempted to destroy production capacity with its rapidly expanding nuclear arsenal (perhaps combined with conventional bombing). Defenses might blunt such an attack, but confidence in that possibility would never be high enough to allow for complete abolition.

Given the destructive potential of even a very limited nuclear attack, no nuclear power could tolerate the possibility that retaliation would be wholly precluded. At some point in a defense-protected build-down, probably at a significantly higher number than Weinberg's posited ten 100-kiloton weapons, decision makers would conclude that going lower—even with a heavily defended retaliatory force—entailed an intolerable risk.

What hard-point defenses alone could not achieve, however, might be approximated by incorporating population defenses. Indeed, if we envision offensive reductions to below one thousand bombs and warheads (as Kissinger proposed), then even the limited population defense arms control plans currently enjoying broad support would approach a defensive potential sufficient to intercept the other side's entire offensive force. (Although most recent proposals have not directly addressed defenses against bombers or cruise missiles, the principle of protection against limited strikes implies the desirability of defense against all types of delivery vehicles.)

Could the nuclear superpowers ever achieve a nuclear relationship that combined low (heavily protected) offenses with population defenses high enough to raise doubts about inflicting any damage in a nuclear attack? First, such a minimum deterrence MDE regime would have to satisfy the two former adversaries that they preserved a sufficient vestige of basic mutual "deterrence." Second, it would require the cooperation of the middle nuclear powers (Britain, France, and China), each of whom has the capacity to disrupt any far-reaching nuclear disarmament regime.

MDE and Mutual Deterrence after the Cold War

To the extent that progress is made toward achieving a minimum-deterrence MDE environment, deterrence would theoretically be enhanced by one new type of uncertainty and decreased by another. It would be enhanced because an aggressor would have to assume that its counterforce offense would be largely if not entirely destroyed by the active defense protecting the victim's retaliatory forces (and command and control centers). It would be decreased because the victim of an attack could never be certain how much damage (with very high levels of defense, if any damage) could be inflicted in retaliation. On balance, these uncertainties weigh decisively more heavily on the aggressor. Thus, although anti-ABM scientists (in the 1960s and today) have often suggested that a population defense may "fail catastrophically,"[84] a rational aggressor would have to worry that *the attack* would catastrophically fail—with the depletion of offenses in a first strike followed by the catastrophic failure of the attacker's population defenses.

War-fighting proponents of SDI often drew on a similar argument: that a unilateral deployment of defenses, whether of forces, populations, or both, would enhance deterrence by increasing the uncertainties associated with calculating the outcome of an attack. Even before Soviet internal change overtook such worst case presumptions of temptations to initiate nuclear war, that argument was erroneous. Its false assumption was that deterrence of a rational adversary is even remotely "delicate" under current conditions of assured vulnerability. (The possibility, even if remote, that the victim might "launch on warning" would deter any rational decision maker from attempting a disarming first strike.) It seems far more reasonable to assume that with offense dominance, defense dominance, or some mixture of the two, no rational leader is ever likely to calculate that launching a nuclear war promises prospective gains that outweigh costs and risks.

Managing a transition to defense is desirable because miscalculation, insanity, accident, or evil cannot be accommodated by any theory or practice of deterrence. War can come by technological failure, by human error, during the panic of a crisis, or at the hands of a leader who is emotionally (and perhaps physically) detached from its consequences. Only if that moment arrives will it matter how effective defenses have become after (one hopes) many years of on-

84. Thus one ABM opponent in 1969 invoked as the "most important" criticism of ABM the "substantial likelihood that . . . the system would fail completely, for totally unexpected reasons." Leonard S. Rodberg, "ABM Reliability," in *ABM: An Evaluation of the Decision to Deploy an Antiballistic Missile System*, ed. Abram Chayes and Jerome B. Wiesner (New York: New American Library, 1969), p. 117. For discussion of the issue of catastrophic failure, see chapter 3.

going improvements, and how far the negotiated defensive transition has proceeded. There is no reason to agree in advance on some ultimately perfect balance between offense and defense, though one should presume that no particular level of offensive nuclear strength is self-evidently too low. The guiding principle of MDE would simply be to move as far toward defense dominance as agreed standards of parity, deterrence stability, and verification allow.

As in the 1960s, few in the mainstream arms control community have seriously examined any of the recent arguments and proposals for MDE. Instead, just as Jerome Wiesner in 1967 momentarily abandoned the ABM debate to concede that ABM's meaning was transformed when placed in an arms control context, similar brief asides appear in critiques of SDI. One example is the widely cited study by Stanford University's Center for International Security and Arms Control. A single paragraph in this otherwise unrelenting repudiation of strategic defense detected one potentially positive contribution: "If defensive systems are to contribute to a safer and more stable strategic relationship with the Soviet Union, they will have to be embedded in a strict arms control regime that limits offensive systems. Technology alone will not solve the political problems of managing the strategic relationship."[85]

Had the Reagan administration presented a coherent proposal for MDE instead of the Star Wars speech, it is possible that such passing references to MDE's feasibility would have yielded to the first serious exploration of such a regime in the nuclear era. Even a technically plausible plan would have encountered opposition, however. The rapid post-Reykjavik retreat from radical strategic arms proposals showed that the U.S. leadership was unwilling to defend its position that nuclear disarmament and European security were compatible. Given that no U.S. leader had endorsed that argument since the 1940s, it is striking that it was even briefly advanced in 1986. *New York Times* columnist Flora Lewis wrote (in welcoming the disarmament talks at Reykjavik):

> And no wonder NATO generals and some allied leaders were aghast . . . that if it weren't for his attachment to the . . . Strategic Defense Initiative, Mr. Reagan might have signed away the nuclear deterrent. . . . There have been no studies of the implications of such dramatic changes for the U.S. and its allies, no alternative plans, no agreed "posture statements." . . . It is natural for people whose whole careers

85. Sidney D. Drell et al., *The Reagan Strategic Defense Initiative: A Technical, Political and Arms Control Assessment* (Stanford: Stanford University Press, 1984), p. 93.

have been built on this . . . to feel they have been asked to jump off a cliff."[86]

Yet though the administration's abrupt policy shift invited accusations of erratic behavior, the challenge to nuclear reliance did not occur in a political vacuum. Despite the long-standing centrality of extended deterrence as a rationale for offense-dominant nuclear policies, that approach had always been open to challenge on its merits. Moreover, changes in the strategic and international environment since the adoption of NATO's flexible response doctrine in 1967 had by the mid-1980s made extended nuclear deterrence far harder to justify.

MDE and Western Security after the Cold War

After years of attributing responsibility for the arms race to the Soviets, the Reagan administration underwent a painful education regarding the fact that the West was ultimately more reliant on the nuclear menace than were the Russians. The process began with Gorbachev's January 1986 proposal for "nuclear disarmament by the year 2000" (which introduced the radical Soviet reversal regarding the need for on-site inspection) and culminated in the series of Soviet concessions that produced the Intermediate Nuclear Forces Treaty.

As early as the 1960s, McNamara had attempted to reduce NATO's reliance on nuclear weapons, but the primary meaning of the 1967 flexible response compromise he achieved was that NATO remained unprepared for any fundamental shifts in policy. The world had changed since the 1960s, however, and every important development had pointed toward the rejection of nuclear threats as the basis for European security.

First, the balance of terror had truly become a balance. In 1967 superpower nuclear parity still seemed remote (far more remote than it actually was); for the moment, the United States had managed to reproduce the same huge preponderance in missiles as it had created earlier in bombers. By the 1980s, hopes that the United States could somehow preclude a completely devastating retaliation following a first use of strategic weapons had long since disap-

86. Flora Lewis, "Now for the Real Issues," *New York Times*, October 21, 1986, p. A31. For a description of European concerns after Reykjavik, see *New York Times*, November 16, 1986, p. A1.

peared. Western leaders found it increasingly difficult to explain why the United States would be willing to commit national suicide in order to punish Soviet aggression in Europe.

Second, Western Europe had grown economically more powerful than the Soviet Union, strengthening the case that the West could afford an effective conventional deterrent. Secretary of State Shultz would likely have found broad domestic support for his proposition that a lack of European "political will" was not an adequate basis for maintaining the balance of terror.

Third, the progressive erosion of the credibility of extended nuclear deterrence had been coupled to a reduction in the perceived Soviet threat. Both superpowers had experienced the costs of establishing control over relatively primitive Third World nations, and the specter of the Soviets starting World War III in hopes of conquering Europe seemed almost wholly incredible.[87] As former president Richard Nixon observed in 1988, "Today the fear of nuclear weapons is greater than the fear of the Soviets."[88]

European support for the 1988 Intermediate Nuclear Forces Treaty both reflected those changes and substantially reinforced their impact. Indeed, the INF Treaty may have represented as significant a turning point in nuclear policy as Harry Truman's tentative 1949 decision to base European defense on nuclear weapons. Strategist Edward Luttwak made the observation in particularly stark terms:

> For once, the importance of an arms control agreement is not being overstated. But the new INF agreement is important for a much greater reason than the withdrawal of a few hundred warheads. It marks, I believe, the beginning of a "post-nuclear" era. . . . Thousands of nuclear weapons may remain in this post-nuclear world. But they will no longer provide a realistic option for defending Europe.[89]

Even though many in the European defense establishment initially preferred to ward off reminders of an emergent "postnuclear

87. By the 1980s some experts were disputing whether the Soviets were capable of successfully invading Europe. For a positive assessment of NATO capabilities, see John J. Mearsheimer, "Why the Soviets Can't Win Quickly in Central Europe," *International Security* 7 (Summer 1982): 3–39. Another analysis concluded: "NATO conventional forces in Europe could probably thwart a Pact conventional attack today and could have done so when the Reagan administration took office in 1981." Barry R. Posen and Stephen W. Van Evera, "Reagan Administration Defense Policy: Departure from Containment," in *Eagle Resurgent? The Reagan Era in Foreign Policy*, ed. Kenneth A. Oye, Robert J. Lieber, and Donald Rothchild (Boston: Little, Brown, 1987), p. 83.

88. William Safire, "The European Pillar," *New York Times*, April 7, 1988, p. A23.

89. Edward N. Luttwak, "Why the INF Pact Means the Nuclear Era Is Over," *Washington Post*, November 29, 1987, p. L2.

era," their anxiety over the particular features of U.S. nuclear arms control proposals was misdirected. Across the range from INF to START to the U.S. Strategic Concept, the new U.S. positions basically reflected the reality that there was no longer any policy that would bolster the credibility of extended deterrent threats.

Concerned European leaders could take comfort, however, in that just as no U.S. buildup could "restore" the credibility of extended deterrence, no imaginable superpower arms control regime would eliminate the inherent inhibiting effect of nuclear weapons. Short of complete offensive disarmament, nuclear parity at *any* level means both that the United States is unlikely to use its strategic forces in the event of war *and* that the Russians could never fully preclude such use.

In his statement to the press immediately following the collapse of Reykjavik, Secretary of State Shultz announced: "As the agreement that might have been, during this 10-year period, in effect, all offensive strategic arms and ballistic missiles would be eliminated."[90] That statement was both wildly unrealistic and unnecessarily alarming. Had the United States not been flirting with a giant leap to the "ultimate objective" of its Strategic Concept, the MDE agreement that "might have been" could have been no more disquieting to Western Europe than the administration's other strategic arms reduction proposals.

Relatively modest initial steps could have countered any appearance of "jumping off a cliff" toward a nonnuclear world. A first stage of negotiations, for example, might have addressed the utility of a defense-protected build-down as a means of strengthening a START agreement, which a number of experts charged would make U.S. land-based forces intolerably vulnerable.[91] That could have been coupled to some version of Senator Nunn's proposal for a light population defense against accidental or unauthorized attack.

More than at any time since the U.S. decision to rely on massive retaliation threats to protect Europe, the late 1980s offered a chance to initiate a restructuring of offense-dominant strategic forces. Europeans were already largely unafraid of invasion and scarcely confident that U.S. nuclear threats were adding to their security. Those preconditions for a shift from MAD existed even before the political liberation of Eastern Europe.

The ultimate key to reshaping the European security environment was the dismantling of the Soviet offensive conventional threat. Al-

90. *New York Times*, October 28, 1986, p. A6.

91. A year before he became President Bush's national security adviser, Brent Scowcroft was a strong proponent of that view. See Brent Scowcroft, John Deutch, and R. James Woolsey, "Come and Get Us," *New Republic*, April 18, 1988, pp. 16–18.

though Gorbachev invoked historical and geographic factors to explain past Soviet military policy, he confronted the fact that his state's defensive intentions could be credibly demonstrated only by a corresponding military posture.[92] The reduction and restructuring of Soviet forces in Europe removed both the chief original cause of the nuclear buildup to MAD and the only defensible rationale for wanting to preserve it.

As those events were coupled to the collapse of Communism inside the Soviet Union, nuclear deterrence in Europe simply became irrelevant, along with rationales for existing nuclear force structures and the corresponding target lists that had evolved for decades. Rationales for preserving the ability to annihilate whole societies had simply disappeared. To the extent that there was plausible danger of deliberate aggression, there was an emerging consensus among former allies and adversaries that the future axis of threats was far more likely to be North-South than East-West.[93]

Nevertheless, the legacy of reliance on a nuclear counterweight to Soviet conventional strength will continue to affect efforts to dismantle the balance of terror. First, after three decades of Western declarations identifying nuclear deterrence as critical to European security, that policy had taken on a symbolic significance independent of its merits. Far more important, by the 1980s the Europeans had the power to do more than complain about calls for comprehensive strategic arms control agreements, as the growth of British and French nuclear capabilities gave those states the power to obstruct any regime involving deep offensive cuts. That power was also shared by China. Given the continuation of ongoing programs at the end of the decade, British, French, and Chinese forces would cumulatively reach a level of about 1,500 nuclear warheads by the end of the century.[94]

If the nuclear superpowers choose to design an MDE regime that

92. For example: "In the West they talk about inequalities and imbalances. That's right, there are imbalances and asymmetries in some kinds of armaments and armed forces on both sides in Europe, caused by historical, geographical and other factors. We stand for eliminating the inequality existing in some areas, but not through a build-up by those who lag behind but through a reduction by those who are ahead." Gorbachev (n. 54), p. 203.

93. For arguments along this line by U.S., British, French, and Russian analysts, see David Goldfischer and Thomas W. Graham, eds., *Nuclear Deterrence and Global Security in Transition* (Boulder, Colo.: Westview Press, 1992).

94. This estimate is from Harold A. Feiveson and Frank N. von Hippel, "Beyond START: How to Make Much Deeper Cuts," *International Security* 15 (Summer 1990): 159–60. Their source is Stockholm International Peace Research Institute, *SIPRI Yearbook 1989: Armaments and Disarmament* (Oxford: Oxford University Press, 1989), pp. 18–20, 28, 30–31, 34.

lessens their vulnerability to nuclear devastation, these middle nuclear powers will confront fateful choices. On one hand, cooperating with such a regime (by agreeing to limit their own offenses) would mean an erosion of their capacity to retaliate. On the other hand, very deep offensive cuts could ultimately reduce the vulnerability of all states.

Should the nuclear superpowers opt (as some have proposed) to pursue an offense-only arms control regime at greatly reduced force levels, the middle nuclear powers have an undeniable ability to derail an agreement. Except for a small number of Chinese weapons, the nuclear arsenals of these states are still aimed at the former Soviet Union. Russia (or the Commonwealth of Independent States), in effect would be exchanging parity with one state for parity with four. An MDE regime involving substantial population defenses could alleviate Russian concerns over that implication of deep offensive cuts, since defensive deployments could compensate for a diminishing advantage in offensive nuclear forces. At the same time, ongoing reductions in overall CIS offensive capabilities—from conventional power projection to nuclear—should increase European and Chinese tolerance for CIS defenses.

Finally, Europeans will likely become at least as interested in their own theater defenses as in their ability to destroy cities in the former Soviet Union, especially given Europe's proximity to radical Third World states. United States–developed systems such as the Theater High-Altitude Area Air Defense (THAAD) system raise the possibility of European inclusion in an overall shift toward defense. In general, improved defenses and reduced offenses should be seen as dual objectives in an era marked by the absence of serious conflict among the states of the developed world.

We are likely never to witness the fulfillment of Freeman Dyson's vision of a world in which the armed forces of all states are "strictly confined" to the mission of defense. Disparities of power in many cases are so vast that states will be simply unable to relinquish the potential for aggression against much weaker neighbors. In coming decades, however, it may not be beyond aspiration to extend MDE to other powers that accept the territorial status quo, as offensive reductions are combined with growing defenses against threats of less than intercontinental range.

Both the U.S. Strategic Concept and the Soviet MDE conventional arms control approach provided glimpses into how post–nuclear era thinking can be translated into arms control practice. After a treaty in which asymmetical cuts in tanks, mobile artillery, armored vehicles, and airpower will ensure the security of both sides against any renewal of tensions, a serious effort to restructure the nuclear balance would strengthen the accurate conviction that unilateral military strategies have been defeated by the nuclear revolution. Indeed, deliberately preserving the ability to unleash a global catastrophe *after* both sides had rejected aspirations to elude the military stalemate would represent a fateful abandonment of political responsibility.

Conclusion: The Future of Mutual Defense Emphasis

This book has examined the evolution of thinking among those who have sought to design an arms control solution to the nuclear danger. In a sense, arms control theory in the 1980s showed signs of returning to its roots, as both conventional and nuclear arms control analysts rediscovered the principle of mutual defense emphasis that had guided the 1932–33 Geneva Disarmament Conference. In terms of strategic arms control, it is significant that renewed interest in MDE came from across the entire spectrum of nuclear policy advocacy. Thus disarmament advocate Jonathan Schell, SALT negotiator Henry Kissinger, and a significant portion of the community of war-fighting strategists[95] joined in agreeing that the only sound long-term policy must combine deterrence, defense, and offensive disarmament.

As I noted in the first chapter, all theories of arms control that aim to supplant war-fighting strategies rely on distinguishing offensive from defensive military capabilities and call on potential adversaries to emphasize the defense. Had the United States been seriously interested in nuclear disarmament in the first decade of the nuclear era, it would have regarded mutual defense emphasis arms control as the only plausible means to approximate that goal. As I showed

95. Four years before the presentation of the U.S. Strategic Concept, war-fighter Keith Payne wrote: "If U.S. arms control policy is to meet U.S. strategic requirements, it would have to permit a free rein on strategic defense and pursue truly effective constraints on offensive weapons. There is a compatibility betweeen pursuing reductions in offensive weapons and leaving strategic defenses unfettered: restricting the former simplifies the task of the latter." "Deterrence, Arms Control, and U.S. Strategic Doctrine," *Orbis* 25 (Fall 1981): 766. Later he expanded on his arms control rationale for SDI in Keith Payne, *Strategic Defense: "Star Wars" in Perspective* (Boston: Hamilton Press, 1986), pp. 141–78. Unfortunately, Payne failed to come to grips with the probability that simply leaving defenses "unfettered" would preclude any negotiated constraints on offenses. Convinced that a "cost-effective" defense can drive the arms race in the direction of defensive supremacy, his sympathetic references to MDE are not accompanied by any effort to show how Star Wars technologies could be incorporated in a negotiated defensive transition.

earlier, those arms control supporters in the United States who recognized "general and complete disarmament" as a utopian objective in a world of sovereign states in fact tried to construct a defense emphasis framework that could somehow insulate the nuclear danger from the deepening Cold War.

That U.S. arms control theorists became fascinated with a theory that glorified offensive weapons may one day come to be viewed as one of many strange episodes in the confusing period when humans first tried to come to grips with the prospect of self-inflicted extinction. The theory would probably have never existed were it not for a unique technological moment of literal defenselessness. It never would have survived had it not turned out to have great value in limiting (though never supplanting) the domestic influence of nuclear war-fighting strategists. Describing MAD as an "arms control theory," moreover, helped obscure the fact that the Western political leaders who endorsed it also endorsed first-use threats, whose credibility required doctrines and deployment policies that were antithetical to meaningful arms control.

I have argued that technology has not been the driving force in creating the current strategic environment of offense-dominant force postures. Instead, MAD capabilities were a creation of unrealistic aspirations to a nuclear victory strategy. Unfortunately, at a point in history when the nuclear superpowers have finally abandoned the competition that produced a balance of terror, the same arms control theory that helped institutionalize that stalemate may now hamper the attempt to make it much less dangerous.

If ideas and theories, far more than technology, have shaped the military environment we now find ourselves in, we may hope that a change in prevailing beliefs about nuclear policy will take us beyond the old debate between offense-only arms control supporters and proponents of nuclear war-fighting doctrines. Thus, in depicting mutual defense emphasis as a philosophy of "live and let live," Freeman Dyson has written:

> Live-and-let-live is not an easy concept to explain. It is at present unfamiliar to the majority of the American people. Standing where it does in the middle, between the hawks and the doves, it will be difficult to defend against political attack from both extremes. Nevertheless, the concept is logically coherent and politically practical, and its central location may in the end be a source of strength rather than of weakness.[96]

96. Dyson (n. 1), p. 283.

For MDE to become "politically practical," however, both strategists and arms controllers (on both sides) will have to reassess the beliefs that have guided their nuclear policy prescriptions for decades. Assuming that centralized control over defense policy endures the transition to a stable post-Soviet political order, several factors suggest long-term Russian receptivity to a serious MDE arms control approach.

First, it corresponds to the Russians' own tradition of arms control thought, which was shaped by historical experience and geography rather than by reasons peculiar to socialist doctrine. In a sense, Moscow's abandonment of MDE arms control in the late 1960s was imposed by the prevailing views in the United States, as American nuclear hawks saw ABM as a means of sustaining nuclear superiority, while even American nuclear doves made it clear that they would spare no effort to overwhelm any effort by the Soviets to protect their people.

Second, MDE offers the only prospect of meaningfully reducing the single external threat they face—the danger of attack by weapons of mass destruction. That the Soviets consistently devoted tremendous resources to deploying anti-aircraft defenses and to improving their BMD technology reflects deep preoccupation with that threat. In the near term, their geographic position will make them far more vulnerable than the United States to potential future Saddams armed with missiles and nuclear weapons.

An opportunity to test their interest in MDE will come, however, only if U.S. leaders reject the strategists' dream of "defense unlimited" and agree to seal off its reemergence by means of verifiable constraints on the SDI program. One might have hoped that those who renewed the drive for a defensive advantage in the early 1980s would have remembered that the last ABM debate ended with a repudiation of both the search for superiority *and* the search for safety. Unfortunately, the only lesson the war-fighters learned from their failure in the 1960s was to take Herman Kahn's tactical advice; that is, to package strategic defense as a "shield to facilitate . . . lasting arms control measures."

The aftermath of the Cold War has produced unprecedented political support for combining defense with arms control. The surest path to undercutting that support would be for U.S. leaders to continue to invoke common interests in defense primarily as a rhetorical ploy to push their bid for a defense in space. As in the 1960s, claims in the 1980s that the United States could unilaterally achieve real safety against the Soviet nuclear arsenal failed to withstand expert scrutiny and public debate, and congressional support for SDI correspondingly waned with each budgetary battle. For the near future, any actual system hardware that might be displayed will provide a very feeble incentive for abandoning a cooperative approach to the nuclear danger.

The impetus for nuclear arms control stems from the assumption that it will be impossible to attain such fundamental strategic objectives as protection of the homeland and victory in war. The nuclear problem imposes two related tasks on those who have reached that conclusion. First, policymakers must be convinced that unilateral efforts to achieve safety are futile. Second, an arms control framework must be devised that inspires confidence on both sides that national security concerns have been adequately addressed. The two tasks are obviously linked, since political support for arms control in general will be affected by how much confidence particular proposed arms control regimes inspire.

The U.S. arms control community became so preoccupied with the first task that it paid too little attention to the second. For two decades, it convincingly depicted the prospects for an effective defense as so remote, and the consequences of an all-out offense-defense arms race as so unpredictable and costly, that it would be foolhardy at best to massively divert the nation's resources for the necessary effort.

Arms controllers were far less persuasive in arguing that the nuclear superpowers should instead embrace an arms control regime that indefinitely preserves the total vulnerability of each to a nuclear catastrophe. In fact, their preferred framework was repeatedly proved precarious, as the common interest of the two adversaries in surviving a failure of deterrence drove them both toward defensive measures that not only subverted the MAD framework but reinforced suspicions that the goal of far-reaching cooperative management of the nuclear problem was illusory.

In light of the fragility of a MAD arms control regime, and given the obvious desirability of meaningfully reducing offensive capabilities in the post–Cold War world, assertions by prominent mainstream arms control advocates that a defense emphasis arms control regime "can contribute to a safer and more stable strategic relationship" cry out for further elaboration. Extensive analysis and informed debate should be directed toward discovering which types of defensive systems might prove compatible with arms control, how and when they could be deployed, and the most desirable ultimate objective of a negotiated transition from offense to defense.

Difficult technical and political questions are certain to arise in such an inquiry. In a world where nuclear offenses will continue to exist, the technological research competition between offense and defense can never be fully halted. Some offensive countermeasures, however, such as maneuverable reentry vehicles, can be precluded by test bans. The utility of decoys and other penetration aids can be circumscribed both by placing limits on tests and by limiting the size of reentry vehicles: the incorporation of such "pen-aids" forces a tradeoff between lowering the yield of warheads and lowering their chances of reaching the target. Both choices reduce the ability to inflicting damage. In the post–Cold War world, leaps to zero or near zero in some types of delivery systems have become plausible and could vastly simplify (and reduce the costs of) a defensive transition.

Although it would be impossible to eliminate the uncertainties of offensive and defensive performance, there would also be no need to do so. Uncertainty over operational performance enhances deterrence; establishing reasonable qualitative limits on the technical design of offensive and defensive weapons need only provide standards for comparability and approximate parity of both sides' forces.

In that regard, the ABM Treaty and the recent START agreement have demonstrated that it is possible to find common technical ground on these issues. Nevertheless, moving toward much lower overall offensive forces will likely test both the ingenuity of arms control experts and the tolerance of both nuclear superpowers (and soon, of other nuclear powers) for increasingly intrusive verification measures.

Two weeks after the Reagan administration proposed its Strategic Concept, NATO secretary-general Lord Peter Carrington suggested that "it will, at the very least, be extremely difficult to devise a system which meets these objectives of balance, no superiority, and enhanced deterrence."[97] Such wholly intuitive speculations may prove correct; but to use them as an excuse for not making the effort amounts to abdicating an attempt to achieve a safer world.

If there is a single critical revision in arms control thought that would pave the way for such an inquiry, it would be a reassessment of the meaning of "cost-effectiveness." Cost-effectiveness is a standard by which strategists decide whether weapons should be designed for the offense, the defense, or, optimally, for both purposes. Because strategic (i.e., war-fighting) approaches can only result in an endless and unwinnable nuclear arms competition, there is no limit to the long-term cost of strategic weapons programs, just as the

97. *Washington Post*, February 14, 1985, p. A25.

weapons' "effectiveness" for achieving the goals of strategy is nonexistent.

Once potential adversaries are committed to avoiding the costs and risks of preparing for nuclear war, the criterion of cost-effectiveness loses much of its meaning. The long-term issue becomes which type of weapons deployment would maximize safety against the common danger posed by nuclear weapons. In an MDE arms control regime with reasonable verification measures, defenses need only be sufficiently effective—and new offensive weapons sufficiently costly—to provide ample time for one side to react to massive cheating by the other side.

Opponents understandably regarded SDI as a direct threat to arms control. In its original design, they were almost certainly right. Yet no debating points will be lost if arms controllers stress that substantial defenses might well prove feasible in arms control, and would almost certainly otherwise remain elusive. The claim that arms control is designed to leave us defenseless was the most powerful—and up to now, valid—rationale for the assault on it in the 1980s. Using arms control to alter the offense-defense balance would be the best way to ensure a long-term consensus in support of cooperative management of the nuclear danger.

The defense-protected world of "mutual assured security" called for in the U.S. Strategic Concept may well be just as utopian as the Soviet proposal for "disarmament by the year 2000." But it is far from utopian to aim at progressively reducing the awesome consequences of a nuclear exchange, in a manner that would not compromise the interests of great powers in a strong national defense. Joint planning toward that end did not have to await resolution of the range of political and ideological conflicts that constituted the superpowers' adversarial relationship. All that was required, in essence, was a realistic recognition of their "solidarity . . . against the total war of which they would be the first victims."[98]

Deterrence—the need to confront a potential aggressor with "a prospect of costs and risks outweighing his prospective gain"[99]—is not inherently immoral. Choosing to base deterrence indefinitely on the threat to unleash a nuclear holocaust *is* immoral; and refusal to

98. This statement by Raymond Aron was cited by McGeorge Bundy, "Strategic Defense Thirty Years Later: What Has Changed?" in *The Future of Strategic Deterrence, Part I*, Adelphi Paper no. 160 (London: International Institute for Strategic Studies, 1980), p. 7.

99. For the definition of deterrence from which this is drawn, see Glenn Snyder, *Deterrence and Defense: Toward a Theory of National Security* (Princeton: Princeton University Press, 1961), p. 3.

explore a potentially viable alternative is bizarre. The leaders of two nation-states presumed to settle their momentary differences by building weapons that could conceivably exterminate the entire species. Having resolved those differences, we can hope that appeals to "realism" that claim this is "the best of all possible nuclear worlds" will be rejected long before the day when deterrence fails.

Index

Cornell Studies in Security Affairs

edited by Robert J. Art *and* Robert Jervis

Strategic Nuclear Targeting, edited by Desmond Ball and Jeffrey Richelson
Japan Prepares for Total War: The Search for Economic Security, 1919–1941, by Michael A. Barnhart
The German Nuclear Dilemma, by Jeffrey Boutwell
Flying Blind: The Politics of the U.S. Strategic Bomber Program, by Michael L. Brown
Citizens and Soldiers: The Dilemmas of Military Service, by Eliot A. Cohen
Great Power Politics and the Struggle over Austria, 1945–1955, by Audrey Kurth Cronin
Military Organizations, Complex Machines: Modernization in the U.S. Armed Services, by Chris C. Demchak
Nuclear Arguments: Understanding the Strategic Nuclear Arms and Arms Control Debate, edited by Lynn Eden and Steven E. Miller
Public Opinion and National Security in Western Europe, by Richard C. Eichenberg
Innovation and the Arms Race: How the United States and the Soviet Union Develop New Military Technologies, by Matthew Evangelista
Guarding the Guardians: Civilian Control of Nuclear Weapons in the United States, by Peter Douglas Feaver
Men, Money, and Diplomacy: The Evolution of British Strategic Foreign Policy, 1919–1926, by John Robert Ferris
A Substitute for Victory: The Politics of Peacekeeping at the Korean Armistice Talks, by Rosemary Foot
The Wrong War: American Policy and the Dimensions of the Korean Conflict, 1950–1953, by Rosemary Foot
The Best Defense: Policy Alternatives for U.S. Nuclear Security from the 1950s to the 1990s, by David Goldfischer
House of Cards: Why Arms Control Must Fail, by Colin S. Gray
The Soviet Union and the Politics of Nuclear Weapons in Europe, 1969–1987, by Jonathan Haslam
The Soviet Union and the Failure of Collective Security, 1934–1938, by Jiri Hochman
The Warsaw Pact: Alliance in Transition? edited by David Holloway and Jane M. O. Sharp
The Illogic of American Nuclear Strategy, by Robert Jervis
The Meaning of the Nuclear Revolution, by Robert Jervis

Nuclear Crisis Management: A Dangerous Illusion, by Richard Ned Lebow
The Search for Security in Space, edited by Kenneth N. Luongo and W. Thomas Wander
The Nuclear Future, by Michael Mandelbaum
Conventional Deterrence, by John J. Mearsheimer
Liddell Hart and the Weight of History, by John J. Mearsheimer
The Sacred Cause: Civil-Military Conflict over Soviet National Security, 1917–1992, by Thomas M. Nichols
Inadvertent Escalation: Conventional War and Nuclear Risks, by Barry R. Posen
The Sources of Military Doctrine: France, Britain, and Germany between the World Wars, by Barry R. Posen
Dilemmas of Appeasement: British Deterrence and Defense, 1934–1937, by Gaines Post, Jr.
Winning the Next War: Innovation and the Modern Military, by Stephen Peter Rosen
Israel and Conventional Deterrence: Border Warfare from 1953 to 1970, by Jonathan Shimshoni
Fighting to a Finish: The Politics of War Termination in the United States and Japan, 1945, by Leon V. Sigal
The Ideology of the Offensive: Military Decision Making and the Disasters of 1914, by Jack Snyder
Myths of Empire: Domestic Politics and International Ambition, by Jack Snyder
The Militarization of Space: U.S. Policy, 1945–1984, by Paul B. Stares
Making the Alliance Work: The United States and Western Europe, by Gregory F. Treverton
The Origins of Alliances, by Stephen M. Walt
The Ultimate Enemy: British Intelligence and Nazi Germany, 1933–1939, by Wesley K. Wark
The Tet Offensive: Intelligence Failure in War, by James J. Wirtz
The Elusive Balance: Power and Perceptions during the Cold War, William Curti Wohlforth
Deterrence and Strategic Culture: Chinese-American Confrontations, 1949–1958, by Shu Guang Zhang

Library of Congress Cataloging-in-Publication Data

Goldfischer. David.
The best defense : policy alternatives for U.S. nuclear security from the 1950s to the 1990s / David Goldfischer.
p. cm.—(Cornell studies in security affairs)
Includes bibliographical references and index.
ISBN 0-8014-2570-0 (alk. paper)
1. Nuclear arms control—United States. 2. United States—Military policy. 3. Security, International. I. Title. II. Series.
JX1974.7.G652 1993
355.02′17′0973—dc20 92-56778